FORBIDDEN HISTORY

by

John Dudley Aldworth

Truthful History Publications

17 Clark Place, Hamilton 3216, Waikato, New Zealand

COVER PHOTOGRAPH

A skull-capped or helmeted statue of a sentinel overlooks a hillside in the Waikato region of New Zealand's North Island. Carved from hard basalt the figure, reminiscent of Easter Island moai, is severely weathered, indicating extreme age. Picture © Bryan Mitchell.

Forbidden History

By John Dudley Aldworth

ISBN 978-0-473-35264-6

Layout consultant: Mike Williams.

The author wishes to thank all those who contributed information, advice and technical assistance to make this book possible.

Published by Truthful History Publications

This book is dedicated to those ancient peoples of New Zealand who, though from different races, lived in peace here for over 1,000 years, to my loving wife Naomi without whose support it would not have been written and to the many helpers who have made it possible.

Why this book?

Studying pre-history, has long been a passion for this author. And as a writer for Hamilton This Week newspaper I wrote several stories about our forgotten past. One report caused shock when it asserted that the Moriori people, thought to have died out long ago, in fact were alive and well in the Waikato where they had lived for centuries.

In 2014 my friend, paramount chief, Te Upoko Ariki Hori Kupenga Manuka Manuka (a.k.a. George Connnelly) asked me to write a book about his life and the history of his people. They are the Waitaha who reached these shores in 550AD.

Later, Max Hill, author of two books on pre-history which I had edited, suggested I should write a book of my own. Max's books provide important artifacts and research indicating non-Māori people settled New Zealand long ago.

Forbidden History is different. It tells the stories of George, the Waitaha chief, and of Monica Matamua, leader of the last few Patupaiarehe descendants, survivors from the 17th and 18th century holocaust of their people.

This book then views New Zealand's history through the Paatupaiarehe and Waitaha traditions rather than the perspective of Māori and latter-day European accounts. In support it cites rock solid artifacts, important world historical research and the undeniable discovery of old shipwrecks that brought pre-Māori people to this 'Far Away Land'.

Contents

Preface
Forbidden history
Introduction A plea to Māori people........................ 13
Chapter 1 The place of peace 18
Chapter 2 Monica's story..................................... 22
Chapter 3 What's in a name?............................... 71
Chapter 4 A convenient mythology..................... 75
Chapter 5 The moa farmers 86
Chapter 6 Seeing the rainbow.............................. 95
Chapter 7 The house of learning 102
Chapter 8 A nation in denial................................ 109
Chapter 9 The great genocide.............................. 123
The ancient burials of a peaceful people................................ 135
Chapter 10 What drove them to it?........................ 141
Chapter 11 Ancient peacemakers 147
Chapter 12 Standing on the battle line 161
Chapter 13 End of the carnage 166
Chapter 14 A high chief's story 173
Chapter 15 Where the trouble began..................... 191
Chapter 16 The Melanesian connection 197
Chapter 17 Whence the Moriori? 203
Timetable for Settlement.. 213
Chapter 18 From Spain with love.......................... 215
Chapter 19 An amazing discovery 223
Chapter 20 Arrivals from afar 250
Chapter 21 The de Gonneville mystery................. 253
Chapter 22 An obsession with maps 268
Chapter 23 The 'unknown' mappers 276
Chapter 24 'Red heads' or ancient Celts?.............. 288
Chapter 25 The *Urekehu* Odyssey 305
Chapter 26 Corn's amaizing story 319
Chapter 27 So what should we do? 330

A chief of long ago, wearing a South American style headdress, peers out from this ancient rock carving found in Taranaki. He has clear European facial features. When did his people first reach New Zealand?

Foreword

by Doug Woolerton

Now a professional political lobbyist, Doug Woolerton was a Waikato farmer for 21 years and a milk company director for nine. He left the National Party in 1992 to form New Zealand First with Winston Peters and was president of the party from 1992 until 2005. He was a Member of Parliament for four terms from 1996 to 2008.

It is important when we research our history that we challenge all of the accepted pre-conceptions upon which today's knowledge is based. Scientists are at the forefront of this and as a consequence our awareness of the world around us and for that matter the heavens is constantly expanding.

Historians and writers the world over keep coming up with new discoveries and explanations for previously unexplained facts that may well be difficult or uncomfortable to accept, but they extend our knowledge and therefore are good for us. Forbidden History is such a book and sets out to pull together discordant and long ignored events and artefacts which simply do not gel with history as we are taught it.

This book will challenge the reader and lead to more questions being asked of our institutions including our Government. The New Zealand Establishment, be they scientific, legal or political like things to be nice and tidy and squared away so that they are not questioned. John Aldworth, Monica Matamua and George Connelly do not subscribe to this train of thought and give good reasons for their alternative views of our history.

There is a saying that history is written by the victorious and these three individuals would go along with that line of thinking. How did the carvings and the shipwrecks get to be where they are and how are we to explain them if not by the acceptance that someone was here before us? To accept that is not to disavow our history but to add to it, in my view.

Forbidden History contends that there were people here before Maori. A great many of us have no trouble with that concept knowing that great seafaring civilisations go back very many thousands of years. In fact, it would be strange if other people had not been here prior to Moriori and Maori. Therefore why would we not pursue that possibility and acknowledge those who are from different tribes be they European Asian Moriori or other? Are we not proud to be multicultural these days?

There is no possibility that the order of today's society is going to be upset by accepting that history may have got it a little wrong here and there; that perhaps there are others who have had land confiscated by battle. Or for that matter had ancestors grievously wronged and killed. The sin is in the denial of these things, surely.

This book will make you think and it will raise as many questions as answers. It will be interpreted wrongly in many cases just as it in turn questions many established "truths" in other historical accounts. I found it a fascinating read and it will surely add to the sum total of our very short history.

Doug Woolerton

Preface

Forbidden history

In New Zealand bones of wrecked ships protrude from the sand, writing is found in cave inscriptions and large, stone monuments are scattered far and wide. And some still living among us say their ancestors left these marks of their existence long before the first Māori set foot on these shores.

Yet accepted New Zealand history and official Government policy insist there were no such ancient first-comers to this far off land. Successive generations of schoolchildren are still taught that prior to the Polynesian arrival there were no earlier settlers at all.

This politically correct view is maintained despite a plethora of artifacts to the contrary. Not to mention a firm tradition that 2,000 or more years ago a tall, white people whose red hair shone like gold came here from the other side of the world. Actually, these voyagers to paradise were among the first to discover New Zealand and to create here a haven of peace and plenty that lasted for over 1,000 years before the coming of the Māori. Yet their history is officially denied because in New Zealand it is illegal and forbidden to explore the true past.

Current law refers all discovered ancient human remains to local Māori elders for their decision. Often such elders respond, 'These people are not our people; they are old but they are not our people. Dispose of them as you wish'.

In this way many skeletal remains of the pre-Polynesian European people said to have once thronged this land have been bulldozed back into the ground, or, in worst case, ground up into fertiliser.

Amateur archaeologists may not dig at contentious sites and little or no effort is made to preserve the precious remnants of stone pre-Polynesian past. It is forbidden to do so.

One important relic that has survived destruction, however, is the 'Chronos Stone', a sophisticated astronomical calendar device carved in solid rock and held to predate both Polynesian and latter day European settlement of this country. The Government has been asked to take this artifact, believed to be the only advanced ancient sun dial of its kind, into safe custody and suitably display it as a visitor attraction. Sadly, its only response has been to refer the matter to the Historic Places Trust which has taken no action at all.

In Northland's Waipoua Forest lie the remains of a stone city, extensive walls, roundhouse dwellings, a temple and altars, believed by researchers to be the work of a skilled ancient people here long before Moriori, Māori or latter day Europeans. However, the site has been placed off limits to investigators. Indeed they have been physically threatened when they have tried to access it.

Occasionally road building contractors dig up ancient pre-Māori burial sites. They then halt work out of respect for the skeletons uncovered. Yet in at least one case they were ordered to bulldoze the evidence back into the ground. Where archaeological digs have been carried out on ancient sites, the dating in some cases has been fudged to make them appear far later than they actually are.

Reports have been excised from the records and others buried out of sight. All, apparently, so that the 'consensus' of archaeological experts, the assertion that no one was here in New Zealand before arrival of the Moriori around 1100AD, can be maintained.

Near Port Waikato entrances to caves found long ago to have contained the buried skeletons of large, European, pre-Māori people are said to have been have been destroyed and the landscape altered to prevent access. What's more historians and archaeologists refuse to acknowledge the existence of 'ooparts' – out-of-place artifacts – that might negate the politically correct paradigm that Māori are the tangata whenua, the first settlers of the land.

So what is the truth? This book has been written so something of the tradition that New Zealand has an ancient, peaceful and

European past can be told. Not so much through archaeological evidence, although that is cited too, but more importantly through the first-hand accounts of the descendants of those who, it is said, first landed here thousands of years ago.

Having read their stories and the cited proof, you the reader can judge for yourself whether such claims are right or wrong.

The Chronos Stone is thought to be the work of ancient Caucasians who lived in New Zealand more than 1,000 years before the coming of the Māori. Found in Northland it is a sundial, calendar stone and star position calculator of unique ancient design. Picture © Noel Hilliam.

An artist's impression of a huge, nine-masted Chinese junk such as those built in the 1400s when China explored the world. Does the wreckage of such a ship still lie buried in the sands of the Kaipara coast? Picture courtesy of Noel Hilliam.

Introduction

A plea to Māori people

This book is not against Māori people, nor written to stir up animosity against them? That is not its purpose. Granted, some hard to swallow things are said about Māori slaughter of the earlier peoples of New Zealand and of themselves. But no more than Māori people themselves admit is true.

Actually, the author has a strong affection for Māori people. He loves their happy humour, their friendliness, resilience, their strong family and community spirit and their excellence in art, music and even politics. For his money Māori Television often provides better viewing than its European New Zealand counterpart and he appreciates their penchant for melodic songs where the words can be heard without screaming and shouting. It puts them way ahead of the raucous offerings more commonly available.

Like many New Zealand immigrants of European origin I formed strong friendships with Māori people; I was married to a lady of Ngati Porou extraction for many years and our two children move in both the Māori and general New Zealand cultures. They are a living embodiment of the phrase, *He iwi tahi tātou*, meaning 'We are now one people'. And to my mind Māori people need and should be given all the help they can get in terms of regional development in such depressed areas as Northland. This, so that alongside and with other New Zealanders, they can prosper.

He iwi tahi tatou was British representative William Hobson's summing up of what was achieved at the signing of the Treaty of Waitangi in 1840. Two peoples became one, albeit not without difficulty and disagreement in the decades that followed. Yet today it is noticeable that while there is pressure from other New Zealanders to sunder the British connection by erasing the Union Jack from the flag and turning New Zealand into a republic, these proposals are resolutely resisted by Māori. It seems they value connection to the Crown more strongly than many of the rest of us.

Fact is there is no way New Zealand would be New Zealand without her Māori people. Yet this book pleads for recognition that New Zealand also cannot be New Zealand unless the pre-Māori peoples who first settled this country are acknowledged in history and their descendants honoured as still living among us. Ignored and unrepresented as separate entities at the signing of the Treaty in 1840, the Waitaha and Patupaiarehe people have yet to be acknowledged for who they are, let alone formally made part of the 'one people' agreement. Our history needs rewriting to include them.

Admittedly, this book takes issue with Māori when they brush aside the legitimate claims of the Patupaiarehe and Waitaha to their ancestral land, their status as separate peoples and their rightful place in history. It may be politically incorrect, but it is not racist, to maintain on the solid facts of proven history, that the Māori people were not the first to settle this land; that they are not the true *tangata whenua* (original people of the soil). As much as Europeans must atone for injustices in wrongly taking Māori land, Māori themselves must also put right the terrible wrongs they have done to the first inhabitants of New Zealand.

Thankfully, the terrible cannibalism and genocidal slaughter of the 1700s and 1800s, which came close to exterminating the original peoples of New Zealand at the hands of the Māori, is long past. Those that perpetrated those dark deeds are long dead and today Māori are a peaceful, forward-looking people rightfully aspiring to a better life as New Zealanders.

The bloody past must be forgiven but not forgotten, for Māori are themselves descended from both sides in the conflict. The history of the Patupaiarehe and Waitaha peoples is also their history because through marriage, forced or otherwise, the blood of these two true *tangata whenua* peoples flows in some Māori veins too. Māori come then, at least in some small part, from the gene pool of the ancient

Caucasians who pioneered settlement in this land and, consequently, they should be proud of the Waitaha and Patupaiarehe achievements as part of their history.

Frankly, it is a pity they have joined with New Zealand academics, archaeologists and historians in denying their own heritage. Māori folklore has largely dismissed the Patupaiarehe as 'fairies', unreal people, while the late New Zealand historian Michael King[1] derided the Waitaha people's account of their arrival in the sixth century AD as 'mere myth' and 'delusion'. He claimed there was 'not a skerrick of evidence – linguistic, artifactual, genetic, no datable carbon or pollen remains; nothing – that the story had any basis in fact'.

Well, that was how he saw it in 2003. Since then much has changed. DNA has conclusively proved that Patupaiarehe descendant Monica Matamua has a predominance of Mediterranean genes, Professor Richard Holdaway has found rat bones beneath volcanic ash proving that the rat, *rattus exulans*, was brought to New Zealand by humans some 2,000 years ago, huge monolithic remains and stone carvings have come to light and a welter of Māori tradition has emerged affirming the ancient presence of both Patupaiarehe and Waitaha people, all of which was ignored by King.

Today the truth must be recognised that we New Zealanders, though people from many lands, are all one in terms of the overriding principle of the Treaty of Waitangi. Fact is that every New Zealander is a migrant or a descendant of migrants. Even the first people to populate this land, most likely Phoenicians were migrants – that is they came from somewhere else, just as we latecomer Europeans did. It is possible that, aside from the Phoenicians and their near cousins, the Waitaha, other ancient Celts, Greeks, Egyptians and even Chinese people, also reached here and settled long before the birth of Christ.

1 Michael King The Penguin History of New Zealand, Penguin Book NZ Ltd, 2003

The Māori people themselves proudly hold that they too came from somewhere else, a far distant homeland, buried in the mists of time and mythology, called *Hawaiki*. But they were not the first to reach these shores and they should not falsely claim *tangata whenua* status by denying recognition to the people they largely, but not entirely, replaced.

The Patupaiarehe and Waitaha are immigrants too but it is notable they are not seeking special benefits as a separate people – only recognition of their true place in history, restoration of some of their ancestral lands and acknowledgement of the legacy of peace they have left to all peoples of this land.

Sadly, political correctness has so distorted this country's pre-history that racially divisive laws are invoked to give special historical recognition and benefits to one sector of the population while denying them to others. When practiced in South Africa this principle was known as *apartheid*.

The bottom line is that Māori have declared themselves the tangata whenua (original people of the land) when clearly they were not and are not. Worse still laws have been passed that forbid open, honest examination of important burial remains and very old artifacts that challenge the Māori claims.

Such laws are undeniably racist, for when it comes to the finding and preservation of artifacts, relics from this country's ancient past, only one race of people decides what should happen to them – the Māori. The rest of us are excluded.

However, it is surely well past time for such differences to be put aside, for Māori to recognise themselves as New Zealanders, immigrants like the rest of us, and for them to cease denying that others were here before them.

Is this an altar stone or what remains of an old sundial and star calendar? Shipwreck explorer Noel Hilliam (pictured) found this important artifact in the 'stone city' ruins of New Zealand's Waipoua Forest. Picture © Noel Hilliam.

Chapter 1

The place of peace

Does New Zealand's ancient past matter? Does this country's prehistory have a precious legacy we have ignored? Did a now all but forgotten people once achieve here, at the ends of the earth, a feat unequalled anywhere else in the world? The answer to all these questions is a resounding yes. Because forgotten in the halls of science, omitted from conventional history, an inspiring human triumph was achieved in this land that towers far above all other efforts by people

No other country can claim such a crowning success. No other people have come anywhere near it. This achievement is unique to this, our far flung country. Because of its isolation, New Zealand as we now call it, was arguably the last significant land mass on earth, except for Antarctica perhaps, to be found and lived in by people. And this was a blessing because the people who voyaged far across different oceans to reach these islands came with a determination.

Their mission was to live as no other peoples on earth lived. To live in peace, forgiving and not taking revenge. They succeeded, this country's isolation helping, in that for many centuries no invaders disrupted their sacred purpose. Their settlement of these two large islands therefore enshrines a mystery that all the world must learn about because, now more than ever, mankind must learn to live at peace.

This secret is that long ago here, in the land once known as *Te Wai Pounamu, Nukuroa*, and *Te Ika a Maui*, or even earlier as 'The Far Off Land', people of various races lived at peace. Not just for a few years before inevitably fighting broke out and war followed, as it has everywhere else on the globe, but for many centuries. Here in New Zealand the first settlers lived, traded and co-operated in peace from one end of the country to the other, for an astounding period of no less than 1300 years without conflict.

This book has been written to recapture something of the message of these early pioneers, to explain who they were and who they still are. To tell the stories of their past, as passed on down the generations and voiced today through the lips of their descendants still living here now. To support where possible their account of this land's prehistory with solid artifacts and proven, scientific evidence.

Because stone buildings, ancient shipwrecks, rock carvings, skeletons, other artifacts and transferred plants really do bear testimony to the past achievements of a people of Northern Hemisphere, European origin who predate the coming of the Māori.

From whence did these brave voyagers come and why did they determine to 'learn the art of war no more'? Why did they leave the lands they were born in? How did they voyage more than half way round the world to reach this uninhabited land? Come to that how did they know it was here?

Beyond all this we need to know how they kept peace among themselves and what they believed that made them the peaceful people they were. For in several ways the first New Zealanders were unique. Among others hatred, bloodshed and killing were the common lot. None have lived in harmony, except, as the evidence shows, the now largely forgotten peoples who first formed the nation of New Zealand, then known as the 'Far Off Land'.

Actually, the true pre-history of these islands reaches far back in time. It predates not only latter day European settlers but also that of Māori and earlier Polynesian peoples. It even goes back beyond the landing of the also peaceful Waitaha people who came to these shores around 550AD. This country's real beginnings belong to a time centuries before the birth of Christ when a brave people seeking peace fled the war-torn Middle East and sailed half way round the world. They did so to find and found a land where no warriors lived, nor would live for over 1,000 years. And they called this land of two great islands, and the sea that surrounds them, *Te Wai Pounamu* (the waters of peace) or 'the waters of the peace stone'.

Break the word pounamu into its constituent parts, as cited in The Māori Dictionary, and we find: *pou* meaning a post, column or standard; *na* is a particle used in relative clauses; and *mu*, fascinatingly, is the Phoenician word for 'water'. The original name for New Zealand, *Pounamu*, may well have meant 'the pole that is from the waters'. And because of their practice of peace, *pounamu* also came to mean peace. Right down into the 1800s greenstone carvings were given by tribes as a seal or sign of peace.

The first New Zealanders knew a creator God who spoke to them through rocks and river, trees and birds, mountain and sea. They told time and seasons by the stars and tilled the ground with prayer to grow crops. In living at peace, they did the will of Him who said, 'Blessed are the peacemakers…'[2]

May his peace be with you as you read the story of the ancient peoples who first settled New Zealand as told by their descendants.

2 Matthew 5:9, Authorised King James version.

Now in her 80s Patupaiarehe descendant Monica Matamua still has the golden hair and green eyes of her ancestors. Today she is the leader of this country's remaining Patupaiarehe people.

Chapter 2

Monica's story

Surviving Patupaiarehe descendant Monica Matamua tells her people's story in her own words. Interspersed comments by the author are in italics.

I'm now 82 and I wonder how long I have to live before recognition and justice is achieved for my people, the Patupaiarehe. Nearly 10 years ago I began a claim process to regain ownership of the Taurewa block on the lower slopes of the volcanic plateau above Taumarunui.

This land was taken from my tribe, the Ngati Hotu, by the Crown for the National Park. Around 2,000 hectares was sold to the Crown by eight tribes of Tuwharetoa for the National Park farm. Only my people of Ngati Hinewai and Ngati Hotu never sold. Now the land is being farmed by Land Corp. But originally it was stolen from us by Tuwharetoa and sold to the Crown. I am told by the Office of Treaty Settlements it will be 2016 at the earliest before our land claim can be settled and meanwhile 20 of my family, the remaining descendants of the Ngati Hotu tribe, have died waiting for justice.

My married name is Matamua, my husband's surname, meaning the 'first born' and, importantly, I am not Māori. I am descended from that ancient people, the Patupaiarehe who came to New Zealand over 2,000 years ago. I was born into a family of 11 and two of us, my brother and I, were chosen to take up our people's fight to restore both our name and the land taken from us.

We Patupaiarehe are a happy people who do not hold grudges or seek *utu* (revenge) but we have been robbed of both our name and our land. It hurt us when the 100-ha block of our ancestral land at Kakahi that my father bought back from European owners in 1935 was lost to us through the devious workings of the Government's railways land confiscation legislation. The Roads Board took Kakahi then sold it to the settlers to generate funds to build the railways.

Our voices were not heard

Our names did not appear on the ownership lists, even though my ancestors were the true owners, having never left the land. Nor were we as an ancient people wiped out on our lands which we held at Taurewa, Kakahi, Owhango, Kaitieke, Tunanui, Taumarunui, Raurimu, National Park and other places. The Crown dealt only with what they called the 'Waka Fleet' people, whereas we now know there was no such thing as the Māori 'Great Fleet'. But they saw this as the easiest way forward to take land they wanted.

The Te Turu Whenua Act of 1993 empowered the Native Land Court to make land decisions without notifying the owners, and that's just what they did. So the *tupuna* (ancestral family) block we once owned and had occupied for centuries was placed into a trust amalgamation. This happened even though not one owner signed any legal document. Review of this court's decisions is under way and the changes that could result could be a real blessing for the Ngati Hotu and Ngati Hinewai people. Return of our land would greatly benefit my people and give us hope for a better future. Our aim is to progress our visions for the future and to leave the land in a better state than we found it.

Despite most owners of that block being absent from the hearing, Land Court Judge Sir Eddie Durie ruled the attendance of the few was enough for the land's fate to be decided. To date the official court attendance list stating just who they were has never been found. Because of this decision a trust was set up and even though we had legally partitioned our ancestral land site at Te Rena, which had been ours for many generations, it was included in the amalgamation. This took place even though our family had built a camper's lodge on the site so we could be self-sufficient and fund rebuilding of our *marae*.

The 'Promised Land': A glimpse of Te Rena and the banks of the Whanganui River with the camper's lodge in the background. A Māori Land Court judge has ruled that the land should be returned to Monica and her people but when this book went to print the ruling had yet to take effect.

The hostel on the Te Rena lot was on land we held on to for many centuries in fear of our lives, risking savage attacks from those who wanted to exterminate us. We stood on that land for some 600 years at least. Te Rena is, or was, the Ngati Hotu *Papakainga* (our last standing place). Here as late as 1800 still stood our ancestral Whakahou Marae constructed underground so as not to be obvious to our enemies. It was rebuilt in timber in 1908 when the timber mills arrived but was later destroyed by an arson attack in 1967.

Years ago when I applied to the trustees to rebuild our marae I didn't know that our grandmother Te Oti MihiTerina legally owned the land. Despite that, in 1991 the trustees let us move on to my grandmother's land and in 1996 we were given the right to occupy. My late husband Ike (Iki Whenua) was a skilled carpenter and builder and in 1998 built the two-storey house which we ran as the Whakahou Campers' Lodge.

Ike drained land for a camp site and we and visiting students and campers planted many native and exotic trees, turning what was bare land into a garden paradise. The idea was to create income to rebuild the marae, employ hapu members and provide quality accommodation at an affordable price.

Forced off the land we owned

All went well for a while and we took out an $80,000 mortgage to extend the lodge. Then in 2002 trouble struck. New trustees took over and ordered us off the land. In 2004 the trust, or someone with a key to the gate, seized all the assets and put the lodge up for sale or removal.

However, it didn't sell. Baches had been built on the land by two of my grandchildren for their families. One was dumped and the other stolen. The children's playground gifted by the Waikato Trust disappeared and the gardens and orchard were bulldozed flat. We were even told we could not visit our *urupa* (cemetery) where many generations of our people are buried. But we breached an injunction to bury Ike and my son Henry there and continue to tend their graves and those of others of my family.

Today cattle still graze the whole campsite and trample the most ancient burial grounds. The trustees later fenced a small part of the Whakahou *Urupa* (cemetery) but have still left 30 graves open to grazing. Even to this day the land is still leased for grazing. Graves are everywhere, just as they are on Taupiri, Tainui's burial mountain. That mountain is sacred to Tainui and you wouldn't want to farm that. Nor should anyone be able to farm our people's sacred burial place.

Our family has spent over $40,000 in lawyer's fees and have been to court six times to get this huge injustice redressed but to date without success. It broke Ike's heart; he was still talking about our dreams of rebuilding Te Rena, when he died from asbestosis of the lungs. That disease came from working with Blue Asbestos which killed many builders during Ike's time. No one knew then how toxic it was. It took 40 years for the symptoms to appear.

Historically, my people held many other blocks of land stretching out from Taumarunui including Kakahi, Raurimu, Retaruke and Kaitieke and the Maungakeke Pa. All these were occupied by Ngati Hotu under our chiefs Te Kakahi, Te Piki Te Pikikotuku, Te Kaaka and others before we were driven off. On our claim for Taurewa, in 2006 it was set aside when in December 2014 the Crown recognised Tuwharetoa's claim to the land. It was then included it in the Tuwharetoa A.I.P (Agreement in Principle), which allows Tuwharetoa to buy back land they claim as theirs, although actually we were and are the real owners.

Our two Patupaiarehe tribes, Ngati Hotu and Ngati Hinewai object strongly to this move. After all we are landless today, we have no *marae*, nothing. What's more today Tuwharetoa hold the Taurewa Forest for the *hapu* Ngati Hikairo when much of it rightfully belongs to us. Actually they were our lands for hundreds of years but we were disinherited by false evidence given by our enemies, the Tuwharetoa, to the effect that we were extinct. It's a terrible thing to experience when at a *marae* hearing you are told to sit down and shut up, because you 'no longer exist'.

The most awful and bloody details of our 'extermination' as Patupaiarehe at the hands of Tuwharetoa were given in evidence by their witnesses at the Waitangi Tribunal hearings held at Otukoa Marae, Lake Rotoaira. The Tuwharetoa witnesses set out to deliberately attack and discredit Ngati Hotu but today they have to live with their wrongs. After all they were only saying what they had been told to say. The massacre evidence was sickening to listen to.

To see this doesn't happen again I've picked up the battle for our recognition as a tribe and as Patupaiarehe people from where my mother Tangi left it and our hopes now rest on re-claiming the last tract of our ancestral land, at Te Rena and the Taurewa 2,000 hectare block at Ruapehu.

If we succeed we can proceed with our own innovative plans for a mountain resort with multiple activities similar to those at Queenstown. We hope to offer tourist attractions year-round through what we have named the 'Mountain to the Sea Iwi Project'.

The true tangata whenua

This claim is for land we once held around Mount Ruapehu, Taurewa plus the Waiu Turoa Ski field side of Ruapehu renamed Rangipo 8. While Te Ururoa Flavell, the Māori First MP and party leader has yet to study both our claim and the Ngati Hotu project proposal, we hope he will support them both as they fit into his vision for Māori Iwi Family Developments under the new Te Ture Whenua Act.

To stand up for our claim, I recently put our case direct to the present Tuwharetoa chief, Tumu Te Heuheu himself, but I didn't get far. So instead I am pursuing our tribal land claim through our tribal relatives at Whanganui also descended from my great, great grandfather Piki Te Pikikotuku.

I know that taking our land happened many years ago. However,

Monica with the obelisk erected to record the burial of several family members whose graves and headstones were destroyed and flattened in a vandalistic attack on this sacred Patupaiarehe burial ground.

the way Tuwharetoa recounted the bloody details again in 2014 was shameful and upset many people. You might ask why anyone should care about it now. Could I suggest that, apart from righting the wrongs done to an oppressed and suppressed people now considered 'extinct' – although we aren't – the reason is that justice should be given us in the interests of true history? We the Patupaiarehe are the true *tangata whenua*, the original people of this land. Not only the Ngati Hotu, but also the other remnants of this once great people, form an important part of every New Zealander's heritage, be they Māori, otherwise Polynesian, European or from other countries and races.

We can only find unity by treating with respect, equality and justice all peoples who live here or who call New Zealand home. And a good first step towards achieving that would be to recognise us as the descendants of the Patupaiarehe, the first settlers of New Zealand, for who we really are, and to stop suggesting that we are extinct or were just 'fairies', figments of Māori imagination.

Persia was our ancient home

We were in this land here long before the Waitaha people. There were many sub tribes of the Patupaiarehe and Turehu but for many centuries we all lived in peace. And that continued after Waitaha arrived, several hundred years after our landing, and they and we still have a lot of respect for each other. In the South Island the Waitaha were badly treated by the Crown and like us lost their lands.

We were peaceful folk. Going back for thousands of years, as far as can be remembered, we lived in peace. The history I received from my mother and grandmother says that long ago we once lived on an island offshore from what is now Iran. And because wars broke out there we left, fleeing for our survival.

I am glad we did, because pursuing peace and avoiding war became the principle we lived by for over 2,000 years – until finally Tuwharetoa forced us to fight to avoid extinction.

My Mum told me that originally we, as a people, were part of Egypt when it was still all one, before that nation's empire was broken up. We kept moving to avoid war. For a time we were in Persia, then in the island off Iran. This is confirmed because the test of my DNA shows I have strong Mediterranean ancestry – it's 28 per cent of my genetic make-up.

Our history says that our original home was in the ancient Persian Empire and that originally we came from an island in the Persian Gulf, offshore from present day Iran.

Rebellion broke out because of the greed of the then Persian emperor, named King Assis. He built the Wailing Wall at the temple in Jerusalem for his people.

We left this homeland when our people were overrun and we could no longer fight the enemy. In the break-up of that empire there were terrible wars and we took to our ships and fled for survival. This occurred when Esther of the Bible reigned as the Queen consort of the Persian emperor.

Author's note:

The Patupaiarehe history Monica recounts is of great interest. The island 'off the coast of present day Iran' may have been Bahrain, or, as it was known 2,500 years ago, Tylos. According to the World Atlas *the ancient island of Bahrain was an important trading centre in existence way before Roman times. The Achaemenian dynasty incorporated Bahrain into the Persian Empire in the 6th century BC, and the island remained under their ruling until the 3rd century when the Parthians took control.*

Bahrain was the key Persian Gulf entrepot for those avid merchant adventurers, the Phoenicians. Farmers, traders, architects, masons, metal workers and, above all brilliant seafarers, these people were the 'Canaanites' of the Old Testament. They occupied what is now Lebanon from ancient times and under King Hiram supplied the hewn stones, timber and builders for the King Solomon's temple. They sailed to Egypt, linked both eastern and western Greece within the

Mediterranean and are believed to have traded with India, and even Indonesia.

According to Michael Streeter[3] *they sailed out from their Persian Gulf homeland and the strategic coastal strip they occupied in present day Lebanon and Syria to trade with the then entire known world. He writes:*

> *They gave the Greeks, and thus modern western civilisation, the alphabet, yet few of their writings have survived.*

Streeter reports that 21st century DNA testing of peoples around the Mediterranean where Phoenicians had settled found little genetic difference between the Canaanites of scripture, the Phoenicians of antiquity and modern Lebanese people. Their DNA was also very similar to their neighbours in the Levant.

Culturally Phoenicians spoke the same language, had a common religion and linked their several city states, each ruled by its own king, co-operatively. Could it be this arrangement was the forerunner of the similar symbiotic co-dependency developed later among the different Patupaiarehe and Turehu settlements in New Zealand? They were the founders of Carthage in North Africa, traded with advanced flourishing cultures in Spain and Sardinia and even brought tin from Britain. Indian chronicles record they were prominent in the extensive trade developed between India, Egypt, China and the Mediterranean.

Wherever they settled the Phoenicians jealously sought to preserve their independence. Although they provided the bulk of the Persian Empire's war fleets, the Phoenician cities of Tyre and Sidon were among the first to rebel against Artaxerxes II, and Carthage's refusal to bow to the later might of Rome caused three Punic (Phoenician) wars.

Clash of the Titans

3 *The Mediterranean – Cradle of European Culture* (2006), Michael Streeter, New Holland, London.

But while they were profitable colonists and successful marine mercenaries for a while in the Mediterranean and Persian Gulf, eventually the clash of the Titans – Greece and Persia – destroyed them. Huge battles were fought as Persia sought to crush Greece. At Marathon the Persian army lost 6,000 men and the Greeks several hundred.

For Monica and her people the crunch may well have come at a decisive sea battle in Salamis Bay when Greeks trapped the vast Persian fleet, largely built and manned by the Phoenicians, then routed it. Many ships and crews were destroyed; others fled and maybe Monica's forebears were among the escapers. Defeat both on land and at sea caused the Persian king Artaxerxes to withdraw, abandoning his plan to conquer the whole Mediterranean and, significantly, it may well be this king who Monica names as the one under which the Persian Empire broke up and her people took ship to seek new life in a new land elsewhere.

It seems the 'King Assis' she refers to could be the Ahasuerus of the Book of Esther. Ahasuerus is Xerxes in Greek and both are derived from the Old Persian name Xsayarsa. Xerxes could well be pronounced Assis.

According to Wikipaedia 19th century Bible commentaries identified Ahasuerus with Xerxes I of Persia. As to building Jerusalem's walls it was Cyrus who, in response to his cup bearer Nehemiah's pleas to do so, initiated the temple re-construction (Ezra 4:3). And it was the Persian king Oarses (Ahasuerus) who stopped the build at the instigation of the 'people of the land' who 'troubled the Jews' (Ezra 4:6).

But it seems Monica's story has it right. For it was Artaxerxes II, king of Persia, who later commanded the walls at Jerusalem to be rebuilt.

And, according to Wikipaedia, an inscription from the time of this king records that 'he was also known as ***Arshu****, understood to be a shortening of the Babylonian form Achshiyarshu derived from the*

Persian Khshayarsha (Xerxes). The Greek historians Ctesias and Deinon noted that Artaxerxes was also called Arsicas or Oarses . And that is as near as you would want to get in pronunciation to 'Assis'. Agreed dating for the reign of Artaxerxes I is 456-358BC and in the reign of his son the break-up of the Persian Empire began when, as Monica says, he became 'too greedy'. Interestingly, he is identified by some ancient scholars as the Persian king Ahasuerus of the Bible's Esther story. Artaxerxes II is said to have had over 115 sons from 350 wives. He also is said to have loved a young eunuch named Tiridates, who died 'as he was emerging from childhood'. His death caused Artaxerxes enormous grief.

Much of Artaxerxes's wealth was spent on building projects. He restored the palace of Darius I at Susa and also the fortifications; including a strong redoubt at the southeast corner of the enclosure and gave Ecbatana a new apadana and sculptures. History records that such extravagance caused the Phoenicians at Sidon to revolt against Persian rule and this accords with Monica's statement that excessive

This silver coin of Persian King Artaxerxes II shows the bearded monarch wearing his crown and on the reverse side holding his sceptre before a lighted altar. Picture courtesy of www.forumancientcoins.com

greed caused vassal states to rebel against Persia, precipitating the empire's break up which began with losing Egypt in Artaxerxes II's reign.

In 343BC Artaxerxes III destroyed Sidon, the vassal Phoenician city state at Sidon (the Tyre and Sidon of the Bible) and invaded Egypt. However, the rot could not be stopped and nine years later in 334BC Alexander the Great defeated the Persian army in the reign of Darius Codomannus at the Dardanelles.

All this lends great credence to Monica's version of events from her people's history and, to my mind at least, strongly suggests that the Patupaiarehe have their origins in Phoenicia, the land in which Tyre formed an important strategic island in ancient times. If this is so it would explain a great deal about the capabilities and character of her people. Importantly, the Phoenicians played a crucial maritime role in the ancient Mediterranean world. Their merchant fleets traded throughout the then known world; they were ship builders and provided the ships, crew and technical skills for the Persian Navy.

Further evidence for ancient Phoenician presence in New Zealand is presented in Ross Wiseman's book, New Zealand's Hidden Past. It includes an ancient, deeply etched rock carving of the mast and spars of a sailing ship said to date back to 300BC. The carving, with others, was discovered after a layer of volcanic deposit (stemming from the 232AD Taupo eruption) on Mount Tauhora was dislodged by a rock slide, laying bare the incisions in the hard ignimbrite rock beneath. Wiseman arrived at his date of 300BC for these important findings by calculating the weathering of similar rock not covered by tephra.

Monica's story resumes:

When they were overwhelmed in the fighting, those who became my ancestors had to flee for their lives. They did so in ships, some having to leave their families behind. These ships, with crews and passengers made up of several Middle Eastern and European peoples, sailed to other parts of the world. From what my mother told me my particular ancestors were glad they left the Mediterranean because eventually we came to a far better place – the land that in our ancient tongue was called the Far Off Land. Today we call it New Zealand.

A people from the Mediterranean

Above all things my people, the ancient Patupaiarehe, prized peace. On our way down to this, the other side of the world, we stopped off often. But always, almost everywhere there was war or the threat of war sooner or later. Rather than fight, we moved on. Among the countries we passed through were Egypt, India and Borneo. We would have also sailed to Carthage that great Phoenician colony established in North Africa. But always we sailed on searching for a land where we could find true peace.

I believe our people knew where they were going because they had maps to guide them. The Phoenicians as merchants traded with India and when my people reached there they would have learned from the Indian seafarers of the lands that lay beyond in the southern half of the world. From what has been handed down it seems we came to live in Borneo for years before again moving on. Then again we have a strong tradition that some of our people were also in Peru. Yes, back then we knew like Eratosthenes that the earth was round and we had the ancient maps that depicted lands in that great southern ocean, the Pacific. We hoped that they would be lands free of war.

On the ships they sailed in all I know is they were substantial, capable of carrying a hundred or more people. We did not land in New Zealand in a single ship but in ships. And I was told that later at least one ship sailed back to our homeland in the Middle East and then returned to New Zealand, leaving some of our people behind.

Long after reaching this land another contingent of peace-loving Mediterranean people joined us here in New Zealand. They were the Waitaha, who were driven out of Peru when they were overrun by Maya or Inca warriors. A temple painting in Yucatan shows these attackers sacrificing white Europeans who may have been my

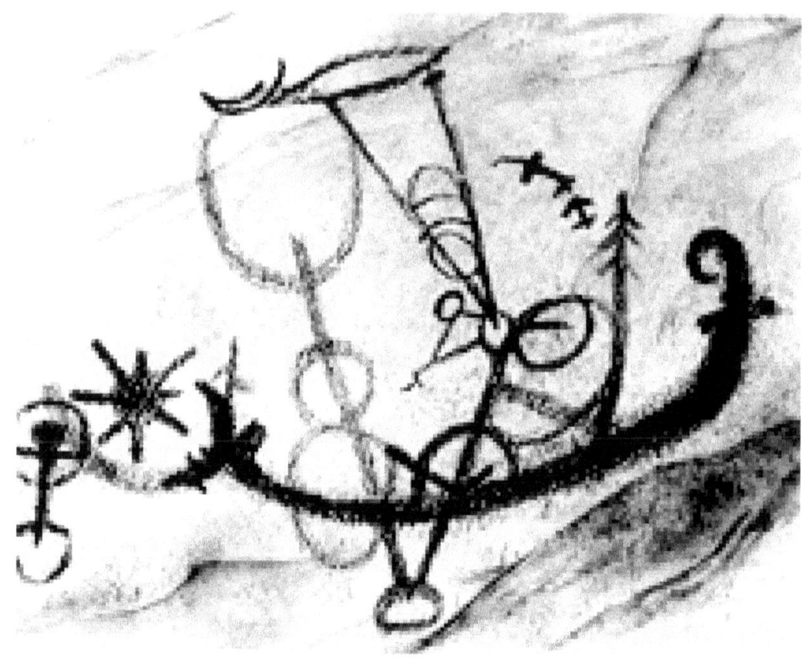

Diagramatic drawing of a ship of the 232BC expedition navigated by Maui, as found on the walls the Cave of the Navigators at McCluer Bay, West Irian.

ancestors, and those of the Waitaha, and otherwise driving them out.

The mural also shows some white people being drowned and others escaping on ships. My DNA shows my ancestry is derived from both the Mediterranean and Peru. My DNA line goes to America twice, so ancient relatives of ours must have lived there for long periods.

My people's history says that long after we had settled in New Zealand the Waitaha fled Peru where they had lived for centuries when attackers broke the peace they had maintained until then.

These people were white Caucasian like us. They sailed to Easter Island, then came down through the Pacific island, inter-marrying with Polynesians on the way, to eventually reach New Zealand as the Waitaha several hundred years after our arrival.

Some writers have suggested that we Patupaiarehe are just Polynesians and came by canoe. Others that we originated from India. But my DNA test proved what we have believed all along, that we were farming, stone building, trading and seafaring people from the Mediterranean.

I believe what I have been told that my people were the first to arrive and that they came in ships. And what a wonderful paradise they found here in New Zealand!

The sea, rivers and lakes teemed with fish, the land was covered with forest and bush and birds abounded everywhere, ample to feed everybody. It was a green and fertile land and, best of all, there was no one here to fight us.

We brought plants and food with us. On board there were marrows, vegetables, wheat, rice and cotton for planting. Wild wheat stills grows in New Zealand today as evidence of this. Later the Waitaha people, to whom we are related, brought from South America the kumara and maize (corn) with the purple, pink and yellow potatoes, now known as 'Māori potatoes' which are still here in New Zealand today. We also brought the karaka tree from Easter Island to New Zealand.

And possibly some animals came with us too. The pukeko, once the sacred bird of Egypt came to New Zealand aboard our ships. Maybe the big bush rat, the *kiore*, also came with us. *Kiore* have died out now but once they were a wonderful food, particularly if you were living inland. About half the size of a big cat they provided succulent meat, feeding as they did only on bush tucker.

Author's notes:

Did you notice, that in sharp contrast to Māori migration legends, which are extremely vague on details, Monica's account of her people's origin in the Middle East cites the real names and places of history? Hers is a credible account and there is supportive evidence for at least two assertions it features:

Maize. See chapter, 'Corn's amaizing story', chapter 26.

Evidence written in stone: *An important background to Monica's story is found in* To The Ends Of The Earth *by Max Hill. Contributor Gary Cook records how Harvard Professor New Zealander Barry Fell, an expert in ancient languages and texts, deciphered 'graffiti' which was visible beneath layers of calcite on the walls of a limestone cave in McCluer Bay, West Irian Jaya.*

Fell's translation, published in 1974, set a cat among the pigeons for modern historians of Polynesia. For the petroglyphs (writings on rock) record a brave, round-the-world voyage launched by Greek-Egyptian Pharaoh Ptolemy III in 232BC, over 1500 years before the accepted date for human arrival in New Zealand. Gary Cook asserted this fleet reached New Zealand nearly 2,300 years ago and planted a settlement of Greek, Egyptian, Libyan and Celtic peoples here before sailing on through the Pacific to South America.

These white-skinned, Northern Hemisphere voyagers left cave inscriptions at Pitcairn Island and in a cave in Santiago, Chile a formal declaration was incised, claiming 'this great southern land' in the name of the Pharaoh. The inscription was discovered only in the 19th century.

According to Fell, the fleet, commanded by Rata, Admiral of Egypt's Libyan fleet and directed by the navigator Maui, set sail to find gold, new lands, and to prove the theory of that great scholar, Eratosthenes, that the earth was round. However, unable to sail past the South and North American continents (there was no Panama Canal then), these hardy mariners could not complete the circumnavigation. While some voyagers settled in South America, at least one ship, it is believed, retraced the route and returned to Egypt.

Where Monica's people fit in

Author Hill maintains these settlers were the 'white race' that built many of Peru and Mexico's pyramids and stone temples. Centuries later they were driven out by the Maya, as evidenced by

Yucatan temple murals showing brown-skinned, head-dressed warriors ritually slaying whites on altars, driving them out and depicting other whites departing by ship to sea.

George Connelly, the last Upoko Ariki (or paramount chief) of the Waitaha people, says his ancestors fled Peru to Easter Island, then sailed from one Pacific island to the next, finally reaching New Zealand around 550AD. They brought with them the staple foods of South America, the kumara and maize as well as the karaka tree from Easter Island. So where do Monica's people fit in this scenario? Answer: Most probably in all of it. There would have been Libyans, Celts and Phoenicians, both men and women, in the Rata-Maui expedition crews. Some 200 years after the expedition master map maker Claudius Ptolemy was drawing world maps in the round that included parts of the Australian and New Zealand coastline. Quite likely they were from charts drawn by ships returning to Egypt from this expedition.

Ptolemy's charts and others were stored in the Great Library of Alexandria and copied widely in the Middle Eastern and Mediterranean world. They would be available to Phoenicians in their principal home ports of Tyre in the Mediterranean and Bahrain in the Persian Gulf, Monica's most likely 'homeland'. Monica says that some ships her people came to New Zealand in returned to the 'homeland' and then sailed back yet again to the new land. It is even possible new ships were built in New Zealand to maintain this connection.

Furthermore, Northern Hemisphere voyagers to the far side of the world may well have reached New Zealand even in the centuries before the Rata-Maui 232AD voyage of discovery[4] *documented in Max Hill's book landed here.*

And while Libyans and people of many Middle Eastern races comprised the Rata-Maui crews, Phoenicians were predominant as ship builders, commanders and navigators in the Persian Navy.

---

4 Pages 45-56 *To The Ends Of The Earth* by Maxwell C Hill (2012), Ancient History Publications.

A Phoenician ship from before the time of Christ is depicted in this ancient stone carving.

'Other ranks', however, would be a motley meld of different races and cultures, having only this in common; that they were all part of the Persian Empire as it broke up.

As to the kiore, Rattus exulans, bones found beneath layers of volcanic ash have been dated by Prof. Richard Holdaway to indicate that ocean-faring adventurers reached New Zealand over 2,000 years ago, although he insists there is no evidence they stayed.

However, this book has been written to show there is abundant evidence that human beings lived here from prehistoric times onward. And among such evidence is the story Monica tells of her people's ancient past.

Monica's story continues:

We Patupaiarehe have been considered primitive by some because, after the Māori arrived, we lived simply in the hills and bush to escape slaughter. But actually we were a technically advanced people for our time. We were clever gardeners and agriculturalists and artisans in stone and wood. However, in New Zealand, rather than create large plantations or fields of crops, we learned to plant in patches in the bush where our staple foods would grow almost naturally. And we cultivated many existing native plants too.

Very different to the Māori

Although our history differs in parts from that of the Waitaha people we found they held the same values we do. We traded with each other and knew of no hatred or war. We lived in peace and cooperation with them for hundreds of years.'

As our ancestors grew in numbers they settled throughout these islands of New Zealand and as different sub-tribes of branches of our people they took many names but collectively we were known, and still should be recognised as, Patupaiarehe, or Turehu, the fair-skinned or white ones. Another generic name for our race is *Urekehu*. That term also means the white-skinned, fair-haired peoples.

We were and still are a people of European and Mediterranean descent. We were here long before the first Polynesian set foot on these shores which makes us the true *tangata whenua* (people of the land). If it's offensive to Māori to learn that a white race were the founder settlers of New Zealand, well that's just too bad, because it's the truth. We are a very different people to the Māori. We spoke another language, did not tattoo our faces and we came on ships, not canoes, bringing with us with a heritage as skilled farmers and seafarers.

We believed in a creator God of peace, not a dark deity of war and cannibalism. To us killing and eating the flesh of others was wicked and cannibalism which, at its worst included *kai pirau* (eating dead, rotting bodies), was utterly abhorrent. Among us only women wore the *moko* chin tattoo with black lips and, a tattoo triangle below each eye, an adornment still in existence in some parts of the Mediterranean.

I've been told that, according to Professor Barry Fell, the Harvard expert in deciphering ancient rock inscriptions, the first language used in New Zealand was a mixture of ancient Libyan and Egyptian. Prof. Fell found written examples inscribed in rock, such as the Tattoed Rocks at Raglan, and said it was an old Mauryan or Libyan script he termed 'ancient Māori' or Hebrew.

Actually, until recently a close relative of mine still spoke the old Patupaiarehe language. Or rather he sang it, because that is how my people used to communicate. Sadly because of illness he can no longer do so. While it is true the old language has connections with Māori, which we believe was in part derived from it, there are many different words in it.

All this fits in with the story of my people as handed down to me. It explains why I and my family have the curved 'Mediterranean' nose and a white, Caucasian complexion. It's the hallmark of the *Urekehu* people called by Māori the white-skinned or 'fairy people' of the mountains. It's true there is also Polynesian or Māori blood in me. After all my grandfather was a descendant of Tuwharetoa and Ngati Maru and so his genetic inheritance has passed down through my mother, Tangi Maria Karauti.

My grandmother, Te Oti Mihi Terina was from the Pikiao-Rotoiti people, and she was a Patupaiarehe descendant through and through. Because my mother told me our people go back for 74 generations in this land I was determined to prove that we, as the original Patupaiarehe, had ancient links to the land and so I took the *National Geographic* DNA Ancestry Project test.

Author's note:

If one takes 30 as an average generation, since Monica's people were and still are notably long-lived, then 74 x 30 = 2220, placing their likely arrival in New Zealand at 220BC.

Pictograph writing found on rocks at Raglan. According to epigraphic expert Professor Barry Fell the language is ancient Mauri (i.e Mediterranean in origin.)

This comes close to 232BC when, according to Professor Barry Fell's deciphering of calcite-covered rock inscriptions in an Iran Jaya cave, the Maui-Rata Greek-Egyptian exploration fleet[5] *reached Indonesia on its attempt to sail round the world and is thought to have come to New Zealand.*

Monica's story resumes:

I just wept when I received my DNA results because they prove beyond doubt I am not Polynesian, nor Māori. They also show the story of my people is true – that we came originally from the Middle East of European stock. This is nothing new.

Early New Zealand painters, such as G. F. Angas, depicted the blond or red hair, fair complexion and green eyes of my predecessors and the 20th century author James Cowan in his book, *The Māori:*

5 *To The Ends Of The Earth* by Max Hill.

Yesterday and Today, featured the picture of a girl with the caption: *'Urekehu girl, of the Urewera tribe at Mataatua (Ruatahuna). This is the ancient, fair-haired type, pure Māori'.* My late husband, Iki-Whenua Matamua (Ike), was of the Tuhoe people from Waikaremoana.

A DNA test proves my European origin

But proving we were and are a separate people from the Moriori and Māori, who came much later, has always been difficult. Especially when so-called scientific experts give evidence you are extinct before the Waitangi Tribunal. Thankfully, my DNA results show that my people are distinct and that they originated from the Mediterranean, Egypt and the Middle East, just as our oral history recounts.

Twenty eight per cent of my DNA make up is Mediterranean, while another 12 per cent is Northern European and another 20 per cent is South-East Asian. Only 18 per cent of my DNA is Oceanian, deriving from the people of Papua New Guinea and Melanesia whereas, this percentage is 91 per cent in a Papuan and very much higher than mine in Māori and Moriori profiles.

Importantly, the Mediterranean, Northern European, Sub-Saharan and South West Asian components of my ancestral DNA history show strong linkages to European peoples in the Neolithic expansion from the Middle East outwards. My DNA description notes that Europeans have mixed with South-West Asian peoples for thousands of years.

Author's note:

According to the National Geographic DNA analysis the highest frequency of Monica's Northern European component is found in people from the United Kingdom, Denmark, Finland , Russia and Germany, 'likely the signal of the earliest hunter-gatherer inhabitants of Europe ... the last to make the transition to agriculture as it moved in from the Middle East... about 8,000 years ago'.

Her Mediterranean DNA component is found in highest

frequencies among people in Southern Europe and the Levant.

Actually Monica's DNA contains only 20 per cent of the South-East component which makes up 57 per cent of the genetic structure of Polynesians. What's more 54 per cent of Monica's DNA structure is taken up by North-East Asian, Mediterranean, Sub-Saharan, South-West Asian and North European components, all of which are linked to either Europe, the Middle East or to both.

The test results also reveal an interesting timeline, pointing to a Neolithic (Stone Age) expansion of peoples from the Middle East and from Europe into Asia and beyond. And they follow an extensive trail of migrations around the globe, including Africa, Europe, China, India, South-East, Indonesia and South America. Likely while some of Monica's far distant ancestors took their ancient culture from the Middle East to Europe, others brought their advanced Stone Age civilisation, traces of which are found in New Zealand, the other way.

And while some of her forebears possibly sailed as a mixed crew of Libyans, Egyptians, Celts and Greeks with the Maui-Rata fleet to reach New Zealand, other peoples such as the Waitaha who arrived later may have travelled to South America first. People with Indian, Indonesian and Chinese genetic backgrounds may well have added to the mix.

But despite these genetic 'interventions' and the fact of Māori intermarriage into Monica's ancestral line, the predominant Caucasian genetic characteristics won through to make Monica truly the person she appears to be and knows that she is – a true daughter of the European-Mediterranean Patupaiarehe people who have lived in New Zealand for more than 2,200 years.

Did Māori originate in Melanesia?

The bottom line is that her genetic make-up is very, very different to that which the DNA researchers say is the typical profile of a Polynesian. To get a little more technical, Monica's genetic structure was extracted from her mitochondrial DNA, which in women is inherited solely from the mother. The smallest chromosome of mitochondrial DNA has coding for 37 genes containing approximately 16,600 base pairs.

And it was mitochondrial DNA that microbiologist Adele White of Victoria University, Wellington, used to trace Māori origins back to mainland Asia. Her supervisor Dr. Geoff Chambers, found an exact match between a variant Māori gene and that of people from Taiwan. However, study of the Y (male) chromosome of Māori revealed that it originated from Melanesia.

In Dr. Chambers' opinion this shows that Māori migrated from China to Taiwan, then to the Philippines, through the Pacific islands and eventually reached New Zealand. Importantly, however, another view holds that Māori reached New Zealand first aboard Chinese ships and interbred with the Moriori people they found already living here.

The strong Melanesian blood lines found in Māori came not by canoe from Micronesia and Melanesia, it is thought, but from impressed crew or slaves who escaped, or were dumped ashore sick, by the several Spanish, Portuguese, Dutch, French and perhaps even English, ships which visited New Zealand, mapped its waters and stayed ashore sometimes for months.

Forced pressing of crew, later to develop into 'black birding', in the Pacific, was a necessity for ships making the long voyage from Europe. On any voyage lasting over 60 days, scurvy set in, taking a deadly toll of crew, already reduced by accident or other disease. From the mid-1500s onwards the Spanish took hundreds of natives as virtual slaves from the Solomons, Papua New Guinea and islands such as Espiritu Santo.

They were then kept as ready crew replacements at the Spanish forward exploration base of Hao Atoll, where ships arriving from Europe could replenish their crews before voyaging on, sometimes to New Zealand. What's more, it is well recorded that in the heyday of European exploration of the South Pacific, Fijian and other islanders bought passages aboard passing sailing ships to travel to other islands and, it is believed, to New Zealand, paying for them in pigs and potatoes. Evidence of such transactions is amply recorded by Captain Cook and the New Zealand missionary Henry Williams.

It can clearly be seen that that the Māori have a strong genetic heritage from Taiwan and Melanesia, whereas Monica's people trace their roots mainly to the Mediterranean, Europe and South America. Elsewhere in this book these Chinese and Melanesian links are traced more fully. Meanwhile, let's note that if the Melanesian crewmen of visiting ships were allowed the sailors' customary shore leave for even only a few days in New Zealand, their amorous proclivities would have engendered enough contact with local women to produce a new race, a new breed of people in New Zealand, one shunned by existing inhabitants and exhibiting the savage warfare and cruelty of the lands from which they had come.

Furthermore, there is direct evidence of the Portuguese taking slaves from Melville Island, off Australia, as far back as the 1500s. Dutch and English explorers tried to colonise the island, dubbed Van Diemen's Land by the Dutch, but were driven off by the fierce Tiwi warriors.[6]

Monica's story resumes:

It's important to understand that after settling here we called ourselves Patupaiarehe or Turehu. Only after the coming of the Māori and their attacks on us did we call ourselves Ngati Hinewai or Ngati Hotu to appear more like the Māori tribes.

My mother told me we lived for many centuries in and around what is now the Whakatane area. My people were then well spread out, living in little settlements based on our farming of the bush and the land. We were there to witness 'Toi the Wood Eater' arrive. He was Polynesian and he and his fellow voyagers inter-married with us and together we became a numerous people, known to later incoming

6 Morris J. 1961, *An Outline Of The History Of The Tiwi*, Historical Society of the Northern Territory.

Māori as *Te Tini o Toi*, or 'the Multitude of Toi'.

We didn't know what war was

Later aggressive Māori people arrived from the North and pushed us off our lands. The truth handed down to me is there was no fighting among the different peoples living in New Zealand for many centuries. To the contrary we all lived peaceably and traded with one another until incoming Māori grew large in number and went on the war path against us, the original people, throughout the country.

We had lived at peace for so long. We did not know what war was. We had no weapons, nor did we know how to fight. There was no need for conflict because there was food aplenty for everybody and, until the Māori came, all the peoples were hard working and industrious. They built villages of thatched huts framed from timber cut from the forest, they planted gardens, grew kumara and caught fish and birds. Leaves and plants from the forest also formed a large part of their diet.

But the people who became Tuwharetoa shattered this busy, happy way of life forever. They were welcomed at first by my Patupaiarehe predecessors, who gave them food and shelter to help them settle. But it soon became clear that the newcomers were not inclined to sow and reap and live off the forest as we did. Nor did they want to build their own settlements. It was easier for them to use threats and bullying to take over our villages and our well established gardens.

Such encroachment was achieved by various means. Where negotiation and intermarriage failed, attack and forcible seizure were resorted to. The sad thing is they did not really need to attack my people. There was plenty of land available elsewhere, unoccupied by anyone else. They could have simply lived there. But rather than do the hard work of establishing their own dwelling places, they preferred to take over our ready-made villages.

This they did by a campaign of intimidation at first. Then

they attacked us. But they were never content with the land they took. They resorted to threats and eventually to outright violence. The intruders forced us step by step to move out from our lands by the sea around what is now Whakatane. Try as we would to reach peaceful agreements we found we couldn't live near or alongside them. They were belligerent, trouble-making, violent people.

Finding themselves driven progressively out from the rich forests and easy living near the Bay of Plenty coast, my people still tried hard to appease the fierce warriors who had come among them, asking them to settle for the lands they had already taken and to leave us alone to live in peace in the villages we had built.

But in vain. We couldn't fight – we didn't know how – so we tried to make peace with them. The history handed down by my mother tells how we tried hard to appease them. We gave way before them and gave them a village here and more land there and hoped this would bring peace. But it didn't. Always they came back for more, and pressed us further. And when we refused to give more they attacked us.

My mother said that over 3,000 Patupaiarehe and Turehu in the land between Taupo and Ruapehu and Taurewa perished in the killing and cannibalism that raged there throughout the 1700s and into the 1800s. This killing and eating, often just for the sake of it, was still going on as late as 1835.

Thank God the European came when he did. If the British hadn't come here there would have been none of us left. Because the rapidly growing numbers of incoming Māori were not planting enough to feed themselves they put huge pressure on our natural resources.

That is why in the end they attacked us. You see we knew how to live off the bush. The trees and plants were our food, as were the birds and there were a lot of native fish. But as the Māori population increased they placed too much pressure on these natural resources in the lands they had taken.

Meanwhile, we Patupaiarehe were now calling ourselves Ngati

The peaceful ones. This ancestral fiigure, which adorns a Maniapoto marae in Tuamurunui, symbolically describes the Ngati Hotu, Patupaiarehe tribe as a people of peace. Thus the spear the figure holds is a fishing spear not a weapon of war.

Hotu and Ngati Hinewai after the two sisters who came here with Toi and married the Ngati Hotu chief Uenuku. We did this to give ourselves some standing as a tribe to be recognised by Māori. And because we now found our territory greatly reduced, my ancestors resorted to a practice that had stood them in good stead when food resources became scarce. This was to reduce the tribe's rate of reproduction.

Our people used a contraceptive from bush. They ate the flax root. It must have tasted bitter but it was better than producing more children than we could feed. By contrast, Ngati Tuwharetoa and other Māori just multiplied and food became scarce. By now the wild birds, once so plentiful were now disappearing and the Māori were starving. So they turned on us and made us their larder. They chased us through the bush, bashed us to death then feasted on us like a pack of rats. Indeed, such an attack was described by the Tuwharetoa court witness to knock out our land claim.

Perhaps real hunger in lean seasons was an early driving force for attacks upon us but my people soon realised they had become the prey in what for Tuwharetoa had become a blood sport. They were attacking us and eating us for the love of doing it and when some of us decided in return to eat them on the one occasion we defeated them – well that was just as bad. No doubt they saw us not as human beings but just another animal food source.

To escape this grim fate my ancestors eventually fled the gentler valleys below and moved up to the higher slopes of Mount Ruapehu. But even then the attacks kept coming. Earlier we had been gradually driven away from the Whakatane plains and eventually settled around Lake Taupo. Here we joined other ancient peoples such as the Waitaha, who at that time were still living there[7]. We all lived in peace and shared the food and other resources together and even today still love each other.

---

7 Ironically, not long ago New Zealand schools taught that before the coming of the Māori a peaceful people called the Moriori already lived here and because they were the original inhabitants Māori had no claim to being *tangata whenua*, the first people of New Zealand.

Several tribes of the indigenous first peoples of New Zealand lived there and co-operated together for many years, but not the Māori. They never fitted in.

So tolerant and accepting of one another were the peoples then that together the different tribes were Taupo Nui Atea or 'The Big Universe of Taupo', because there were so many of us from different sub tribes.

But with the coming of Tuwharetoa, who attacked and destroyed most of us to get their hands on the land, the region became Taupo Nui Atia, meaning 'The Big Taupo We Seized"; Atia means to seize in Samoan or to 'break' in Cook Island Māori. So from being a region of peace with room for everybody it became the land seized by Tuwharetoa.

It went from bad to worse. We, as the tribe Ngati Hotu now, were so frequently attacked and hunted down by Tuwharetoa we moved first to Taumarunui and then were driven up on to the slopes of Ruapehu and along the Whanganui river, finally to be massacred nearly to extinction first at the battle of Pukekaikiore (The Hill of the Meal of Rats), then again in the Battle of the Five Forts at Kakahi.

But at the end of it all a handful of us hung on at Te Rena. They were my great grandparents Mihi Terina and her husband Te Kaaka Tamakeno and their three daughters, Te Oti, Tamara and Kataraina.

Te Rena includes parts of Whangaipeke, especially Block 7B2, which for generations was farmed by our Ngati Hotu ancestors and today is worked by my brother Jim Ham and his sons and grandchildren. Others of our tribes escaped slaughter from the many attacks upon us over the years by fleeing far away. I learned this from my grandfather Mahinui Te Araroa Karauti. He told us that long ago after our people after our people were attacked by Ngati Maru of Taranaki at a place called Pipiriki near Patea, some of those who had escaped fled to what became our last homeland, our final refuge in the most rugged part of Taurewa on the slopes of Ruapehu.

Still others of our people moved to Kakahi across from Te

Artist's impression of Māori warriors preparing to fend off attackers to defend their pa. Photo courtesy of newstangata.whenua.com

Rena, 15 kilometres south of Taumarunui, or to the bush around the Waimarino River south of what is now Turangi. When things became more peaceful in the 1850s many Ngati Hotu came back to their main *marae*, which was called Takapuna, meaning 'Falling Spring'.

However, that *marae* was later destroyed, leaving us with no meeting house at Kakahi when the Crown forces took it over while trying to catch Te Kooti in 1868 after the battle of Te Porere. Part of this is in the 100 acres my Dad bought back in 1935.

Now we have no *marae* and that's very sad for all the Ngati Hotu and Hinewai descendants because, like any family, we need to have a *turangawaewae*, a place to stand where we can get together.

It's true we were nearly exterminated by Ngati Tuwharetoa, but the fact is we survived against all odds and we clung on to our land through thick and thin by staying on it. We've been nearly destroyed as a people then robbed of our land by the Crown.

You might think Ngati Tuwharetoa would be ashamed to admit

their savagery and the genocide they practiced upon us. But far from it. In the Waitangi Tribunal hearings they recited their massacres of us in great detail to show that we were extinct.

One Ngati Tuwharetoa witness, stated how his tribe had massacred Ngati Hotu and feasted on those slain. The place was the Mangatepopo Pa of Ngati Hotu called *Nga Hautepo* or 'The Gateway To Hell'.

I was present at the hearing to defend our claim to the Taurewa Block and had to listen as this person recited that Ngati Hotu had been 'completely wiped out", that 'they are no more'. Even the judge looked sick hearing how the stream ran red with blood for five days.

This witness said his warrior ancestors stacked up the bodies of our slain tupuna that they weren't able eat during the attack, and left them to rot. They came back again and again in later weeks to feast on the corpses.[8]

But contrary to Tuwharetoa's claim they had killed and 'eaten out' Ngati Hotu, some of us survived. The problem is there is no proper recognition of us as a people. Apparently, officially, we don't exist – that is why it is so hard to get back even a small part of the lands we lived on and cultivated for many centuries.

All along the way, on travels that have taken us more than half way round the world, we lived in peace and tried our best to get along in friendship with other peoples, but in one country after another we were forced to leave because of the threat of violence or outbreak of war.

It's sad that the Patupaiarehe path of peace came to an end in the 1800s some years after the cruel lesson of the Battle of the Five Forts in which thousands of my people were slain. You see any hope of peaceful co-existence ended when the Ngati Hotu from this battle, who had taken refuge in hills and caves along the Whanganui River, were then ruthlessly slaughtered by invading war parties from Māori

8 The practice of feasting on rotten human flesh is known as *kai pirau* and may be the reason some Māori to this day suffer an illness known as Mate Māori.

tribes which had seized lands from Whanganui and Taranaki.

This was the last straw. For us the worm turned and we abandoned peace to fight for our lives in one last stand. If we hadn't then truly we would not exist as a people today; there would be no Patupaiarehe descendants such as my family.

My people were desperate but just when they most needed it they found help from an unexpected quarter. One of the Tuwharetoa themselves took pity on us. He was appalled at his tribe's treatment of us and, leaving his own people, came to us, saying he had come to teach us to fight.

His name was Rereao, a man who like Maniapoto, saw we had a right to live and from that day no more battles took place. Rereao then returned to his people.

Under his guidance we made *mere* and *taiaha* (clubs and fighting staffs). Then he taught us how use them, and my ancestors practised in mock battles until they got the hang of fighting with them.

Ngati Hotu's 'last stand'

With this battle-hardened warrior as their tutor the last 800 survivors of Ngati Hotu regathered to defend the last of their land. They must have shivered on the cold and windy Ruapehu mountainside but kept themselves warm by frantically practicing manoeuvres. We had to become a skilled fighting force in our own right. It was that or die.

Thankfully when the great battle came Ngati Hotu did not stand alone. Ngati Apa and Ngati Tama, fellow Patupaiarehe supported us. After the battle 600 Ngati Hotu survivors left with them to find safety in the Manawatu district.

The fight took place amid the rocks and tussock grass of what is now the Turoa ski field in Mt Ruapehu's south-western slope. Tuwharetoa came on with more than a thousand warriors and my ancestors and our allies fielded almost as many. Our women stood behind the men to urge them on and themselves battled enemy stragglers.

They must have shivered on the cold and windy Ruapehu mountainside as but kept themselves warm by frantically practicing

Tuwharetoa threw themselves into the fray expecting us to break and run as on previous occasions. Instead we rose up to fight with our allies. Tuwharetoa reeled back and although they recovered soon found themselves in retreat and giving way before us.

It was the first time in their history that Tuwharetoa were defeated. After the battle they signed peace with us and that peace has held from that day until now.

Today the battle is not for our lives but to establish our identity and for us to be given our proper place in New Zealand history. It is also to fight for the return of at least some of our land.

Our *papakainga*, our ancestral land at Te Rena, should be given back to us so we, the last few of the true descendants of the Patupaiarehe Taurewa people, so we can rebuild a marae and have a place to live and garden. Let me be very clear about this. I am not and my people were not Māori or Polynesian.

We were and are very different. We are from a white race of ancestors and we're not ashamed to say so. If others don't like that or it causes them offence, well so be it.

We had no war dance, we had a dance of peace, of joy and celebration when kumara were harvested, or a good catch of fish landed. We also celebrated marriages with a dance.

We had our own language and still spoke it until recently. It was a different language to Māori and was usually sung. It's a language like no other that I have heard. Unfortunately, I can't speak it and those that can have passed on or become too ill to pass it on to others.

However, I can say it sounds like singing and is delivered in a continuous stream with no full stops and no pauses. Furthermore, the words are different.

In the Patupaiarehe language the word for eel is *kaa-ka*, which is also my great grandfather's first name. And an indication we lived closely and harmoniously with the Waitaha people is that in their language *kakaaka* also means eel, whereas in Māori the word for eel is *tuna*.

We had chiefs but our history says that Uenuku was the first leader, the 'Father' of the Patupaiarehe people. We take our name from him and like him we are white-skinned, red or fair haired and have the same green or blue eyes you find in Celtic and other European peoples to this day.

It is wrong for Māori tribes to claim Uenuku as their ancestor when he was ours and the first chief of the Patupaiarehe tribe to arrive here. In the 1600-1700AD period the Ngati Hotu chief Uenuku–Tope lived at Whakapapa on Mt. Ruapehu at the *marae* Te-Ringa-Kawai and Piritoa.

All this adds up to the fact we were and are a very different people, the first and original New Zealanders.

We should not be told that we don't exist every time we claim our land back or seek *wahi tapu* (sacred burial rights) for places where our ancestors fell in battle or were otherwise buried. Why, even at Te Rena our burial mount, Hena Hill – which to us is as sacred as Taupiri Mountain is to the Tainui people – access is denied to us.

We visit the graves of our dead in secret because our land was swallowed up in an amalgamation ordered by the Māori Land Court and we were evicted by trustees who neither acknowledged who we were nor our rights to be on our own land. Such denial still persists today in 2015 among the existing Taurewa Trustees. Their latest email re-states the principle of 'domination, conquer, rule' on which they hold our land.

We had our own beliefs. While some of my ancestors were absorbed into Māori tribes and others adopted Māori ways and customs, even tattooing themselves, this was only adopting the fashion of the day to fit in. And you find Māori people doing just the same thing during the European settlement. Look at the photographs of yesteryear and you find Māori wearing bowler hats and suits because they were the English fashion of the day. In the same way some of my forebears were tattooed while others refused to do so.

One important difference you can see to this day is that while Māori meeting houses are ornately carved ours are not. They are unadorned and much simpler. Actually, the Māori learned the design and art of building *whare* and *whare nui* (the meeting house) from us.

We constructed our *whare* (homes) in the same gabled roof design still employed in meeting houses to this day and the Māori learned how to do this from us. Our houses, thatched with Nikau palm, raupo and flax were built together in village clusters.

Ngati Hotu were a gardening people who planted crops in many places throughout the forests so that wherever they went, near or far, there would be ready-grown food for them to harvest. That is why large tracts of land were so important to us. We needed a large area to plant farm and forage so we could harvest and catch birds and rats continually on a sustainable basis.

My people ate the fruit and berries the birds fed on and harvested the *raureki* or *puha* (watercress) and the plentiful *pikopiko*, the fern shoots. To preserve them, potatoes and kumara were buried in sandy pumice soil, or placed in caves where the air could get at them.

From ancient times we had ground maize corn for bread and I believe that the maize or sweetcorn, along with the kumara and potatoes were brought from South America long ago by my ancestors. That connection is proved in my DNA test. The results show there is a strong link, at least twice, to people with the same inherited genetic make-up in South America.

The closest inherited genetic match to mine is that of people living in Hawaii and, secondarily, in Vietnam. But again, importantly, there is a low Polynesian contribution to my DNA.

As we have learned from those related to us still living there, some of the earliest Patupaiarehe to reach New Zealand sailed back to our Middle East homeland. While some of these stayed on the other side of the world, others of our people made return voyages to New Zealand, bringing other sources of foods with them. These included peach, plum, apple and quince trees.

This ancient wood totem pole once stood at Te Koutu Pa, Lake Okaitana, near Rotorua. It depicts Bes, the flat-hatted Egyptian dwarf god who protected hearth and home. Compare this New Zealand version with an Egyptian original on the next page.

Supportive of that is the fact the existing native population of New Zealand supplied peaches and other fruits to missionaries and other late European settlers and that the much sought after Louisa plum is indigenous to this country.

It may be also that peanuts were brought here long ago by the first arrivals here of my predecessors. Many generations of the Patupaiarehe grew them right around the Taupo region because they thrived in the pumice soils. My mother grew them on the lower slopes of Ruapehu at Te Rena.

From what I have been told I believe that, like the Waitaha, we fled from Peru on the outbreak of war against us. That does not preclude some of my ancestors having arrived in New Zealand much earlier on a more direct route from the Middle East.

Māori tribal lore well records they learned how to make fishing nets and to use them from my Patupaiarehe people and the finding and carving of *pounamu* (greenstone) originated with my people too.

We constructed the stone walls, stone buildings, trigonometry sites and rock carvings that can be found in many areas of New Zealand. Such remains can still be found in New Zealand with drawings and some stone inscriptions, such as those found on the Tattooed Rocks at Raglan.

Our ancestors dressed themselves in garments woven from flax fibre, reeds, long grasses and *houhera*, sweet smelling bark taken in long strips from the Lace Bark Tree. These clothes were dyed with dyes made from berries, sea weed or clay, just as we had done in the ancient homeland.

Blue cosmetic jar in the form of the Egyptian god Bes (c.664-525BC). Reproduced courtesy of the Cleveland Museum of Art, Ohio, USA.

Above all, we had a very different, peaceful, industrious way of life that allowed us to live in peace with others. This most definitely did not come from Polynesia. It was in our blood and culture long ago when we left the Middle East.

What we believed

On our beliefs, we knew and prayed to the Creator God. We knew Him as Tiki. We had carved images of our most important ancestors but they were for remembrance, much the same as the statues erected to honour important statesmen or rulers anywhere in the world. We did not pray to them. We also knew Bes, the Egyptian dwarf god who protected children, families and home, whose appearance is commemorated in the *Tiki* pendant design. So much of what the Māori now claim as their own was taken from us.

An important part of our experience is that occasionally a big white light appears to us to guide us at events of crucial importance.

When I experienced this it really knocked me back. It happened when my husband Ike and I were deciding where to build the backpackers hostel and camp at Te Rena on the 100 acres of our ancestral land.

The light grew brighter the closer it came. Then it retreated back into our tribal burial hill, Hena. So we built our camp and lodge there in front of the hill where it hovered for a few minutes before disappearing back into Hena. We believe this to be the same bright round white light that guided Te Kooti when he fled the Government forces in the Ureweras.

My mother told me that the lights of the Ngati Hotu people slaughtered in the many attacks upon us used to dance along the river cliffs at Kakahi. They also appeared, my mother said, at the Ngati Hotu marae, Takapuna, which no longer exists today. The night my mother died in Taumarunui Hospital my father after being alerted by his dog barking, witnessed the light leaving the Takapuna Marae site, coming up the hill, then remaining all night hovering above the homestead. At 7am it disappeared and he knew mother had died and told my sister Eva who cared for them both.

I'm a Catholic. I became a believer through my parents and my wonderful husband Iki-Whenua. I'll never forget how Ike and I first met at a dance. He was of Ngati-Hotu-Tuhoe from Ruapani extraction and as a child had been adopted and brought up by Presbyterian missionaries from four-and-a-half years old. He came to Taumarunui as a carpenter. His adopted parents, a deaconess in the Presbyterian Church, were Sister Janet Kearney and a school teacher, Miss Olive Harvey. Ike and I married at St Patrick's Catholic Church, Taumarunui, in August 1955.

But importantly, I live by what my Mum and Dad Tangi and James told us as kids, that we as a people, like Jesus, were hated without a cause but that we should never hate. When we were mocked and bullied at school because with our fair skin, red hair and green eyes we were physically very different from the Māori kids, they told us to just let it be and to be proud of who we were.

Somehow hatred is foreign to our nature. It's just not born into who we are. Mum and Dad hated no one; they got on well with everybody. God made us the way we are, always carrying a smile. My mother always said, if people hate you it's because there's something you've got that they can't have.

Some things hurt but they don't make me angry. That was so when I was told at a lands claim meeting to sit down because I and my people were 'extinct'. They called me a crazy woman. I was hurt but I didn't feel angry. Rather the affront made me more determined than ever to tell my story and that of my family and people, to destroy the lie with the truth. These criticisms gave me strength to keep going although there were times I wanted to throw in the towel but somewhere deep inside me the ancient ones wouldn't let me rest, so it was back on the job. God loves a trier.

Perhaps it's because from ancient times we knew God as Creator. Perhaps it's because for thousands of years we as a people have sought peace and determined to live in peace among ourselves. Whatever the reason, peace and not hatred, firmness but not anger, is hard-wired into our genes. Despite all the evil and personal abuse that has happened I don't feel hatred for anybody at all.

Despite that, the ongoing battle to be recognised as a people and to reclaim our rightful lands has taken a heavy toll of my family. My mother, whose maiden name was Tangi Maria Te Araroa Karauti, but who was better known as Mrs. James Hoani Ham, grew sick in the fight for our land claim and preservation of our uniquely God-given culture.

She died in 1970 but not before she had passed on to me the task of continuing the struggle.

So when my father died in 1984 my mother had already given me all her papers and grandfather Te Araroa's records, saying I was the right one to have them. Little did I know in 1970, when I was given them, these records would become my lifeline, bringing to light the history of the Ancient Ones and I am so proud to have completed the history of our great, great grandfather, Tipuna Piki Te Pikikotuku. Piki, I love you.

As a child I had always wanted to learn more about who I was and who we were as a Patupaiarehe people and our history as the Ngati Hotu tribe. My mother took much time to impart the true story of our people as handed down to her from many previous generations.

Among my brothers and sisters it seems it was only I who had such an intense interest. The one exception was my late brother Dean Waretini Haami but he died and so could not support me when we put our case to a Waitangi Tribunal hearing in 2006.

My mother and grandfather Mahinui Te Araroa sought redress through the Native Land Court in 1930s and after their deaths it fell to me to spend over 30 years in painstakingly researching, then writing up our case before presenting it before later Waitangi Tribunal hearings in 2006, 2008, 2010 and 2012 and 2014. Today we are still fighting what seems to be an inbuilt prejudice against us based on our people having been overrun by our enemies and the massacre of large numbers of us.

Twenty of my family have died while these court hearings dragged on and on and are still ongoing today. The upshot is that Ngati Hotu have been dispossessed of their ancient homelands which once totaled many thousands of hectares. Under the Te Turu Whenua Act of 1993 the Native Land Court did not notify owners of hearings and so we, and Ngati Hinewai, a neighbouring tribe we are related to, both being of Patupaiarehe descent, found our lands at Te Rena comprising the E2B1 250 Papakainga Block acres were lumped into common ownership with some 3,000 other owners.

But we are making progress. I have established who I am and who my people were and still are. I believe we will win back the land on Mount Ruapehu we fought for and that Ngati Hotu will be re-established on their land with a home base and economic future for our descendants.

I am determined not to give up even though my mother grew sick in the fight. My grandfather Mahinui Te Araroa Karauti died

Monica beside the grave of her much-loved husband Iki (Ike) who died while standing with her in the battle to regain historic recognition of her Patupaiarehe people and the return of their lands. It was Ike who built the camper's lodge on the Te Rena land Monica is now battling to have returned to her family.

contesting it as did my dear husband Ike after doing so much to help us forward.

He took up the Ngati Hotu cause as his own and together he and I determined to rebuild Ngati Hotu's Whakahou marae at Te Rena, the ancient papakainga of my family. History shows this meeting house, dug out underground, was still there in the early 1800s and was rebuilt in timber in 1906. Then in 1967 some wicked person burnt it down.

Also long gone is Takapuna, once the main Ngati Hotu marae

near the Whanganui River and Whakapapa river confluence. This building survived the terrible massacre of Ngati Hotu by Ngati Maru and later some of my people who fled to other parts returned to it.

But today only 100 acres remain in the family. The rest of the Kakahi Township and other places were taken to settle for European inhabitants and we seek full compensation for our losses which can only be the Taurewa Farms owned by the Crown and taken from us in 1905.

Ten miles from Taumarunui, Mangakeke, another pa of my people, was long held by our chief Kakahi before he and his people were forced out. To recover possession my family bought back about half of this land, held for many generations by Ngati Hotu and leased more in 1964.

Eventually by buying from other owners we regained about 100 acres and my brother Jim's sons farm these ancestral acres to this day.

We shouldn't have had to buy our land back but when it is pretended you no longer exist it is what you have to do. Sadly, most of our historic *pa* sites had been destroyed by 1935. That's when my family began the long fight to re-establish ourselves on our land. Now we're still fighting for our last bastion, the land at Te Rena in the Taurewa block. This 250 acre site is all that is left of land that my people had occupied continually since the 1400s. It was owned by my grandmother Te Oti Mihi Terina, and legal title proves it.

Happy days with my husband Ike

However, I did not know this when in 1996 Ike and I applied to the trustees of the Taurewa block for permission to move on to Te Rena to rebuild the Whakahou marae. Not one of the owners of this family land ever agreed to it being amalgamated. The amalgamation meant that we had to apply to trustees for permission to move back on to my grandmother's land. It was our *marae* and *papakainga* but they built their *marae* on it in 2004 and called it Hikairo for their hapu Ngati Hikairo. Yet Hikairo was never known as a name on the Taurewa Block.

Ike was a skilled builder. He built the large, two-storey house which became our new home and the Whakahou Campers' Lodge. The land was drained to provide ground for tents and caravans.

The venture was a great success. Many visitors came to stay to learn about traditional Patupaiarehe ways of gardening and growing and using native plants. We welcomed schoolchildren, hundreds of overseas students and our rates were so low they could be afforded by the under-privileged.

The camp was run by a Charitable Trust which meant our guests gave what they could afford, according to the old ways, instead of having to pay a set charge.

Before Ike died he drew up the plans for the camping ground *marae*. The amazing thing is it closely resembles the photo of the 'House of Learning', Miringa Karaka, featured in a later chapter in this book. These were happy days. Our guests dubbed Te Rena a 'Garden of Eden' and, to encourage conservation, in 2002 I became a voluntary Department of Conservation ranger, the first woman at the time to do so in Te Rena.

But all too soon it came to an end. New trustees took over the amalgamation and in 2004 ordered us off the land, regardless of earlier promises we could stay. Today the lodge stands empty and almost derelict, the land gone to waste. Worse still payments on the $80,000 mortgage we had borrowed to extend the lodge were no longer being met by income from the campers and we had to continue to service it out of our own pockets. Eventually we paid it off with God's helping hand and by selling investments.

With their hand on all the assets the trustees put the lodge up for sale and removal, even though it didn't rightfully belong to them. We battled that decision and the eviction in court and while the lodge stayed, to this day we still cannot return.

The whole battle cost tens of thousands of dollars in legal fees and broke Ike's health. The jealousy still lingers on. We are a hard working family of savers and look to a better life for our people and families.

Yet he made me promise never to give up the fight for the land where he with my father and brothers had run our stock. Even when dying he still urged me to fulfil the vision of regaining our land and rebuilding the marae. '*Whakahou*', he said, which means 'Forge on and never give up'.

I believe we were made to be seen as 'extinct' by Tuwharetoa through their evidence which they gave to Angela Ballara, a writer of Māori history. Sadly she could have got the story right had she tried to find us but she didn't. Instead she testified that we were extinct with express purpose of excluding us from negotiations about land settlement. Tuwharetoa took this stance because they knew that once we regained out land we would never sell it.

Our historic lands were taken from us by the Crown and our heritage sites desecrated. Ngati Hotu had occupied Taurewa Te Rena from ancient times and held onto it until forced off recently. If the Crown had not bought it out we would also have continued to occupy our *whenua* (traditional land) at Raurimu, Kakahai, Kaiteke and at Retaruke and all of Taurewa.

Camping out to stop the sale

To rub salt in the wound the recognised histories written about these lands and about Tuwharetoa and other tribes hereabouts also dismiss us as a conquered, annihilated race when we are nothing of the sort. However if fighting by legal and peaceful means to win back our rightful place and land is what it takes, then we've plenty of fight to give. We proved that in 2006 when we camped out high on the windy slopes of Ruapehu to stop the sale by Land Corp of the Taurewa block to a mixed consortium for what was believed to be a sum of $10 million.

There came a phone call which told us we might prevent it going through by a mounting a strong protest. And this we determined to do.

Twenty of us Ngati Hotu stuck it out in caravans and marquees

Treasured memory: Monica Matamua holds a picture of her great great great grandfather Piki-Te-Pikikotuku. A prominent peacemaker in troubled times he tried unsuccessfully to prevent the sacking of the peaceful Parihaka settlement near New Plymouth founded by Te Whiti Rongomai (whose name means 'good news' or the gospel) and Tohu Kakahi, a Patupaiarehe leader related to Ngati Hotu, from whom Monica's ancestral land gets its name. Both men were believers in the Patupaiarehe peace faith augmented by the Christian gospel.

They offered only passive resistance to the land-grabbing Government forces sent against them. Indeed the invading troops were met by troupes of singing children and were offered food. Te Whiti and Kakahi insisted that not a hand be raised against the invaders. Yet 1600 of their people were seized and jailed and the settlement was burnt to the ground.

for two months to stop the sale. And stop it we did. We maintained that Land Corp had no right to sell it because the block, 2,000 hectares in all, was land banked, reserved for compensation.

It was I, Monica Matamua, a claimant in the Northern Whanganui Cluster, who led the occupation and we were joined by others at a *hui* (meeting) at Wharauroa Marae supported by Uenuku of Raetihi, Tamakana and Tamahaki.

Once all this land, and more, was Ngati Hotu's but Tuwharetoa sold the 2,000 acres and the Crown put nine tribes into it. My near relatives the Ngati Hinewai tribe would have had one ninth of the proceeds but rightly they refused to sell, as after all Ngati Hotu were the rightful owners.

Before we gave up the occupation it was agreed that the land remain land-banked and a cash offer to buy back would be made at a 1987 (or thereabouts) valuation – that is, much less than the then current 2006 valuation.

Later in 2014 we felt so cheated when we learned that the Crown was making an A.I.P. (Agreement in Principle) with Tuwharetoa to allow them to buy back the land but with us, the people who originally owned it, excluded from this and the other treaty settlement gains won by Tuwharetoa under the A.I.P.

Earlier some 20,000 acres had been taken by the Crown under the Railways Act but we didn't agree to it. Worse still the Te Rena side of Taurewa is so steep only the deer and goats can live there; it now forms part of the DOC lands. As far as Tuwharetoa is concerned, sub-tribes held to be within their iwi, such as Ngati Hotu and Ngati Hinewai, have no rights. And this is what is so terribly wrong with the whole land claim settlement process.

We believe as non-Māori, who find it hard to fit in anywhere, the Crown have an obligation to give us a fair deal with a discreet settlement of our own Taurewa farms and some compensation.

Then in 2014 the Crown offered to sell this land back to Ngati

Tuwharetoa, again leaving Ngati Hotu and Ngati Hinewai out in the cold. So it turns out that Ngati Hotu saved this block from the American Consortium only to have it offered to Tuwharetoa on a plate.

But all is not lost. My hopes rest now on this Taurewa block, comprising 2000 acres being returned to Ngati Hotu as its rightful owners. We've been waiting 10 years for the Waitangi Tribunal to rule on our claim.

We hope that the compelling evidence of who we are, how we lived, the extent of the lands we once owned, and the atrocities visited on us by Tuwharetoa, plus the fact we were in continual residence on this land until wrong court decisions threw us off, will all work in our favour.

Author's note:

Monica's story raises many challenges to the conventional accepted history of New Zealand and the world. Some of these are addressed in subsequent chapters.

Chapter 3

What's in a name?

Patu-pai-a-rehe is the ancient name of the first people to arrive and settle in New Zealand. They were here first and their whole way of life was based on peace. Yet today even their most prominent surviving descendant, Monica Matamua, is hard put to define the meaning of this collective name.

'*Patu* means an ornamental weapon, *pai* means good or peace and *arehe* means something that flies,' she muses. 'Perhaps it means a weapon that flies for peace.'

Dictionaries, encyclopaedias and learned works on New Zealand's pre-history and the meaning of Māori language throw little light on the matter, although they describe the *Patu-pai-a-rehe* as the inhabitants Māori found living here when they arrived in this land.

They also state they had red or fair hair, were of light complexion and had green eyes. According to Māori lore they hid in the mists of the mountains and were rarely seen.

Although they are still dismissed by some as mythical 'fairy people', undeniable evidence on many fronts shows that the *Patu-pai-a-rehe* truly were the First Nation of New Zealand. What's more their descendants are still here in their hundreds to prove it.

As to their arrival before Māori, take the evidence of a gentleman belonging to the Tainui Māori *iwi* (or tribe) I encountered. Learning he was from Raglan, one of the North Island of New Zealand's favoured seaside resorts in the Waikato region, I asked him if his family had lived there for long?

'We came on the Tainui *waka* (canoe),' he informed me. "And where did your *waka* come from?" I inquired. 'Up north,' was his reply. I then asked if there were other people already here in the Waikato when Tainui people arrived in the Waikato.

'Why of course there were,' he responded. 'We would have had a hard time if they hadn't shown us what to eat from the bush and what plants could be our medicines. They were here all right.' But when I asked what had happened to these people since then and where they were now I was met with silence.

Closer to our time history records that the women of these ancient folk, were so beautiful they were described as "waka blondes' by the latter day Europeans reaching this country in the 19th century.

What's more, a few years ago a respected Māori elder gave evidence that in his lifetime these ancient people lived on Mt Pirongia and that their last refuge against Māori tribes hell bent on destroying them was at Moehu Mountain in the Coromandel.

So the *Patu-pai-a-rehe* were the original *tangata whenua* (first people of the land) but what did, what does, their name mean?

Thankfully, words can be broken down to their constituent parts to give greater meaning. If the English word *atonement* is separated it reads *at-one-ment* and it immediately becomes clear it means 'reconciliation", the process by which sinners are reconciled to God.

And this is where it gets exciting. Breaking down *Patu-pai-a-rehe* into its constituent parts yields a meaning that truly describes the distinctive features of these ancient people. The words making up the collective noun are: *patu*, *pai*, *a*, *rehe*. Now, while to Māori *patu* means a war club, according to the Māori Dictionary, its other and evidently earlier meaning is that of a wall, hedge, or protective screen.

And the *Patu-pai-a-rehe* were indeed builders in stone as old walls and the remains of stone houses attest in various parts of New Zealand. Examples include the remains of stone houses in the King Country, extensive stonework in a pa near New Plymouth, miles of walls, remains of stone houses, platforms and carved slabs in Waipoua Forest and even pyramids.

The Kaimana Wall with its large and apparently accurately cut stones has every appearance of a man-made structure. Excavation shows the stonework continues more than a metre below ground. The visible part of the structure is said to be only the top, or cap, of a large and high pyramid beneath that was buried in the great Taupo volcanic eruption of 232AD.

Stone fields, stone walls, stone gardens, stone altars and stone carvings are found in several parts of both the North and South islands of New Zealand. Ignored by archaeologists and conservationists because they challenge the conventional scientific mantra, that Māori were the *tangata whenua*, first people to settle New Zealand, such archaeological remains dating back as much as 2,000 years bear mute testimony to the truth that a stone-building, stone carving people lived here long, long ago.

But back to our word puzzle. Again, according to the *Māori Dictionary*, *pai* means that which is 'good, excellent, suitable, agreeable and pleasant'. This accurately describes the character of these happy, fair-haired, green-eyed and skillful people that were, and still are, the *Patu-pai-a-rehe*, or Turehu. Their outlook on life is best summed up in the phrase *He aroha kit e pai* – love that which is good.

Throughout their history the *Patu-pai-a-rehe* did love that which is good; peace and kindness were ingrained in their nature. But their hospitality to later peoples arriving in New Zealand was cruelly repaid. Far from honouring and respecting these first settlers of New Zealand later arrivals such as the Māori turned on their erstwhile hosts and killed and ate them.

As now noted, *patu* refers to building walls and *pai* refers to that which is 'good". *Arehe* means either a buzzing insect or something which flies. However, separate out *a*, which is Māori for 'and' or 'to', and the word *rehe* appears.

And rehe means trade or craft or skill. A rough translation then might be: 'The good and skillful wall builders'. Or, more mystically, perhaps: 'They that with great skill build walls of peace'.

So why has the story of these skilled and peaceful people disappeared from the pages of recognised New Zealand history? The next chapter seeks to provide an answer.

Monica Matamua with a copy of her land claim which, at the time of writing, was being considered by the Māori Land Court.

Chapter 4

A convenient mythology

What do you do if you want someone you hate to go away but they stubbornly stay put? Answer: you pretend they don't exist. And, to be blunt about it, that's just what the Māori have done with Patupaiarehe and other original indigenous people of New Zealand. They have turned the real existence of the Patupaiarehe, Turehu and other indigenous peoples of New Zealand literally into a fairy tale; they call the Patupaiarehe just that – fairies.

Ask one's Māori friends about the Patupaiarehe and they will tell you they don't exist, except as mythical creatures of the imagination, a New Zealand version of the English delusion about 'fairies at the bottom of the garden'.

The original peoples of New Zealand, believed to have numbered 100,000 prior to the Māori, have been so successfully converted into myth that now most New Zealanders do not believe they really existed at all. Yet not only did they live then but they also live now. Thousands of their more direct descendants are among us as New Zealanders today. Yet denial of their existence, either in the past or now as still present, is rife.

I well recall years ago interviewing an archaeologist undertaking a survey of Māori archaeological remains and sites in the Waikato. 'What about non-Māori archeological remains that predate the Māori arrival?' I asked. 'Will you be protecting them too?' 'No need,' he replied. 'There aren't any'. And no citing of examples, such as the 'Tattoed Rocks' at Raglan, the stone fort near Wanganui, the ancient rock carvings at Taupo and elsewhere, the skeletons of pre-Māori people in New Zealand, could dissuade him.

Furore erupted when I published in the *Hamilton This Week* paper an article stating that Morori, then believed to have died out on the Chatham Islands had lived in the Waikato since the 1100s and were still here now.

The story ran with a picture of Moriori chief Philip Ranga who lives at Raglan and told how his people once owned land stretching from Raglan to Tauranga. Philip told me his people were overrun by the Māori and had to pass themselves off as Tainui to survive. Far from being 'extinct' he and his descendants still live in the Waikato, land which once was all theirs.

Now, if you ask a Māori person about the ancient Patupaiarehe people, although his own history records they were the first to reach these shores, he most likely will tell you these people are the creatures of legend, the subject of tribal fairy tales told to children to prevent them wandering off on their own. 'Stay safe, stay at home lest the fairy folk of the forest get you' succeeding generations of Māori told their children. And not just Māori. That the Patupaiarehe were the subject of make belief, people of the night who vanished when other folk saw them, is the view of many in academia and even in Government. The online *Encyclopaedia of New Zealand* in its chapter 'Patupaiarehe', says that:

> In Māori tradition Patupaiarehe, also known as Tūrehu and Pakepakehā, were fairy-like creatures of the forests and mountain tops.
>
> Although they had some human attributes, Patupaiarehe were regarded not as people but as supernatural beings (*he iwi atua*). They were seldom seen, and an air of mystery and secrecy still surrounds them. In most traditions, those who encountered Patupaiarehe were able to understand their language. But in one account they were unintelligible. Patupaiarehe had light skin, and red or fair hair with blue or greenish eyes. Unlike Māori, they were never tattooed. Patupaiarehe were generally found deep in the forests, or on mist-covered hilltops. In these isolated places they settled and built their homes, sometimes described as forts. In some stories their houses and pa were

built from swirling mist. In others, they were made from *kareao* (supplejack vine).

The chapter says these ancients were said to live mainly in the Waikato–Waipa basin, the Cape Colville–Te Aroha range, the hills about Rotorua, the Urewera ranges and Wairoa districts, and the Waitakere ranges in the Auckland region. South Island traditions had them living mainly in the hills around Lyttelton Harbour, Akaroa and the Takitimu range, and in the hills between the Arahura River and Lake Brunner.

Patupaiarehe were hunters and gatherers, the *Encyclopaedia* states, surviving on raw forest foods and sometimes fishing from the shores of the sea or a lake. Their canoes were made of *korari* (flax stalks). Cooked food was offensive or foul to some of them.

Fearing the light, they were active mainly in the twilight hours and at night, or when the mist was heavy enough to shield them. They wore flax garments (*pakerangi*), dyed red, but also rough mats (*pora* or *pureke*). They were also known for playing *koauau* and *putorino* (flutes).

Evidently the incoming Māori learned much from the 'fairies', including the art of net-making. A Māori ancestor, Kahakura, is said to have beguiled the fairies (*pa-tupaearehe*) into leaving their nets behind. Hokianga Māori were taught similarly by the Parau, a mountain tribe, who used to come down to the shore at night to fish.

The fairies (*turehu*) on the East Coast, Bay of Plenty, were tricked out of their nets by Titipa, Weaving and wood-carving were taught to Rua, an old Māori ancestor, by the 'Wood Fairies'(*Hakuturi*).

Why did Māori mythologise the Patupaiarehe, you ask? The answer to my mind is their guilt for having killed, eaten and driven them off their land into the higher hills. Also involved is the Māori belief that once an enemy is conquered they, as a people, exist no longer.

That is, they become subject to widespread amnesia on the

Describing this 1990s postage stamp, New Zealand Post says that every New Zealand region has stories telling of encounters with supernatural beings such as taniwha, fairies (Patupaiarehe) and giant reptiles. The Patupaiarehe, it says, were 'handsome, uncanny people who lived on hilltops and in remote places. The men were expert flute players'. But you might ask, where did the koauau (flutes) they played come from? Pipes and flutes are not part of Melanesian or most Pacific island culture. But they are found in every Celtic-originated culture from the Middle East through to South America and in Spain, France, Ireland and Scotland, usually in the form of bagpipes. In New Zealand they seem to have been preserved as pipes but without the 'bags'. Perhaps because there was no large, hairy bellied animal from which to make them.

part of their destroyers. Thus the Patupaiarehe were first considered tapu (out of bounds and off limits), then deemed wife snatchers; finally they were relegated to status of 'fairies', not at the bottom of the hill, but in the high mountains.

You see, to the traditional Māori, *mana* (prestige, standing) was highly important. A chief that no longer had people to rule, slain enemies to gloat over or land to occupy had no *mana*. And a people conquered and driven out, especially if they did not fight back, in Māori eyes had no *mana* at all. Indeed the heads of slain chiefs would be hung up before the conquering chief's *whare* (house) and their bodies cooked and eaten to swallow up their *mana*.

What were Māori to do then, when it later came to writing up tribal history, with that persecuted, peaceful but still persisting people, the Patupaiarehe? How were they to account for them in the annals of tribal lore recorded in the late 19th century and later?

One answer, according to the several accounts I have read, was to treat them as mythical beings, as 'fairies', as spiritual beings that only came out at night and could be dismissed as figments of one's imagination, or who were not really there at all. Another was to largely ignore them altogether.

Once consigned to the realm of folklore such people could be largely forgotten or dismissed in as few words as possible when recounting tribal history. In land claim matters any evidence of their existence could be dismissed as the stuff of legends.

That is exactly what happened to stalwart Patupaiarehe descendant and campaigner Monica Matamua, whose story is featured earlier in this book, when she attended a Tuwharetoa *hui* (meeting), to discuss pursuing land claims against the Crown.

Monica stood to speak of her own people, the Ngati Hotu's claim for land and was asked by an elder 'Who are you?" When she explained that she was 'of Ngati Hinewai, of Ngati Hotu', the elder snapped, 'Sit down and shut up. You are nothing', with the clear implication she and her people did not exist, at least as far as Tuwharetoa was concerned.

Accordingly Māori literature has some oblique, enigmatic and brief references to the earlier inhabitants of New Zealand but tells at length folk tales about the 'fairy people'. In his book *Takitimu* J. H. Mitchell (p. 66) says that Māori, as immigrants from Eastern Polynesia, had not been builders of *pas* defended by earthen ramparts and stockades, yet seem to have adopted this practice when they landed on these shores:

> This could only mean that being numerically weak, they stood in fear of the original inhabitants, and probably put to their own use this aboriginal mode of defence. Assuredly, those few newcomers must have lived here on sufferance, their wellbeing depending on the good will of the local people.

So there were original inhabitants here before the Māori. That is the first point clarified by Mr. Mitchell's statement. The second is these first settlers in this land extended goodwill to the Māori arrivals. Fact is they showed them how to fish, how to gather food from the bush, when to plant, how to build homes that would withstand winter and much more. But there was one lesson the First Nation sought to teach that the new arrivals never learned or, it seems, wanted to learn – how to live in peace.

Mr. Mitchell suggests fear of the original inhabitants as the reason that incoming Māori built *pas*. I disagree. There was another, far more likely, reason for such action: the need for the incomers to protect themselves from each other – not from 'original inhabitants', who are well recorded, both in *Takitimu* and elsewhere in Māori lore as being peaceful. Only paragraphs later Mitchell records that 'trouble arose' among the immigrants shortly after their arrival at Whakatane.

According to this story, come planting time, seven months after the landing, the jealous Puhi (eponymous ancestor of the Ngapuhi tribe of Northland) insulted his elder brother Toroa as they sowed seed. The quarrel became so bitter, Mitchell says, that Puhi took the canoe *Matatua* on which they are said to have arrived and with most of its crew members sailed north, leaving only six members of the Toroa family behind.

While not actually saying so, this story implies that Puhi reached New Zealand from overseas, i.e. the Pacific islands. However, this cannot be so because research by historian Max Hill[9] has shown from Māori records that the canoe *Matatua* was built in the upper North Island. Puhi then was merely sailing back to where he had come

A famous photograph of three young Patupaiarehe ladies, members of the original indigenous peoples of New Zealand, taken in the 19th century. Note the fair, delicate hair and fair complexions. European settlers encountering these fair maidens dubbed them 'waka blondes'.

9 Max Hill, author of *To The Ends Of The Earth* and *To The Ends Of The Earth And Back Again*.

from, that is Northland. Again fear of the original settlers cannot have been the reason for building forts because as Mitchell says on page 70 '…the immigrants met with very little opposition from the peaceful inhabitants of the land'.

That the Patupaiarehe, Turehu, Kapupungapunga, Waitaha and other early tribes comprised a large and peaceful population living here before Māori arrival is further evidenced by a Takitimu entry on page 187 which says that before the Māori migration 'two main tribes of the original people of this (Whakatane and Opotiki) district were Te Hapu-oneone and Te Tini o Toi. Mr. Mitchell goes on:

> These were the two primal stock from which sprang the various old-time tribes that held the lands of the Bay of Plenty from Matata to Opotiki. The title of the Hapu-oneone may be taken as meaning 'the earth-born people' or 'the People of the Land'.

So here we have the official tribal history of *Takitimu* stating that preceding the Māori arrival there was a widespread numerous people in residence called 'the People of the Land' or in Māori, *tangata whenua*. So much for Māori claims they and their descendants are *tangata whenua*. For the record *Te Tini o Toi* means 'the Multitude of Toi'. So there were plenty of them. Further proof is supplied in one of the Transactions of the Royal Society of New Zealand Vol. 37 1904 entitled '*Rangimatoru*'. It says:

> Another tradition of Ngatiawa contains a singular statement which would seem to mean that the canoes "Rangimatoru" and "Te Paepae-ki-Rarotonga" belonged to these original people of the Bay of Plenty, and that they accompanied "Te Aratawhao" to Hawaiki in quest of the coveted kumara. Whether Hape was or was not the origin of the Hapu-oneone tribe, it is certain that those people were some of the ancient inhabitants of the Bay of Plenty district, and were a numerous people when the historical fleet of canoes, "Te Arawa," "Matatua," &c., arrived from Hawaiki. They occupied the district from Ohiwa across to Ruatoki.

Again on page 188, Mitchell tells how Tu-whare-toa, the eponymous ancestor of the powerful present day tribe of that name, and his family settled at Kawerau near Te Teko in the Bay of Plenty and says that:

> At this time, the **whole** of the country around, extending from Mapouriki (a pa on the range north of the cheese factory Waimana) to Taupo and to Hei-pipi pa at Petane (now known as Bay View) near Napier, was held by a **numerous** tribe called Maru-iwi, who were the **original inhabitants** of the land. (*Emphasis mine*).

Over the next two pages Mitchell records how Tu-whare-toa's sons led war parties 'searching the Kaingaroa plains for someone to kill'. They attacked Maru-iwi but were repulsed, then invoked dark spiritual powers to bring about their victims' end when, in a nocturnal stampede, they fell over a cliff. Takitimu laconically records:

> Most of Maru-iwi perished in the *waro* (chasm) and their tribal name became lost to the world… After this Tu-whare-toa took possession of all the Taupo lands. Before doing so they had to overpower a small tribe named **Ngati Hotu** and this was done by peace and inter-marriages.

Ngati Hotu survivor Monica Matamua begs to differ. She agrees that peace was preserved by inter-marriage at the outset but insists that the truce did not last long. 'They kept wanting more. Although we gave them more land it was never enough. They took to raiding and attacking us. In the end we became their meat larder.'

And it was worse in the Waikato. According to Tainui tribal historian Pei Te Hurinui Jones in *Nga Iwi of Tainui*, Tainui first entered the region about 1400. (However, other evidence shows it was not until the late 1600s that Tainui arrived). He stated that by about 1450 they had 'conquered the last of the indigenous people' in a battle at Atiamuri. The 'indigenous people' were the Kapupungapunga who were wiped out to the last member of their tribe, making Tainui's conquest genocide.

Since the Patupaiarehe people were dedicated to a peaceful lifestyle the *patu* to them was a symbol of peace, not in the abstract but as a conscious, constant practice. Carved in bone or greenstone the *patu* spoke of the authority to insist on and maintain peace. It would be carried by the chief or venerable ancestor as a symbol of his authority in much the same way as the mace bespeaks the authority of Parliament in both Britain and New Zealand and the sceptre symbolizes the peaceful power and authority of Queen Elizabeth.

Importantly, even among Māori the greenstone *patu* was kept largely for ceremonial use only. Even for them it was a symbol for peace. Thus a *patu* carved from greenstone, is recorded in Takitimu (p. 164) as given as a peace offering in a vain attempt by residents in a Ngati Kahungunu *pa* to dissuade a hostile Tuhoe war party from attacking them. J. H. Mitchell records:

> The two forces (of a war party of warriors combined from five tribes), proceeded on the warpath. On reaching Nuhaka (near Wairoa), Te-Ra-taau, a chief of that place, offered them a greenstone adze named Te Rama-apakura as a peace offering (*whakauto pahi*).
>
> The weapon was accepted but peace was spurned. When the raiding party reached Puke-Karoro pa at Te Awa-pata North, Te Ra-taau again attempted to make peace by presenting the raiders with two other greenstone weapons (*meres*) named Kahawai and Kaue-hurihia but even this failed.
>
> The raiders were determined to both capture the *pa* and keep the historic weapons which Te Ra-taau must have given up with a severe wrench to his pride. The siege of the *pa* went on until the people were overpowered. Many were slain when the *pa* fell.

Thus the emblem of peace was accepted but the aggressors attacked and slaughtered those living in the *pa* anyway. But that is not the end of the story. The greenstone adze, Te Rama-apakura, was carried away to the Bay of Islands by the Ngapuhi section of the raiding party. There it was seen by a previously captured Kahungunu warrior, Te Whare-umu who had fought for his captor Te Wera. Seeing his prisoner weeping over the heirloom Te Wera was moved to return both it and Te Whare-umu to their home and people. Thus peace won out in the end.

In that *patu* also means to strike, an alternate or additional meaning may be these ancients were those who struck a blow for good by keeping the peace. And as a later chapter will show these cheerful, people were not only peaceful themselves but also strove to make peace among others. And the mute testimony of stone built *pas*, stone cities and stone dwellings certainly attests that they were expert stone builders.

But how long have the Patupaiarehe lived in New Zealand, you might ask? Was it for hundreds or thousands of years before the coming the first Polynesians, the Moriori?

Conventional archeology and history hold that in the 'archaic period' which began Polynesian settlement of New Zealand and which, according to the conventional wisdom began between 900AD and 1100AD, the incomers were 'moa hunters' largely exterminating what had been a large ratite population.

However, there is evidence, forbidden though it may be, that an earlier people, the Patupaiarehe, far from hunting these large birds to extinction, actually farmed and preserved them. This is addressed in the next chapter.

Chapter 5

The moa farmers

Most people know of the moa hunters. They are said to have been people of the first phase of Polynesian settlement in New Zealand. But what about the moa farmers – did they come first?

Now, it's a no brainer that birds are among God's greatest material gifts to hungry mankind, especially if there are no cows, sheep or pigs to provide a meal, as was the case when the first settlers of New Zealand arrived here over 2,000 years ago.

Consider the chicken. Easily tucked under one arm it provides a rich meal for four if killed, or if kept alive produces an egg a day and you can make pillows from its feathers. Yet the chicken was a latecomer to the New Zealand isles, arriving only with latter-day European immigrants. Not that a beneficent Creator left the first people to reach this land bereft of good protein. Arriving on these unsullied shores they could choose from a larder overflowing with birds and fish of many kinds. Seals and rats provided mammalian meat but 2,000 years ago this South Pacific landmass was unequalled on earth for the quantity of the 'poultry' nature provided. Ducks, geese, large swans, a gamut of sea birds and, above all the moa, provided such a large meat resource one cannot imagine such a bountiful supply being exhausted.

Yet eaten out it was. In less than 100 years no less than nine major specie groups were eaten into extinction on these shores, the large swan, geese and the moa among them.

However, the original European settlers of this country, the Patupaiarehe and the later arrivals, the Waitaha people were not to blame. Latecomer Polynesians were. In a *Nature Communications Journal* article University of Canterbury and University of Otago researchers Professor Richard Holdaway (from Canterbury) and Chris Jacomb (Otago) say it took only a few hundred Polynesians to bring about moa extinction in a time-frame of little more than a century.

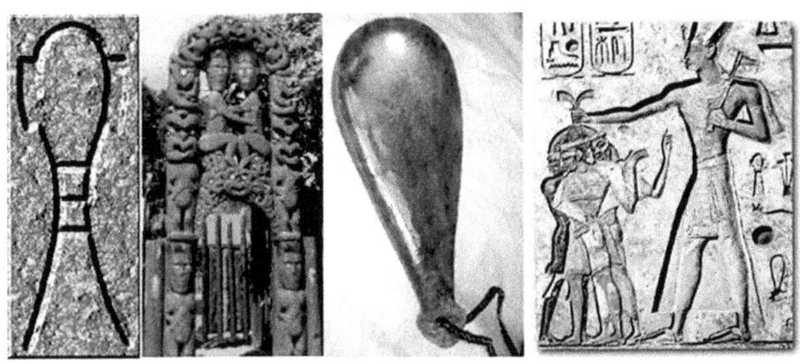

A symbolic club or 'patu', as inscribed in ancient Egyptian depictions and in the form of the hieroglyphic 'Sa' signifying protection. (2) The same motif (picked out in green) is seen in this carved gateway to a Māori village. (3) A greenstone patu carved in New Zealand. (4) Pharaoh Rameses II threatening to slaughter enemies with the 'Sa' or 'patu' symbol of protection depicted twice below his elbow. Pictures courtesy of Martin Doutre, author of 'Celtic New Zealand'. Retrieved from www.celticnz.co.nz

During the peak period of moa hunting, probably within a decade either side of 1425, there were fewer than 1,500 Polynesian settlers in New Zealand, or about one person per 100 square km, compared with a New Zealand population density today of 17 persons per square km, the researchers assert. Moa then, were eaten out by this small population barely a century after East Polynesians first settled the earliest well-dated moa eating site, at Wairau Bar near Blenheim.

Importantly, Prof Holdaway and Mr. Jacomb say such rapid extinction of the New Zealand terrestrial megafauna of moa, giant eagle, and large geese by so few shows that population size can no longer be an argument against human involvement in extinctions as it often has been elsewhere in the world.

Regrettably Holdaway and Jacomb's valuable contribution to our knowledge does not examine how New Zealand's earlier inhabitants conserved this country's well stocked avian larder for over 1400 years before the coming of the Māori. But our prehistory does, as we will detail shortly.

First though it should realised that in New Zealand it seems nature compensated for the lack of sheep, cattle and pigs by providing the biggest and best eating birds to be found. Kilogram for kilogram the now extinct moa of New Zealand had no equal, even outclassing the ostrich for the quantity of meat it yielded. The bird was a walk-in larder, a fierce but spearable butcher's shop of choice cuts that fell easy prey to human hunters.

Consider, then the huge dietary contribution this struthious (ostrich-like) ratite made to the repast of the people who first settled on these shores. They had arrived with the rat (*Rattus exulans*) but a prime specimen of that animal would yield only a 3kg carcase. Contrast that with the 75 kg of meat yielded by the South Island Giant Moa, *Dinornis giganteus*.

One leg alone provided 25kgs of high protein flesh. And even the Little Bush Moa, *Anomalopteryx didiformis*, weighed in with 24kgs of meat, enough to feed several families at a single sitting. These meat weights, deduced from skeletal moa remains, are cited by Ian Smith of the University of Otago's Department of Anthropology in *Otago Archaeological Laboratory Report No. 8*. They can be compared with an average meat yield for a sheep of 30kg, for a pig of 79kg and of a cow of 356kg.

Now scientists say that in ancient New Zealand the several species of moa with geese, ducks and the succulently large wood pigeon, the kereru, took the place of mammals in the meat diet of the first settlers in this land. Which raises a question. Were the first settlers of New Zealand poultry farmers on a grand scale? Oral history and the evidence of archaeology strongly suggests that they may have been. For instance, Patupaiarehe campaigner Monica Matamua says that for hundreds of years her people farmed the moa.

'My ancestors were clever, they were skilled farmers,' she explains. 'They were used to farming poultry and other stock in the lands they had dwelt in before reaching New Zealand. So when they settled here and discovered the moa they kept them in pens and conserved them. There was no wholesale slaughter. Rather we bred them as semi domesticated birds and killed them selectively for food when needed'.

Much as you might breed ducks or turkeys, it seems. According to Monica, the ancient Patupaiarehe were practicing conservationists. "We were careful to never take too much, whether of plants and fruits of the forest, birds, or fish in the sea. We saw the bush as our garden,' she says.

And there's not just Monica's word for that. In a *Journal of the Polynesian Society* report on the 1957 annual conference of the New Zealand Archaeological Society 1957, Mr. J. Golson, Anthropology Department, Auckland University College, referred to a paper, *The Habits, Distribution and Ecology of the Moa and Contemporary Bird Fauna* by Dr. R. A. Falla, Director, Dominion Museum, which contrasted the moa's natural nests with evidence of their egg-laying in captivity. He states:

> Unfortunately we have little precise information about moa eggs and nesting habits. Pyramid Valley provided a skeleton of *Emeus crassus* with an egg still in the body. More recently good work has been done by Mr. W. H. Hartree who has provided evidence for the nesting habits of *Anomalopteryx* in rock shelters in Hawkes Bay.

Mr. Hartree himself was able, during the discussion that followed Dr. Falla's paper, to explain his work. He said:

> The nests are small scoops in the dry pumice of the latest Taupo shower (300 A.D.) two feet wide and several inches deep. There appears to be one egg per nest. Some shelters have one nest only, others are used for long periods and one shelter recently discovered has produced evidence for nesting in the pre-pumice horizon.

Dr. Falla contrasted this Hawkes Bay data with Frost's evidence for a nesting colony at Doubtless Bay where closely spaced skeletons were discovered each covering one or more eggs.

Such a concentration, Dr. Falla suggested, might result from seasonal corralling of the birds by man, a semi or temporary domestication.

The above evidence is important for two reasons. First is that it shows moa survived the huge Taupo volcanic blast of 232AD and subsequent eruptions since they were found and hunted for many centuries afterwards.

Second, that Dr. Falla's suggestion they were farmed is likely, given that no bird by choice nests near other birds, as the Doubtless Bay discoveries showed was the case. Importantly, it points to an early people domesticating these large birds for meat production. The 1966 edition of *The Encyclopaedia of New Zealand* edited by A.H. MacLintock, contains this description of Doubtless Bay:

> To the south it is joined to the mainland by a belt of sand dunes rising to a height of about 120 ft. This belt is fronted to the east by Tokerau Beach, which extends in the form of a concave arc from Whatuwhiwhi in the north to the Awapoko River in the south, and is about 8 miles long. Among the sand dunes, wherein moa bones can be found, are extensive swamps with several shallow lakes, of which Ohia and Rotokawau are the largest.

Monica Matamua is insistent that her people did not 'eat out' the moa. 'We valued them far too highly to do that. But later arrivals to this land thought otherwise.' They went on an unchecked moa hunting and binge eating spree without thought for the future. Scientists today are united in their conclusion that Polynesians arriving in New Zealand brought about the extinction of the moa.

Their view is set forth in the paper, *Some Thoughts on the Extinction of the Moa* by Dr. C. A. Fleming, Geological Survey, Wellington and read at the 1957 conference of the New Zealand Archaeological Society. Dr. Fleming outlined the problem in New Zealand ecological history constituted by the disappearance of a complete order of birds, the moas, and several carinate birds associated with them (*Aptornis, Cnemiornis, Harpagornis*, etc.):

> Over forty species, diversified to occupy many different ecological niches in New Zealand from lowland lake and swamp to sub-alpine upland and including grazers, carnivores and scavengers, disappeared in a geologically short space of time. The avifauna under discussion successfully survived the climatic vegetational fluctuations … and was abundant in the post-glacial period. Its dramatic disappearance in the centuries preceding European exploration requires an explanation in terms of a fundamental change different from the climatic vicissitudes of the previous millennia. That change came with the arrival of Polynesian man, New Zealand's first mammalian predator.
>
> This explanation in terms of human activity, direct and indirect, has received substantial support of recent years with the demonstration that Dinornis survived into the human period in Southland and in North Canterbury and the inference that *Megalapteryx didinus* lived on in Fiordland into the seventeenth and eighteenth centuries.

The author begs leave to disagree with the above assertion that the Polynesians, in the form of themselves, brought the first mammalian predators to New Zealand.

They didn't because other 'mammalian predators', the Patupaiarehe people, were already here long before the first Polynesians arrived. However, Dr. Fleming does usefully explain how the coming of the Polynesians resulted in the sudden slaughter of many bird species allowed to thrive until then.

Another paper by a Mr. Lockerbie asserted:

> From the point of view of sequence the most important site investigated was Pounawea. Three distinct levels with associated cultural remains were excavated and carbon dated. At the base is a thick black layer with plentiful moa, bones of

An artist's impression of moa peacefully grazing near a water hole.

whale and seal, and a few shells.

This horizon has produced quantities of massive flake knives, two types of slate knife, one piece fish hooks, shanks of composite lure hooks and numerous adzes, including the tanged quadrangular and side hafted types.

The date is 1145 A.D. Above this comes a grey layer composed of dry ash and sand. Moa is less plentiful and fish more common. The date is 1455+/-60 A.D. Finally, by 1665+/-60 the character of the site has changed completely: moa is very scarce and the relevant layer is a midden of the shell fish which now form a principal item of diet.

The important point here is that while incoming Polynesians had no history of farming the Patupaiarehe here long before them did. Coming from the Middle East their agricultural skills included poultry and stock management and growing crops. However, this assertion, and the very existence of the Patupaiarehe prior to Māori arrival, is rejected outright by New Zealand anthropologists, archeologists and academic historians.

One reason they disallow other evidence of a pre-Māori people living here is that archaeological investigation, they assert, has failed to uncover radio carbon dated evidence of such settlement prior to Polynesian arrival about 1,000 years ago. This is because they say no charcoal or burnt remains from cooking fires have been found to denote early Patupaiarehe settlement sites.

A 19th century 'mock-up' of how latter-day Europeans thought moa hunters might have posed with their prey

However, several historical sources point out that the Patupaiarehe 'lived off the bush', ate their meat and fish raw (as the Japanese do) and often did not cook with fire. Why that should be considered so unusual I don't know. We eat oysters and sweetbreads raw. What's more my grandfather loved 'jugged hare' – that is a hare or rabbit eaten raw after it had hung in a tree for two or three weeks.

Confirmation that the Patupaiarehe cooked without fire is found in a paper by James Cowan, published in the *Journal of the Polynesian Society* (Vol. 30 1921 and Volume 30, No. 119, p 142-151) entitled, *The Patu-paiarehe. Notes on Māori folk-tales of the fairy people. Part II.* He writes: An old man Tohe-te-Matehaere, of Weriweri, Waiteti, whose *hapu* of the Arawa is Ngati-Ihenga, speaks as follows on the subject of these fairy mountain-dwellers:

> The name of the tribe of Patu-paiarehe at Ngongotaha and other places in this neighbourhood was Ngati-Rua, and the chiefs of that tribe, in the days of my ancestor Ihenga, were

> Tuehu, Te Rangi-tamai, Tongakohu, and Rotokohu. The people were very numerous; there were a thousand or perhaps many more on Ngongotaha. They were an *iwi atua* (a god-like race, a people of supernatural powers). In appearance some were very much like the Māori people of to-day; others resembled the *Pakeha* (or white) race.
>
> The complexion of most was *kiri puwhero* (reddish skin), and their hair had the red or golden tinge which we call *uru-kehu*. Some had black eyes, some blue like fair-skinned Europeans. They were about the same height as ourselves. Some of their women were very beautiful, very fair of complexion, with shining fair hair. They wore chiefly the flax garment called *pekerangi*, dyed a red colour; they also wore the rough mats *pora* and *pureke*. In disposition they were peaceful; they were not a war-loving, angry people.
>
> Their food comprised the products of the forest, and they also came down to this lake Rotorua to catch *inanga* (whitebait). There was one curious characteristic of these Patu-paiarehe; they had a great dread of the steam that rose from cooked food. In the evenings, when the Māori people living at Te Raho-o-te-Rangipiere and other places near the fairy abodes opened their cooking *hangis*, all the Patu-paiarehe retired to their houses immediately they saw the clouds of vapour rising, and shut themselves up; they feared the *mamaoa* (steam).

This is strong evidence from a convincing witness of the sizeable presence of the Patupaiarehe at Ngongotaha in comparatively recent times. It also speaks of their beauty, their peace and of the fact that apparently they did not cook with fire!

Fact is that they ate their food mainly raw. And they farmed the moa rather than just hunting and slaughtering it. And the difference doesn't end there. When it comes to prehistoric seafaring and the voyages that brought the first settlers to New Zealand we find evidence of an important navigational tool used by the ancients buried within a Māori tradition, as the next chapter explains.

Chapter 6

Seeing the rainbow

Nobody's found a pot of gold at the end of the rainbow but if you were an ancient mariner you might just have found New Zealand there instead. For both in Māori lore and ancient Patupaiarehe tradition the rainbow features both as a leader of people and seemingly even as a supernatural navigator that led peoples of old to these shores.

Interestingly, we are told by *Wikipaedia* that Uenuku, the 'god of rainbows' is especially sacred to the Tainui Māori people. This major tribe also revere a carved, four-pronged post and consider *Te Uenuku* (literally 'The Rainbow) a *taonga* (priceless treasure).

And it was this relic, the supposed personification of the 'Rainbow God', that Tainui believe pointed out the way to go as their ancestral canoe supposedly voyaged from the Pacific islands down to New Zealand. And the importance of *Te Uenuku* does not end there. This wooden carving, in stylised form, is the logo of the Māori Broadcasting Agency, *Te Māngai Pāho*. What's more, so sacred is this relic to Māori that artists are advised to great care in its use for fear of causing offence to those who hold it in such reverential awe. Indeed, Māori regard for it is so high that the carving was made the centre piece of the *Te Māori* exhibition which toured North America and New Zealand in the early to mid-1980s.

But just what really is this relic? And who or what is Uenuku? Well, according to Patupaiarehe history teller Monica Matamua, Uenuku definitely wasn't Māori. 'He was an early leader of my people. He was the father of the Patupaiarehe and he led us to this land. He was not Māori, still less of Tainui. He was one of our most important ancestors,' she says.

And Monica is not the only one contending for Uenuku's ancient, non-Māori past. Waitaha paramount chief, Te Upoko Ariki,

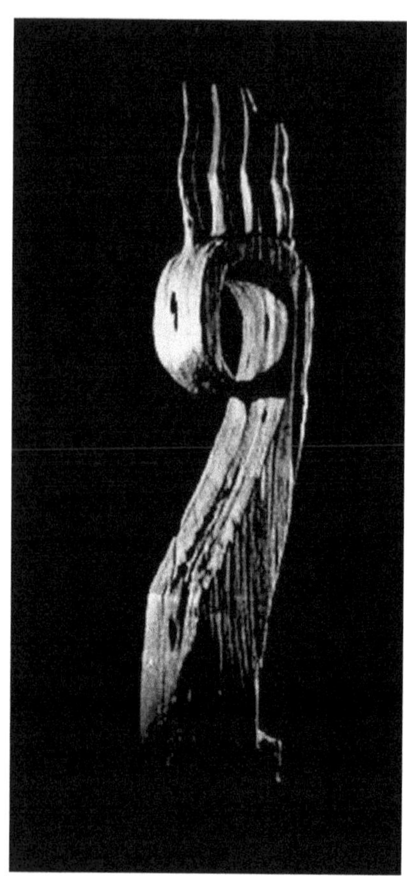

Te Uenuku.

Hori Kupenga Manuka Manuka, or George Connelly as he is known to his friends, insists that the wooden carving, far from being the 'sacred treasure' that steered the legendary *Tainui* canoe to this land, is a Waitaha 'hand-eye' boundary post, known as the 'Manuka Post'.

'Anciently, the "eye" of such a marker warned off intruders or attackers,' he explains. ''It would also mark the boundary for my people's land. It can't have come on the supposed *Tainui* canoe because it has been found to have been carved from New Zealand totara timber and that doesn't grow in the islands. No, it was carved here and set up as a boundary post in the Waikato by my people to denote land that belonged to us, not to Tainui'.

For years this artifact was held in Te Awamutu Museum until Chief George visited it and through a ceremonial prayer sought to reclaim it as an icon of his Waitaha people. Author Max Hill was refused permission to photograph the wooden carving and, apparently to prevent further controversy *Te Uenuku* was shipped off to New Zealand's national museum, Te Papa in Wellington. In 2014 when it was deemed the fuss had died down it was brought back to the Te Awamutu Museum where it still resides. *Wikipaedia* says that Te Uenuku (literally 'The Rainbow') carving represents the tribal god Uenuku and states:

It is 2.7 metres in height and comprises a simple upright post, the top of which has been carved into a spiral form. From the top of this spiral emerge four waving verticals, reminiscent of the teeth of a comb. The form, though simple, often causes a powerful reaction in viewers of the artifact. In appearance the carving is very striking and different from the style of carving seen in the later Classic period.

Again, according to *Wikipaedia*, Māori verbal history has it that around 1800 the Waipa District of the Waikato was invaded by a strong force led by Ngati Toa chief Pikauterangi. In the Battle of Hingakaka near Lake Ngaroto, between Tainui and Ngati Maniapoto warriors, the carving of Te Uenuku was lost. However, in 1906 the carving was found buried close to the lake's shore and was in the R.W. Bourne collection before being acquired by Te Awamutu Museum.

The online encyclopaedia considers the relic's form resembles Hawaiian carving styles. 'Tradition would suggest that it dates from circa 1400 CE, an era known to New Zealand ethnologists as *Te Tipunga* or the Archaic period, although recent work by the museum has shown that it is made from New Zealand Totara, a common native New Zealand hard wood,' it says.

If the 1400 CE date is correct then that dating alone would preclude the carving as of Tainui origin, for the first members of that tribe did not reach New Zealand until the 1600s. That late dating is proved by Max Hill[10] who debunks Tainui's claim to have arrived from the far Pacific by canoe in the North Island in 1340 and 1350AD. Hill notes that Tainui records at one time asserted that the supposed Tainui canoe first landed in New Zealand on the west coast at Kawhia, but later changed their story to say that their canoe landed on the East Coast in company with the legendary Te Arawa waka.

That being so, and since Te Arawa maintain their ancestors reached the North Island 18 generations ago, he calculates that (a

10 Page 198, *To The Ends Of The Earth And Back Again* by Maxwell C. Hill, Ancient History Publications 2015.

generation being counted as 20 years) the Tanui and Te Arawa arrival would have been around 1645AD, not 1340AD.

He further found that Tainui maintain in their story they arrived 300 years after the legendary early explorer of New Zealand, Kupe, who is recorded as sailing around the North Island of New Zealand in 1325. That would mean that Te Uenuku, the carved wooden 'hand eye' post, would have been in place in the Waikato denoting Waitaha owned land long before they got here, he maintains.

There is not a single mention of the Waitaha people in Tainui's tribal history. There is, however, mention of the indigenous original inhabitants being exterminated by the invading Tainui in the 1600s. These early settlers are believed to have been the Kapupungapunga people, comprising both Waitaha and Patupaiarehe people.

Again this is evidence pointing to a late arrival for Tainui. On the marker post, far from being called Te Uenuku, its real name according to Hori Kupenga, is 'Manuka', his name and that of his people.

Further to all this, the Te Awamutu Museum exhibits a large stone, in which according to local legend, the spirit of Uenuku was brought to New Zealand by the people on the Tainui canoe.

It is recounted that when they landed, they made a carving with a round opening at the top, in which the stone was placed so the spirit of Uenuku could inhabit the stone. The museum says that, 'Due to his spiritual significance, photographs of the stone figure of Uenuku are prohibited without the permission of the Māori sovereign'.

But what if the legend of Uenuku, the 'Rainbow God', actually recalls a real occurrence? What if, like the marker post now found to be of actual historical Waitaha usage rather than of supernatural origin, the 'sacred stone' can be traced to a practical truth now buried in superstitious legend?

To be blunt the Tainui arrival story of being 'led by the rainbow god' is a doubtful concoction.

Max Hill proved the tribe's ancestors did not arrive on the mythical canoe Tainui, supposedly buried at Kawhia.

Cordierite, the 'rainbow stone', used by Vikings and other ancient mariners as a navigation device. Was it used by the Patupaiarehe ancestors to steer their ships to New Zealand?

Firstly because it is far too small to have carried more than a handful of people. Second, because it is only a fair-weather, inshore fishing canoe unsuitable for ocean-voyaging. Third because it is made of New Zealand timber which does not grow in the islands and, fourthly, because it didn't belong to Tainui, but to the Moriori people living here when Tainui arrived.

So where did Tainui get the 'rainbow' story from? I suggest that they 'borrowed' it from the original indigenous people of New Zealand, the Patupaiarehe, for their tradition is that they were led here by their great leader, Uenuku.

Could the 'stone' held in the Te Awamutu Museum represent a badly garbled version of wisdom acquired from the Patupaiarehe who came here by ship, a sophisticated people who, according to Monica Matamua, read charts and navigated by ancient Greek technology?

It is an historical fact that ancient Greeks and Phoenicians had sophisticated navigation devices, among them the cross-staff, the torquetum (an ingenious predecessor to the sextant) and, almost certainly, one other directional aid that could keep a ship on course even when cloud obscured the sun.

This latter device comprised a stone but a very special stone. Known today as cordierite it was known to ancients as the 'sun stone' or, wait for it, the 'rainbow stone'. Greeks and Phoenicians called it 'iolite' from the Greek word from the violet because of its purple colour. It was called the 'sun stone' by the Vikings, as recorded in their literature, because it could detect the sun's presence through even thick cloud.

This feat was achieved through the crystal's polarizing properties, for the stone changes colour when it detects a source of light, even through the clouds. Using it ancient navigators could detect the direction in which the sun lay and keep their vessel on course.

To be more technical, according to *Wikipaedia,* it has 'birefringent and dichroic properties, changing color and brightness when rotated in front of polarised light. With an adequately cleaved crystal it is easy to tell the direction of skylight polarization: its color will change (e.g. from blue to light yellow) when pointing towards the sun'. Optical calcite does much the same.

But did ancient mariners really use it? Danish archaeologist, Thorkild Ramskou, asserts that the Vikings employed the stone, found as pebbles on Norway's coast, for orientation when clouds hid the sun's position. And Patupaiarehe descendant Monica Matamua maintains that it was Uenuku, the 'rainbow god', who helped steer her people to these shores. And Tainui would have learned all about it from the ancients they found living in the Waikato when they arrived.

Further support for this proposition is found in the oft told Māori legend of Uenuku who, while hunting early one morning encounters a beautiful maiden who 'appears' out the **mist** or cloud. They fall in love and each **night** she comes to him but as a **mist maiden** returns at day break her home in the sky.

They married and a baby girl was born to them but still the maid stayed only at night, vanishing with the **mist** in the morning. Uenuku told his friends of his wife but since they could not see her they did not believe him. So to manifest her in daylight he blocked the doors and windows of their home so she could not see the **sun**. But on discovering this trick the Mist Maid left him for good, taking their child with her.

In vain Uenuku wandered the world searching for them, until lonely and bent with age Rangi the Sky Father took pity on him and turned him into a **rainbow** so he could join his family in the sky.

What a delightful, poetic way to explain how a 'rainbow' lodestone can find the image and whereabouts of the sun even when it hides behind the clouds? What better way to preserve orally the memory of an important navigational tool that appears to have brought the Patupaiarehe people, and perhaps the Waitaha too, to the shores of New Zealand.

In my view, before Māori 'borrowed' it, the story of Uenuku was a First Nation story told by the ancient Patupaiarehe people to explain how they first came to New Zealand.

According to Monica Matamua, Uenuku's legendary 'Mist Maiden' is actually the Patupaiarehe lady Hinewai. She was one of two sisters who came with Toi and married the Patupaiarehe tribal chief Uenuku, as Minica explained in her earlier account of her people's tradition. The sub tribe Ngati Hinewai is named for her.

Chapter 7

The house of learning

If you want tangible proof that what has been said about the Patupaiarehe, both in Monica's story and elsewhere in this book, is true then you find it in the Cross-house of Miringa Te Kakara.

Researchers hold that for centuries this was a school to train the wise men of the Patupaiarehe in the arts of studying the stars in relation to earth.

Stretching out from this *whare wananga* (house of learning) on the ground surrounding it was a map of the heavens and their stars denoted by posts and extending to a 50-kilometre radius. Each peg denoted a star of importance and the whole was aligned to project the 'Great Triangle of Heaven' upon earth. This cruciform building, with four corner entrances and windows aligned to the sun, moon and the seasons, stood until recently at Tiroa under the shadow of the domed mountain of Pureora. The location is 12 miles east of Mangapehu, south of the main road leading to Mangakino in the centre of New Zealand's North Island.

It was burned down in 1983 in what is thought to have been a deliberate act of arson by activists determined to wipe out one of the last and most important pieces of evidence for the existence of the Patupaiarehe.

Thankfully before flames engulfed this ancient *whare wananga* (House of Learning) it was extensively surveyed and photographed. Looking at the pictures of this extensive and unique structure featured in this chapter, even at a glance, several things become clear.

The first is this **not** a Māori meeting house; nor did it stand on a Māori *marae*. It is devoid of the carvings that typify a Māori meeting house. No malevolent warrior spear in hand scowls from its rooftop, no dark gargoyles are carved into its main posts. No carved figure of a

Wrongly thought to have been a Māori construction, this building was actually a Patupaiarehe temple of worship to the Creator Io and a place to find peace through study of the stars. Picture courtesy of Janine and Ron Raison.

tattooed ancestor stands to support the main upright.

Second, it is, or was, old, very old. Some photographs feature this building roofed with flax and raupo tied down with manuka. Later it was re-roofed with corrugated iron but not by those who built it.

Third, it was not designed or built like a Māori meeting house. The barge boards and side posts of each of the four gabled entrances are massive slabs of timber. The doors slide, there are no centre posts supporting each gabled entrance, the windows are much smaller than those of the traditional Māori meeting house and the walls beneath the entrance porch are not plain but bear a chevron pattern of wood slats. The centre pole in the interior is a massive six feet in diameter.

The sliding doors of this impressive building were each hewn from a single timber slab 4ft. high, 2ft. wide and 2ins. thick. The window ports each closed by sliding slabs 18ins. square and 2ins. thick

What you are looking at, ladies and gentlemen, is not Māori. It is, or was, the last remaining major example of Patupaiarehe

An old black and white picture of Warenga a Kakara showing the original flax and raupo roof before 19th century rebuilding attempts replaced it with a corrugated iron roof. Picture courtesy of the website Forgotten New Zealand.

building construction extant in New Zealand and its design is ancient European. The ancient Egyptian cubit (18 inches) and the British standard inch (Egyptian, Sumerian, Babylonian in origin) predominate in its measurements. The building is oriented to ancient worldwide astronomical codes and could determine equinoxes, measure the earth's circumference, calculate the winter and summer solstices and the phases of the moon.

Monica Matamua says the building was undoubtedly constructed by the Patupaiarehe of old. 'It was how we built our homes of solid timber without carving. Structures like *Te Miringa Kakara* were temples for our worship of *Io* (Jehovah) the Creator God. 'This was where we conducted our sacred rituals and where we were taught our traditions and essential truths.

'The amazing thing is that years ago when my late husband Ike drew up plans to build a marae on our ancestral land at Te Rena, which, hopefully, will now be returned to us, he designed a cross-house structure very similar to that of Te Miringa. We still intend to build a house like that for our people, for a meeting place, to house our history and to worship God in a Christian way'.

According to notes published on the internet by W. Hugh Ross, Pei Te Hurunui Jones, surveyor C.G. Hunt and C. Royal, *Miringa Te Kakara* is a recent name given by Māori to the cruciform house.

Originally it was called *Waerenga a Kakara* meaning the 'Secret Garden in the Forest'. *Waerenga* is a cultivated forest clearing and *kara* is a secret or conspiracy.

Importantly, these notes and those of Martin Doutre[11] confirm that the Patupaiarehe were said to be the original builders of the temple. According to a cleric, Bishop Thomas Herangi, guardian of the Cross-house until the 1980s, this 'Star Temple' was built in 1682 and then renovated in 1788 and again in 1887.

Both Ross and Doutre speak of confusion among Māori tohunga and historians about the origin of the building. They disagree about whether the Cross-house was rebuilt by adherents of the strange Māori *Pai Marire* religion of the 19th century or merely renovated.

Today Māori people run and owned the *Pa Harekeke* eco-adventure tourism business, which organises walks and cycle tours of the Pureora National Park. Its brochure has this to say about *Miringa Te Kakara*:

> Sacred Marae Experience – by arrangement – Cost $95 per person: Miringa Te Kakara is an ancient place of higher learning established in pre-European times to ensure the ancient **Māori** traditions were retained and passed on to the next generation … The guide will talk about this special place and show you why it is revered by **Māori** around the country as a place to learn the ancient traditions. Although many buildings are in a ruinous state and some long gone, the atmosphere remains.
>
> Today Miringa Te Karaka is a place of pilgrimage as the original Cross-house, built in the 1600s, was found to have been built to the same triangular patterns and forms used … in the pyramids of Egypt and the Stonehenge of England. The tour package includes morning and afternoon tea.

Not a word about the Patupaiarehe, you notice. Only **Māori**

11 *Ancient Celtic New Zealand* by Martin Doutre.

are mentioned. Yet the several buildings which once stood on the site, including 'round houses' said to have been special dwellings for the Patupaiarehe 'king' and 'queen', totally differ from Māori construction.

Originally, the Ross notes say, there were four temples to Io in the Pureora Forest. Each was a house of learning. They were at Whenua Tapu on the Waimihia Stream, about three miles north-east of the Waimihia railway station on the Main Trunk Line, at Papaawaka on the Ongarue River a mile above its junction with the Waimihia Stream and at Kete Maringi, or Hurkuia, on the Hurkuhia Range at the head of the Ongarue River.

The history is confused because the Patupaiarehe were killed off or driven out of this their mountain stronghold and Māori taking possession of the land absorbed these sacred sites into their culture. So much so, it is said that in 1863 the fierce, cannibalistic Hau Hau movement, known for decapitating its victims, tried to rebuild *Miringa Te Kakara*. The Hau Hau had emerged as a warlike splinter group from the *Pai Marire* religion, a mix of Christian and Māori folklore, leaders of which believed that the Māori were one of the lost tribes of Israel and that God would give the earth to them.

Evidently, the Hau Hau had deep misgivings about the cruel treatment of the Patupaiarehe by Māori and reportedly tried to rebuild the Cross-house to bring the Patupaiarehe back to this their ancient dwelling place.

It is believed they held that the sin of exterminating the ancient First Nation of New Zealand had to be expiated by summoning their spirits to reoccupy their ancient temple. This so that Māori could receive respite from the 19th century Land Wars steadily stripping them of their land. And you couldn't summon such spirits back to a dilapidated building, could you? Hence the necessity to rebuild it.

The re-building appears to have consisted largely of replacing the original flax and raupo roof with corrugated iron; the walls and internal structure were left as they were. The Ross notes state this 'rebuild' was 'by directive of (Māori) King Tawhiao to Chieftaness

Interior of the Cross-house showing star viewing bench.

Ngaharakeke' (and) is said to have been completed about 1865 under the direction of Te Raa Karepe and Rangawhenua, leaders of the Pao Miere (or Pai Marire) movement'.

Part of an ancient worldwide pattern

The notes insist that the Cross-house of *Waerenga a Kakara* was not 'some form of orphan dwelling' unique to New Zealand, as historians and anthropologists might suggest, but 'was built according to an internationally distributed parcel of astronomical codes, in accordance with a measurement standard that migrated throughout the ancient world and spanned the oceans'.

Those who have studied it say the temple's geometric and measurement attributes replicates astronomical and navigational knowledge also found in ancient stone circles and other structures found from Egypt to Great Britain and through to North and South America.

One commentator opines that such knowledge was obtained

by and recorded in monuments by a very ancient, highly mobilized, migrating group, who set up colonies all over the globe. Many appear to have begun as metal ore mining operations. (See chapters 22 and 23, 'An obsession with maps' and 'The 'unknown' mappers' for further thoughts on this conjecture).

The Ross notes state that the Mt. Ranginui peak is the benchmark for the Cross-house's north orientation from its centre pole. Two wings mark the lines of the winter solstice sunrise and the summer solstice sunset positions. An observer seated on benches at the centre pole viewing upward through the north-east window would observe the major northern standstill position of moon rise and through the south-west window the major southern standstill moon set.

Moonlight beams were reflected by paua shells onto incised symbols in the building and there were also marks and lettering on the extensive pattern of posts surrounding the Cross-house.

Note the solid slab doors at left and the very unusual and pre-Māori wall construction throughout.

Chapter 8

A nation in denial

There is nothing good or bad but thinking makes it so, wrote the great Bard. However, were Shakespeare living in New Zealand today, he would conclude that not thinking about some things, even denying their very existence, is just as effective in bending the facts.

The truth is that most New Zealanders live in denial. They don't or won't admit the proven facts of this country's history and pre-history. Worse than that many, even at an official level, positively assert that such things never happened.

They also deny that peoples still alive here exist at all, or just as bad, assert that they are not the people they say they are. Forgive me if this sounds like Alice's excursion into Wonderland but such are the lengths that politicians, historians, tribal leaders and archaeologists will go to hide what to them is inconvenient truth.

Just as neo-Nazis today deny or minimize the Holocaust in which Hitler's Germany murdered six million Jews so New Zealand officially turns a blind eye to its own historic 'ethnic cleansing'. Against this denial trend Britain has apologised for some atrocities and massacres it executed in colonial years in India, and Japan has admitted guilt over its savage mistreatment of Second World War victims and abuse of 'comfort' women in that conflict.

However, it is notable that no Muslim country or major Islamic leader has ever admitted wrong or said sorry for the numerous murderous atrocities followers of this religion have perpetrated in the 1500-year history of their hatred and persecution of Christians and Jews. Rather they have rejoiced in them and celebrated such slaughter. Turkey, for example, refuses to admit its deliberate campaign of genocide against Armenian Christians killing 3.7 million of them during the First World War. But what has all that to do with New Zealand, you ask? Answer: much in every way. Because New Zealand has deliberately hushed and covered up its own appalling genocide.

George Santayana famously said, '*Those who cannot remember the past are condemned to repeat it'*. And in New Zealand, if the lesson of this country's own genocide is not acknowledged nor remembered, repetition is a real possibility.

The two holocausts

The deliberate slaughter of six million plus Jews by Nazi Germany in the Second World War is rightly called 'The Holocaust', but the same word could be applied to the planned and cruelly executed extermination of the original, indigenous peoples of New Zealand in the 1700s and 1800s. Whole tribes of peaceful, living indigenous people, like the Ngati Kapupungapunga, who once lived in the Waikato, were mercilessly wiped out, killed and eaten, down to the last babe in arms.

Some of my friends have argued that the word 'holocaust' should not be used to describe the concerted nationwide campaign by Māori war tribes to wipe out the Patupaiarehe, Waitaha, Turehu and other first settlers in this land. They say that because it means a burnt sacrifice the word should be reserved for Hitler's attempted genocide of the Jews. However, the Collins Dictionary definition is:

> **Holocaust**: a burnt offering, the whole being consumed by fire; hence wholesale sacrifice, destruction or slaughter.

In its secondary meaning then, that of destruction and slaughter, the word 'holocaust' embraces the many Jewish victims of Hitler's hate religion not consumed in the Auschwitz gas chambers but instead shot, clubbed or by other means put to death.

Similarly, not all of the estimated 100,000 plus Patupaiarehe, Turehu, Waitaha and Kapupungapunga peoples who perished at the hands and teeth of bloodthirsty Māori during the unspeakable horrors of the 17th and 18th centuries in New Zealand were fed into the *hangi* fires to be cooked, although many were, but perished instead through slaughter in other ways. It seems then that 'holocaust' is a fitting word to describe their fate.

One reason for not being squeamish about using the word 'holocaust' is that today Germany itself isn't. In sharp contrast to New Zealand, which hides from succeeding generations the awful truth about this land's comparatively recent genocidal cannibalism, Germany now makes teaching about the Holocaust and the horrors of the Nazi era compulsory in all its schools. The German Government also requires that almost all students visit either a wartime concentration camp where such atrocities were carried out or a Holocaust memorial museum.

However, this honest admittance by Germany of its dark past has not come easily. It took a struggle to bring it about. Lars Rensmann, an educator who teaches political science at the University of Munich and the Moses Mendelssohn Center for European-Jewish Studies at the University of Potsdam, says it is only in the last 20 to 30 years that Holocaust education has gained impetus in Germany.

Prior to that it was a 'taboo' subject. The breakthrough in acknowledgement of the nation's darkest days was sparked by screening of the TV series '*Holocaust*' in German, which, he says, created a new kind of awareness and stimulated major debate.

On the impact on succeeding generations, Israeli Professor Gideon Greif, who lectures thousands of German students each year, says that most now express deep empathy over what happened to Jews during the Holocaust and ask intelligent questions that show familiarity with the subject. 'I meet such great German teenagers', he told a German newspaper reporter. 'What wonderful young people they are. But where were they then (i.e. during the Nazi era)? Why weren't their voices heard then?' he asks.

Admitting an awful past

New Zealand students, however, are told nothing about the dreadful massacres of tens of thousands of this country's first settlers. The obliteration of 'The First Nation', comprised of different pre-

Māori tribes that lived peaceably together for over 1,000 years, is not even mentioned in school history lessons. This is so because New Zealand students are still taught today that such people did not and do not exist.

History education in our schools begins only with the arrival of the Māori when in fact it stretches back beyond the time of Christ. Consequently our children are taught nothing of this country's true pre-history or its wonderful legacy of peace. They are also told little or nothing about the violent and hateful nature of the Māori prior to latter day European settlement, fueled as it was by a desperately dark and blood-thirsty religion. In the view of interdisciplinary research scientist, Dr. John Robinson, Māori culture of the 1700s was 'not just dysfunctional but mad, criminally insane'.

Having all but exterminated the ancient peoples of this land Māori turned on each other and then, according to Dr. Robinson's figures, killed, enslaved or drove out between 50,000 and 60,000 of their own people.

The important question to ask is: What made the Māori go that way? Answer: the Māori nature and character shaped by their chosen religious beliefs, a worship of dark spiritual forces that inculcated hate, treachery, cruelty, fear and bloodlust in those that worshipped them. The historian of the Takitimu tribe J. H. Mitchell[12] states: 'Tu was the supreme god of war and was treated as the most important offspring of Rangi and Papa (heaven and earth). All male children were dedicated in the name and service of Tu'. And Tu, full name Tumatauenga, is of ancient evil origin. The syllable forms part of an alternate name for Marduk, the principal god of biblical Babylon.

And respected 19th century New Zealand ethnographer Elsdon Best had the following to say[13]:

---

12 Page 34, *Takitimu* by JH Mitchell, 1972, facsimile edition, published by A. H. And A. W. Reed, Wellington.

13 *The Maori – Volume 1*, chapter VI 'Religious Beliefs and Practices of the Maori' published 1924 Wellington, (part of the published works of Elsdon Best, retrieved from New Zealand Electronic Data Base, Victoria University of Wellington.

In Tu we have the tutelary deity of the war department of Māoriland. Tu represents war, bloodshed, and the present writer is inclined to hold the view that Tu personifies the setting sun, which is ever associated with death. If Fenton's statement that one Tu held the same position in Babylonia be correct, then it is a very remarkable coincidence, especially when viewed in conjunction with the parallels pertaining to Ra and Sin. Inasmuch as Tu was the chief war god of the Māori, it was his tapu that lay heavy on fighting men when on active service.

> *His mana was over the warrior, and any who infringed the many restrictions imposed by his tapu were indeed in parlous plight. Offerings of the hearts of slain enemies were made to him. He was the presiding genius of war, but, at the same time, any fighting force was also under the sway, mana, and guidance of one at least of the many beings who may be termed tribal war gods. These latter belonged to the third and fourth classes of atua Māori, or native gods.*

And on page 241 of the same work Mr. Best explains how sorcery and possession by evil spirits was the driving force behind Māori warfare. He writes:

> *It would be of no interest or service to give a list of names of these ancestral spirits, but a few cases known to myself may be mentioned as illustrations. When, in the "sixties" of last century, the Tuhoe tribe was in a disturbed state owing to fighting proceeding between certain tribes and the fair skinned Pakeha from far lands, it was decided to protect the tribal lands from invasion. During the guerilla-like bush warfare that followed the decision, a Tuhoe woman named Maraea felt herself called to a higher sphere of life, and so decided to become a poropiti. This is the Māori form of our word prophet, a tohunga matakite (second sight expert) in Māori.*
>
> *Our prophetess now cast about for an atua whose medium she might become, one that would endow her with the necessary*

Sketch by John Philemon Backhouse 1845-1908: Old mill near Mt Eden, Onehunga Road. Once a flour mill, this windmill was later used to grind many generations of Patupaiarehe and Turehu skeletons into fertiliser. Tens of thousands of skeletons of these ancient people were removed from Auckland burial caves to be ground up and scattered as powder on farms. While some skeletons still remain around Auckland and on offshore islands proper, open-minded scientific examination of their age and ethnic origin is still not undertaken because officialdom does not recognise their existence.

powers enabling her to foretell events, and lead her people to victory. Being possibly desirous of making it a family affair, she did not placate any of the known supernormal beings, but decided to evolve a new atua for her own use. Happening to be delivered of a stillborn child, she resolved to utilise the spirit of that child as a war god, or, as anthropologists would say, as a "familiar." Now in Māori belief the spirits of stillborn children, termed atua kahu, are exceedingly malignant beings who ever delight in afflicting the living.

Thus it will be seen that they are useful creatures to employ for the purpose of harassing and destroying one's enemies. Even so Maraea set about conciliating the spirit of her own child by means of offerings and appropriate ceremonial, in which task she would probably be assisted by a priestly expert. She now became the waka or kaupapa (medium) of this spirit god, which received the name of Te Awanui.

Stirring up the bloodlust

Fact is that the Māori deliberately invoked evil spirits and danced to stir up bloodlust. Thus the book *Takitimu* on page 6 records: 'The tohi riri or tutu-ngarehu (war dance) was performed to inspire enthusiasm and bravery and to create savagery'.

Given that evil was deliberately sought and invoked one must ask, did Māori consider they were the children of God, that is the God of the Bible, the Creator, sustainer of life, the Redeemer and Saviour, or by their own choice the children of devils?

Their own literature answers that. An online webpage entitled *MAORI ART Symbolism and Surrealism: Te Ao Tawhito*, cites this extract from page 80 of the book *Māori Artists of the South Pacific*, by Katerina Mataira, published by the New Zealand Māori Artists and Writers Society:

> *At Tatahoata Marae, Ruatahuna, there is a carving of a large male figure sexually connected to a small female figure. I was told by a man, who should know better, that it was a disgusting carving showing a man having incestuous sex with a child. In fact it depicts the sacred union of an atua (big) with a human woman (small) so symbolising our divine heritage. This art record parallels the Hebrew book of Genesis 6v4:*
>
> *'In those days, and for some time after, giant Nephilim lived on the earth, for whenever the sons of God had intercourse with the daughters of men they gave birth to children who became the warriors and heroes of ancient times.'*
>
> *In Māori mythology our most famous cultural hero, Maui Tikitiki-a-Taranga was of this Nephilim type. Judging from the size of some of the taiaha held in Te Papa Museum's*

collection, the wielders of these weapons must have been giants – perhaps evidence of the veracity of ancient legends of the interbreeding of an extra-terrestrial race ('sons of God', Atua) with humans.

So was Maui a misbegotten giant, the hybrid progeny of a devil and a woman? According to at least one Māori that is so and he believes his race can trace its very roots back to the incarnation of evil spirits in mankind. Now, lest you think, as some do, that the 'giants' of Genesis 6:4 perished in Noah's Flood which their sin caused, read the verse again. It says there were 'giants in the earth in those days and also after that'.

Descended from fallen angels?

Evidently, Genesis teaches that further eruptions of fallen angels produced the same evil offspring after the Flood. They are mentioned often later. We are told that the children of Israel entering the Promised Land went to great lengths to kill and destroy such giants but apparently did not totally succeed, lending possible credence to the Māori claim to be their descendants.

Be that is it may, the message from this Māori writer is clear: Some Māori do believe they are descended from fallen angels, the Nephilim, hybrid half-angel, half-human beings which, according to Genesis, so wickedly corrupted mankind that God determined to destroy man from the earth in Noah's Flood.

Notably, this consequence, the triggering of God's judgement by their great sin, is left out of the writer's statement. So, to clarify I will quote Genesis 6:4-8 from the King James Bible in its entirety:

There were giants in the earth in those days, and also after that, when the sons of God came in unto the daughters of men, and they bare children unto them, the same became mighty men which were of old, men of renown.

And God saw that the wickedness of man was great in the earth and that every imagination of the thoughts of his heart was only evil continually. And it repented the Lord that He had made man on the earth, and it grieved Him at his heart.

And the Lord said I will destroy man whom I have created from the face of the earth; both man and beast, and the creeping thing, and the fowls of the air, for it repenteth Me that I have made them. But Noah found grace in the eyes of the Lord.

Fact is that a few of the Māori people knew of the true creator God. They called him 'Io', which may well be a contraction of the biblical Yahweh or Jehovah. However, the knowledge of Io was strictly reserved for the elite who kept it a closely guarded secret. And while Io's creative power was acknowledged, his edicts were not. The sixth commandment, 'Thou shalt not kill' (Exodus 20:13) was honoured by the Patupaiarehe, the first settlers of New Zealand, who did their best to live in peace, but deliberately and persistently disobeyed by the Māori.

Worse still, while Io was worshipped by the elite in one part of the *whare wananga* (house of learning), human sacrifices were regularly and commonly made to Tu, the Māori war god, and other *atua* in others. J. H. Mitchell[14] in *Takitimu* (p. 50) explains:

The building faced east and had three compartments. In the easterly portion, the mahau, sacrificial offerings were killed. In the oblong courtyard named Mua, in front of the mahau, the sacred offerings were made to the gods and all attendant ceremonies performed.

In the centre of the courtyard there was usually a flax bush or fern tree growing, and nearby, a shrine. Here was erected a footless statue of the rainbow god Kahukura. All human sacrifices were buried close to the spot while the blood of the victim was offered to Mua and the heart to Tu. Owing to the presence of the gods, the whole locality and all it contained, animate or inanimate, was highly charged with an extremely potent tapu.

---

14 Page 50, *Takitimu* by J H Mitchell, 1972, facsimile edition, published by A. H. And A. W. Reed, Wellington.

Now some say that 'we are what we eat'. Also true is the dictum that 'we become what we believe'. Māori believed they were descended from devils, 'that is, according to Jude 6 '… angels which kept not their first estate (as unmarried beings, that is) but left their own habitation (heaven) (in order to come to earth)'.

They also believed that such evil spirits could continue to possess them down the generations and, should they be absent, they could be summoned up by prayers, sacrifices and incantations. The *haka* (war dance), was practiced specifically to arouse hatred, rage and bloodlust in the *tuau* (war party) before it set off to attack, kill and eat those selected as the tribe's enemies.

Cruelty, bloodlust and treachery became the hallmarks of Māori behaviour under such influence. According to a *Wikipaedia* entry:

> Perhaps the most important outcome of the Musket Wars was the bitter legacy of inter-hapū and iwi mistrust stemming from the extreme violence with which they were fought. The constant use of **treachery** as a battlefield tactic, coupled with the enslavement of so many, left a long legacy of mistrust.

The third to last battle of the Musket Wars took place just a few months before the Treaty of Waitangi was signed and shows that savagery and cannibalism were still rife then . A *tuau* (war party) from the Te Awamutu area attacked and slaughtered Te Arawa people in the Rotorua area and brought back 60 basket-loads of human flesh to eat.

Thankfully, in a later chapter we can turn to the huge spiritual change which brought light into the savage darkness of New Zealand in the early 19th century.

Today, sadly, this development and its role in bringing about such a radical improvement, is also largely ignored in both school curriculum and recognised history. Yet actually the preaching of the gospel of Jesus Christ is the very foundation stone of modern New Zealand.

History warts and all

This gospel, along with the genocide of the original peoples of this land, and the rampant Māori killing of themselves make up the key threads that woven together form the tapestry of who and what this nation became as Christianity shed light on its darkness. It shaped who and what we have become. Today to be a New Zealander is to be a descendant of our nation's past along with its present. We are what our history has made us.

Just as young Germans must learn the horrors of the Nazi past to discover who they are as Germans today, so New Zealanders of all races must know this land's past in order to truly be New Zealanders. And that means uncovering, not suppressing, the evidence and history of the past.

Thankfully I grew up in a Britain which had learned to do this. In the United Kingdom the past is cherished, each artifact treasured; ancient remains are explored, preserved and celebrated.

British history with its ancient battles, cruel conquests, bitter repressions and glorious victories is taught and appreciated warts and all. Historic defeats and conquests, repressions and freedoms are re-enacted to preserve their significance. As a result succeeding generations know, because they have been told so, that to be truly British they partake of and are a part of all that has gone before.

Human presence in Britain stretches back over 5,000 years. The sophisticated Neolithic dwellings, circle and temple at Scalla Brae, Stonehenge and the complex stone architecture of Ireland all speak of an ancient past.

They were followed by the technically advanced Celtic civilisation, then by Roman iron and might. As a lad I tasted history at first hand, walking the Roman road that crosses the Pennines and visiting several stone circles. And you can add to the British mix the culture of the Angles and Jutes, then the Saxons, to whom I owe my ancestry, followed by that of the Danes and the French. Refugees like the French Huguenots, to whom I am also related, also contributed to the combined English, Welsh, Scots and Irish character mix.

We students, our teachers told us, were the collective legacy, the cultural outworking of all that history, the cumulative results of all best traditions, the courage and the lessons learned all along the way, from the first Stone Age settlers, through Boadicea who trounced the Romans, via Alfred who conquered and converted the Danes to Christianity. Then there was Drake who humbled the Spanish, Nelson who crushed the French at Trafalgar down to the World War Two fighter pilots who held back the Nazi invasion of England.

Brave stuff, but there were also dark deeds, the many blots on the British and English escutcheon. Among them bloody civil wars, crushing of the poor, persecution of religious dissenters, the merciless crushing of the Scots – remember Culloden? – and the oft cruel history of the British Empire, built, as a significant part of it was, on slavery.

No Englishman escapes the bitterness of that past, myself included. I am descended from a line of forebears which includes a Lord Mayor of Bristol who was prominent in the slave trade. But also, thankfully, I come from a line of more humble farmers and artisans who braved Catholic persecutors to worship the God of the Bible as their consciences dictated.

And there is much in British history to be proud of too. In contrast to continental jurisprudence, English law was based on biblical precepts that led to Magna Carta and a progressive curbing of the tyranny of kings. Importantly, Celtic missionaries converted much of Europe to the gospel long before the Roman Catholic Church came to Britain to undo their work.

Years before the Mayflower set sail for America seafaring Aldworths were sailing ships across the Atlantic, carrying passengers seeking a new and freer life outside of the religious and economic repression of England. Against that there were those among my predecessors who owned American plantations worked by slaves, shipped slaves themselves, and cruelly drove the Irish from their lands to occupy them.

Whether good or ill, the Aldworth family history is my legacy. And so is the chequered past that forged the British nation. Every part of it contributed to a greater society and forged a resilient, freer character in its people. Their tenacity is attested by war and endurance, their sense of who they are by their full acceptance of many different peoples and all the history they have sprung from.

Let's celebrate our true past

This much has been said to make the point that the truth of who we really are as New Zealanders can only be found by fully exploring, acknowledging and celebrating this country's past. To ignore or exclude the contribution made to our nationhood by the ancient voyagers of European and Middle Eastern descent who first peopled these shores is to cut ourselves off from our most important cultural roots.

The peaceable nature and culture of these first New Zealanders is as an important contributor to the national psyche as is the fighting bravery of the Māori and the fortitude of the latter day European settlers. Add in the influences of the Moriori, the Chinese, East Europeans and Asians to the mix, each with their own particular characteristics and we have the ingredients to create a unique New Zealand.

But history, an honest and fully acknowledged account of all the peoples of this land, both ancient and modern, must be the crucible in which it is forged. That means the story of this land must be told in full, warts and all. Where there has been wrong it must be acknowledged. Where possible it must be set right. Where not it must be remembered and publicly atoned for.

So why has the Government refused to recognise the shame of New Zealand's holocaust? Why did it allow tens of thousands of skeletons of the Patupaiarehe and other ancient dwellers in this land to be ground up as fertiliser at Robinson's Auckland mill in the 19th century?

Answer: Because in its 'divide and conquer' strategy to secure the land the British New Zealand Government favoured the large and powerful tribes at the expense of small minority sub tribes and groupings.

When it came to subduing Te Rauparaha they cared little or nothing about the ancient Waitaha people he had slaughtered and even less about compensating their descendants? On the Chatham Islands though they had largely killed off the Moriori people it was the Māori who were recognised as owners of the land by right of conquest, not the Moriori.

Monica Matamua asserts that evidence presented to a Whanganui hearing conducted by the Waitangi Tribunal has detailed how 19th century war chief Te Rauparaha killed off many Turehu and Patupaiarehe tribes during his lengthy war campaigns in the North Island.

In pursuit of this devious policy Governor George Grey 'dug' around the Māori King' until he became effectively powerless, opening the way for widespread land seizure by the Crown. And the fierce Tuwharetoa tribe, having taken and largely lost much land around Lake Taupo, was tamed yet again by the Crown when it subsequently recognised the tribe's land claim to 40,000 hectares of land between Taumarunui and Ruapehu but took back 20,000ha as a surveying fee.

Little thought was given to rights or wrongs in the latter process, still less to the valid claim of the Ngati Hotu people and the many other tribes and peoples of the Patupaiarehe whose links to the land go back over 2,000 years.

And the Ngati Hotu claim, still before the courts, is just one of the many matters that must be addressed to do justice to the first settlers of what to them, having sailed half way round the world, was the 'Far Off Land'.

Chapter 9

The great genocide

Monica Matamua will look you straight in the eye and say, 'Thank God the white British settlers came when they did. There would have been none of us left, if they hadn't'. Now that's a provocative thing to say in 21st century New Zealand but this gentle lady, with soft, golden hair, green eyes and rosy complexion, means it from the heart.

In New Zealand, she says, there has been a huge social, academic and political cover-up of the wholesale slaughter that destroyed her own tribe and many others of the original, pre-Māori peoples who first occupied these lands. She believes that only 'genocide' can adequately describe the ferocious attacks conducted across the country by Māori to eradicate the true tangata whenua, the first settlers of New Zealand.

On p. 62 the book *Tainui*, by Lesley Kelly, says that the tribe's warfare 'saw the final extinction ... of the aborigines known as Kapupungapunga (which) were the last remaining remnants of a once numerous people'.

And this is why, in sharp contrast to Māori complainants in the ongoing (Waitangi) Treaty industry process, who often say that European colonisation is largely to blame for their ills, this gracious Patupaiarehe lady is glad the Pakeha came when so many others apparently are not.

Far from blaming them for Māoridom's often self-inflicted ills, Monica says that but for European arrival, and a tentative peace won after her people, the Ngati Hotu, finally learned to fight for the first time in their history, 'we would have been killed and eaten down to the very last one'.

Of course, to say so is politically incorrect. It goes against the grain of our amoral, multicultural New Age, 21st century New

Zealand, brainwashed as it is by an academically sanitised version of this country's prehistory. Monica, however, is talking about massacres that raged throughout New Zealand in the 1700s and the first 40 years of the 1800s in what Māori tribal history itself records as a concerted campaign by the major *iwi* (tribes) to entirely wipe out the indigenous settlers of the land.

As a voice from the past, the descendant of a family that barely survived such genocide on a massive scale, she speaks out with feeling about the grim slaughter of her once numerous people, the Ngati Hotu. 'If the Pakeha had not arrived the carnage would have gone on until none of us were left. Fact is we were, and still are, Pakeha too; *Pakepakeha* and we faced extinction.

'It was only the influx of the European and the preaching of the Christian gospel that stopped the bloodshed and spared us at the end of the day'. Her ancestral history says that as late as 1835 there was still killing and eating of her people by warrior Māori.

But today, adding insult to injury, it is Tuwharetoa, Ngati Hotu's ancient foe, which has been awarded guardianship of Lake Taupo and are still negotiating for the return of surrounding lands, not Ngati Hotu who, says Monica, are still 'trying to pick up crumbs that fall from the table'.

Back in 1833 the Ngati Hotu were then still a tribe of considerable number, a branch of that peaceful living people, the Patupaiarehe. It is estimated that, despite over the centuries, having been driven up from the fertile lands around Whakatane, first to Lake Taupo, then to their last refuge on the slopes of Mount Ruapehu, between 2,000 and 3,000 still remained when the tribe was largely slaughtered at the Battle of the Five Forts.

Earlier, according to the *Wikipaedia* entry *Ngati Hotu*, the tribe had suffered a major defeat at the battle of Pukekaikiore ('Hill of the Meal of the Rats) to the southwest of Lake Taupo where Ngāti Tūwharetoa devastated them, causing the few remaining survivors to flee.

Worse was to come. Some Ngati Hotu who escaped alive from the Pukekaikiore pogrom regrouped on the lower slopes of Mount Ruapehu at Kakahi, which means 'freshwater mussels'

Here, some 30 kilometres west of Lake Taupo, they hid themselves in the bush. Years later, however, their refuge was stumbled on by a party of Whanganui Māori journeying up the Whanganui River. These returned to their pa, called in reinforcements, then returned to attack the settlement.

In defense Ngāti Hotu, for the first time in their history, according to Monica, set up a ring of five forts around the Kakahi settlement and determined to resist, at least with their hands, for they had no weapons. It was a major turning point for a people who had hoped against hope that peace and keeping a low profile would protect them.

'We had no weapons, we believed in doing good and peace,' Monica explains. Despite this pacifist stance, the *Wikipaedia* Ngati Hotu entry records that the Whanganui Māori still attacked in force and took the forts one by one until finally the last two, Otutaarua and Arikipakewa, fell. The citation concludes:

> The final, brutal episode of the Five Forts Battle was played out on the flats between Kakahi and the Wanganui River when the now victorious when the now, effectively victorious Whanganui Māori hung the legs of fallen Ngāti Hotu warriors from poles mounted in the forks of trees – a gesture at which their remaining enemies broke and fled off into the depths of the King Country to vanish from history.
>
> The battle is estimated to have occurred circa 1450 and its story has since been handed down through 15 generations to the Whanganui *kaumatua* Takiwa Tauarua, who related it to prominent New Zealand artist Peter McIntyre in the 1960s.

But vanish from history the Ngati Hotu did not. In fact, this well recorded conflict was a further departure point for Monica's

Pukekaikiore (Hill of the Meal of Rats), the bleak mountain high on the volcanic Central Plateau was the scene of a ruthless slaughter centuries ago of the fair-haired Ngati Hotu, Patupaiarehe people. Towering in the background is the active volcano Mount Ngauruhoe. Photo: Roger Wong.

Patupaiarehe people. It was the last major battle in which they would fight weaponless with bare hands. It was also the last fight from which they would run away.

'Up until the Battle of the Five Forts that's what we'd always done – resist non-violently, plead for our lives, fight with our hands; if all else failed run away,' Monica says.

'There was no warrior tradition among us, we did not make war, nor did we know how to. Ours was a peace loving tradition. It was how we lived and what we lived for. Our ancestors first came to these shores with the very purpose of finding a place where we could live in peace.

'Going back to the start of it, when the Māori arrived and multiplied they began pushing us off our lands. We treated for peace, offered help with growing food, even inter-married in attempts to keep the peace.

'But nothing was ever enough for them. They broke the treaties and forced us out. Gradually we were pushed back from our lands around Whakatane and went to live around Lake Taupo.

'But peace didn't last there. Tuwharetoa attacked us and other tribes there and eventually we the Ngati Hotu were driven up from Taumarunui onto the slopes of Mount Ruapehu itself, to Taurewa, the land that is ours and, rightfully, still should be ours today'.

There in the bush-clad slopes the tribe had made its peaceful earlier stand. The tribespeople had built the forts as shelter, evidently knowing that Ngati Tuwharetoa in alliance with other tribes would launch a concerted effort to wipe out this stubborn remnant of the once plentiful *Urekehu* (red or fair-haired and green-eyed people) who first voyaged to this land.

'We were all but killed and then eaten out on that day. Some of us ran away but most couldn't and were slain where they stood on the last stretch of land we owned.' So great was the slaughter that the Mangatepopo stream at Taurewa ran red with blood for five days, as a Tuwharetoa witness testified at a Waitangi Tribunal hearing into his tribe's claim for the return of land taken by the Crown for the main trunk line and National Park.

Monica was present to present Ngati Hotu's counter claim for the land. But to 'prove' that no such people as Ngati Hotu still existed the witness described in such detail Tuwharetoa's massacre of the Patupaiarehe that, according to Monica, 'even the judge looked sick'.

Once on the witness stand he 'went on at length about how Tuwharetoa chased us through the bush, bashed us to death and then fed on us like a pack of rats. All that detail just to try to show that we as a people did not exist – that Tuwharetoa had exterminated us as a people. When they hadn't.

'After that hideous attack my ancestors fled to hide in the bush and on the cliff tops along the Whanganui River. Others took refuge near Lake Taupo and yet more journeyed to the Waikato to take shelter on Mt Pirongia where their presence is well documented in history.'

But what made this gruesome evidence at the Waitangi Tribunal even harder for Monica to bear was the fact that he was a distant relative.

'Because of past marriage between Ngati Hotu which we had agreed to in a futile effort to bring about peace, it turned that he was a distant cousin of mine,' she says.

Appallingly, the horror of the massacre of the Five Forts did not end with the slaughter, Monica states. The victors indulged in a huge, on the spot, cannibal feast, gorging themselves on the carcasses of those they had slain.

'And the bodies they couldn't eat, because there were so many of them, they stacked up in rows or hung them up in the trees. Then for weeks and months afterwards they came back to feast on the rotting remains. No wonder the tribunal judge felt ill.'

But, one might ask, why did this grisly practice come as any surprise either to the Waitangi Tribunal judge or to any else conversant with history as recorded by Māori themselves? Books of tribal history such as *Takitimu, a History of the Ngati Kahungunu People*, by J H. Mitchell (Tiaki Hikawera Mitira), record that victory in taking a *pa* (fort) and killing its inhabitants was almost routinely followed by a cannibal feast.

For example, *Transactions and Proceedings of the Royal Society of New Zealand* (1868-1961), Vol. 38, 1905, records:

> In regard to cannibalism, and the fierce lust for revenge which so often animated the Native mind, a dreadful illustration is that of the kai pirau – namely, the ghoulish custom which formerly obtained of exhuming the body of a buried enemy, cooking and devouring the same, even though decomposition had set in.

And should you wonder why there are few if any ancient Māori gravestones to be found, although by contrast Patupaiarehe dead have been found decently wrapped in shrouds and buried in dugout coffins, the Society's record offers this explanation:

> On account of the savagely vindictive nature of Māori warfare, their eating the bodies of their enemies, and the delight they look in treating such bodies with every foul indignity, as also the custom of utilising the skull and other bones of the such bodies where from to manufacture various implements, it was necessary for every tribe to bury their dead in secrecy, and to take every precaution that enemies should not discover the resting-place of the bodies or bones. Hence nothing was done to make a grave where a person had been buried.

Further evidence of *kai pirau* is found on p.288 of S. Percy Smith's book, *Māori Wars of the Nineteenth Century* (2011) where he records that the East Coast tribe of Ngati Manawa, ousted from their homes at Galatea and Te Whaiti, sought refuge with Ngati Kahungunu sub tribes living at Te Putere. Sadly, one of their women died en route and was buried at Te Putere, only to be dug up by their hosts the Ngati Kahungunu, cooked and eaten.

Not only was there *kai pirau*; there was also the practice of

Human sacrifice as practised by the Aztecs of South America. It is said that as many as 84,000 victims were slain at the rededication of the Temple of Teotichlan. Detail above from a page of the Codex Mendoza, the scene as painted by Aztec artists themselves. Picture courtesy of Wikipaedia.

kai huaka or 'eat relative'. History records that sometimes children raised in a whanau were taken out and killed by near relatives, then cooked and eaten by 'the whole family'. The book *Kahungunu* records that when a young warrior died in combat his tribe took him home, mourned him, then ate him.

Māori committed wholesale and deliberate genocide against

the several ancient peoples who had first settled this land, the very people in fact who had nurtured them on arrival.

Monica says the tribal history account handed down to her insists that between the early 1700s and 1834 over 3,000 Ngati Hotu alone perished in successive murderous onslaughts by Ngati Tuwharetoa and other warring tribes as they drove these people of ancient lineage from their lands around Lake Taupo to take refuge around Taumarunui, then forced them up onto the bleak slopes of Mt Ruapehu itself.

All up, according to careful estimates by interdisciplinary research scientist Dr. John Robinson, in the decades before 1800 inter-tribal warfare accounted for 35,400 killed in a New Zealand population numbering around 127,000 in 1800, with many more dying from wounds.

The grim 'ethnic cleansing' of Ngati Hotu was a pattern for similar cruel carnage inflicted on the true indigenous people of this country throughout the land. And it didn't stop with the Turehu, Patupaiarehe and other tribes of ancient, pre-Māori lineage. Māori also slew and enslaved their own people on a vast scale.

Then between 1800 and 1840, tribal warfare, accelerated by the introduction of firearms, reached the crescendo known as the Musket Wars. Sadly, governments of New Zealand have been loath to recognise that it was this inter-tribal bloodbath and determined genocide of the indigenous inhabitants of this land that hugely reduced the 19th century non-European population. Instead they have given abject heed to the chorus of complaint voiced by the Māori Treaty grievance industry.

Thus the blame for the steep and rapid decline in native numbers in this period has been laid on colonization by incoming European settlers. Consequently, the havoc wrought by tribal war and the vicious slaughter by Māori of the numerous people of ancient European origin that preceded the Polynesians as New Zealand settlers has been swept under the carpet and ignored.

Did the Government hide the truth?

So determined has Government been to hide the truth of the Great New Zealand Genocide that archeologists have bulldozed, smashed and destroyed precious historical artifacts, buildings and burial sites to wipe out all evidence or remembrance of the Patupaiarehe and other ancient peoples. Reports on such remains have been locked away by classifying them as secret and, as we will see, one eminent demographist was ordered to rewrite a report to tell absolute lies about the alleged 19th century decline in Māori population.

All this was done to wrongly validate both the Crown's own seizure of large swathes of New Zealand and the bloody land grabs of the big chiefs who murdered their smaller tribal counterparts, exterminated all but a handful of the ancients and blamed European New Zealand settlers for the results of carnage they carried out themselves.

Now, if you doubt that the Government deliberately hid the truth from the public on this matter, distorted the facts and bent scientific reports to say the opposite of what really happened, then read John Robinson's book, *The Corruption of New Zealand Democracy*.[15]

This book exposes at first-hand how the state will lie to deceive the public into believing that a national Treaty guilt trip is necessary and that the Māori grievance gravy train was and is justified. Dr. Robinson freely confesses that, to his shame, he gave in to an ultimatum by his state agency clients to doctor his findings on the cause of Māori 19th century depopulation 'to fit the Government's politically-correct pro-Māori, anti-Pakeha, Brit-bashing myth', as one reviewer of his book put it.

For the record, Dr. Robinson has Master of Science degrees in mathematics and physics and is an interdisciplinary research scientist who has written reports for the DSIR, OECD, UNESCO, UNEP and

15 *The Corruption of New Zealand Democracy* by Dr. John Robinson, Tross Publishing, 2011

UNU. However, when he worked for the New Zealand Government he was asked to lie about his findings. In an online excerpt from his book he says that in researching the 19th century Māori population decline he sought to identify the cause. He states:

> The answer is easy to find; indeed it is blindingly obvious. And it is not introduced diseases as stated in my reformulated report. Those diseases existed and were harmful, but they were not the dominant factor. That was war.
>
> The period 1800-1840 was the time of the musket wars, when Māori groups attacked one another – killing, eating, enslaving and taking the land. Many of the captured were kept as slaves and held like cattle on the hoof, to be killed and eaten later. Frequently crops were destroyed or not adequately tended. And in the direct loss of life, the social fabric was devastated. The horror of the times is well documented, the slaughter extreme.
>
> Of about 100,000 – 150,000 Māori living in New Zealand at or around 1810, by 1840 probably somewhere between 50,000 and 60,000 had been killed, enslaved or forced to migrate because of the wars (working from estimates generated by Ian Pool and others). In the main that occurred in the short space of twenty-five years from 1815 to 1840.'
>
> According to Travers, this was a period of slaughter unparalleled in any country. On occasions around one thousand or more perished in the fighting, to be feasted upon thereafter. The cruelty was severe and cannibalism was considered glorious, leading on to the most dreadful atrocities.
>
> Europeans witnessed captives being lined up and standing silently, with the utmost stoicism, while the victors hacked them to death with tomahawks, cut them into pieces, and cleaned, cooked and ate them 'with greedy delight'.
>
> In this atmosphere of fear and foreboding a captured chief, Te Maiharanui, strangled his daughter to prevent her from an

These wooden coffins (stone-hewn) were found in a Maori burial cave high in a cliff face near Atene on the Wanganui River. Mr T.W.Downes, then (1919) in charge of the River Trust, photographed the coffins and their grim contents and then re-interred them.

Photo: courtesy of Rob Graham, Whanganui Photo News.

The ancient burials of a peaceful people

Pictured on the opposite page: The remains of Ngati Hotu people buried in a cliff-face 'cemetery' above the Whanganui River many centuries ago.

The location of this isolated burial cave or shelter was about 100 kilometres away into the badlands interior from where the Ngati Hotu tribe were defeated and many were cannibalised in the 'Battle of the Five Forts' which took place on their homelands around the lower slopes of Ruapehu.

The 'dug out' coffins, each cut from trees, show the respect and care the Patupaiarehe people showed their dead. Each coffin has its own tight fitting lid, cut from a single plank, as were the lids of the coffins of ancient Egypt.

With their 'square', not 'rocker' jaws the pictured skulls speak clearly of a non-Polynesian Northern Hemisphere origin. They were already many centuries old when they discovered in the last century.

The remote location near Atene, some 30 kilometres inland from Whanganui along the course of the river, supports the Ngati Hotu history that these ancients of Mediterranean origin, the first settlers of New Zealand, fled to the farthest hills and remotest bush locations to evade their cannibal enemies in the battles of the 16th century.

This grave in the Ngati Hotu urupa (burial ground) near Te Rena contains the remains of Apatata 'Jim' Hepopo. Alongside there is a hidden, grisly secret. In the mid-1600s in the time of Hena the Patupaiarehe prophetess, the Ngati Hotu chief Tamakana was killed by a Tu Wharetoa war party at Lake Rotoaira because he refused to give up his tribe's land. His brother Tieketahi went to reclaim his body but could only find his head. The rest of his body had been eaten. Tamakana's head was brought back and buried at the Te Rena cemetery, overlooked by the high hill on which the prophetess Hena is buried. In 2004 the memorial post which stood to mark her grave was torn down and in the urupa Tamakana's grave was bulldozed. The culprits, Monica believes were Tuwharetoa. But his head was recovered and buried alongside the grave of Apatata Hepopo.

> even crueler death at the hands of their enemies. He and his wife were later tortured until they both died in considerable agony.
>
> When a slave girl, apparently about fifteen, infuriated an old chief woman, she was promptly killed and eaten. The head was thrown to the children as a plaything.

Not even in the deep south of the USA was the treatment of slaves as brutal as that. Even within a community, and even toward the most vulnerable, death could be inflicted with apparent ease. Infanticide was said by some early European visitors to Māori settlements to be widespread, particularly killing babies. Dr. Robinson concludes that:

> Māori culture was not just dysfunctional but mad, criminally insane. The consequences of those decades of killing, social disruption, destruction of crops, infanticide, fear and uncertainty was a society in shock. There was widespread desolation and devastation among Māori communities.

As I wrote this chapter in April 2015 especial efforts were being made to commemorate the 100th anniversary of the First World War Gallipoli campaign. Thousands of New Zealanders flocked to Anzac Cove to attend remembrance ceremonies.

Remembering the fallen

Thanks to British military blundering, the attempt to conquer Constantinople via landings at Gallipoli cost the lives of 2,779 New Zealand soldiers and another 5,212 were wounded. That is something to be remembered, a terrible mistake that cannot be forgotten.

This brave sacrifice may have cemented us as a nation but in reality it was an unmitigated military tragedy which New Zealanders vowed should never be repeated. In the Second World War New Zealand troops refused to serve under British officers and were commanded instead by General Freyberg. They would 'wave but not salute'. Appropriately, 'Lest we forget' is the slogan as each Anzac Day New Zealand remembers her fallen in two great world wars. Pakeha and Māori rightly pay great attention to honouring those who died in these conflicts. Yet, remarkably, little or no effort is given to commemorating those who died in the dreadful carnage of wars fought in New Zealand itself. And these savage conflicts were many.

Dr. Robinson's tally of 50,000 to 60,000 for the Māori killed, wounded or expelled during the Musket Wars between 1825 and 1840 takes no account of the tens of thousands who perished in the earlier massacre of New Zealand's truly indigenous people, the Patupaiarehe, Turehu and their associated sub tribes.

Successive pogroms were waged against these peoples progressively throughout the 1700s and 1800s. The total slain in this country-wide genocide is thought by some to run into several tens of thousands. Māori also turned on Māori, hugely killing each other.

It is arguable that perhaps 100,000 of the descendants of the earliest settlers in New Zealand lost their lives in the bloody conquests that followed arrival and establishment of the Māori in this land. That, of course, is many times more than the 18,000 New Zealanders who perished in the First World War or the 12,000 who died in the Second World War.

Nevertheless each year Anzac Day rightly reminds us of the sacrifice these soldiers made and of the senseless waste of life and futility of war.

Yet one must ask why is there no similar commemoration or memorial to remind us to weep also for those who fell in the country's darkest days when Māori slaughtered the peaceful Patupaiarehe, the Turehu and the now extinct Ngati Kapupungapunga, the latter being people who occupied the Waikato before Tainui Māori swept them from the land?

An un-bandaged wound

Why are there no monuments to this incredible tragedy, or to the terrible toll Māori tribes inflicted on themselves as they sought to kill and eat each other? Why is the massacre of this country's first settlers all but absent from our popular and accepted history books? Why is there no national day of peace when we remember with respect – because it truly is part of our heritage – the hundreds of years in which the first New Zealanders lived in peace?

But if New Zealand politicians and academics won't officially recognise an historical genocide when they see one, Pope Francis, present head of the Roman Catholic Church, will. In April 2015 he marked the 100th anniversary of the slaughter of 1.5 million Armenian Christians by the Muslim Ottoman Turks, urging the international community to recognise the prolonged atrocity as 'the first genocide of the 20th century'. It was his duty, he said, to honour the memory of innocent men, women and children 'senselessly' murdered by the Turks.

In a message specifically to Armenians the pope called on all heads of state and international organisations to recognise the truth of what had transpired to prevent such 'horrors' from happening again.

In my view New Zealand needs to do just the same in officially recognising the genocide of this country's peaceful first inhabitants.

What's more, Pope Francis spoke truth New Zealand politicians and academics must learn when he said: 'Concealing or denying evil is like allowing a wound to keep bleeding without bandaging it.'

In the upshot the Associated Press reported that the pope's comments were praised by Armenian President Serge Sarkisian, but immediately caused a diplomatic rift between the Vatican and Turkish Government which, in a huff, withdrew its ambassador to the Holy See.

Turkish Foreign Minister Mevlut Cavusoglu decried the pontiff's statement as 'unacceptable and far from historic and legal truths'. This shows that to this day Muslims remain unrepentant about the slaughter of Christians and the genocide of these and other peoples they have practiced in various countries over the last 1500 years.

And, judging by some of their recent pronouncements, Māori, rather than admit they all but wiped out the Patupaiarehe and other early settlers of New Zealand prefer to deny that they ever existed.

Which to my mind puts some Māori leaders in much the same category as Turks who deny the Armenian massacre, neo-Nazis who deny the Holocaust and Russians and Chinese who won't own up to the mass slaughter of multiple millions they wreaked on their own peoples.

Whatever latter-day European colonisation of New Zealand did, and admittedly much of the land grabbing and the ensuing Land War was wrong, it was neither systematic extermination nor genocide. Nor were such depredations largely responsible for the oft alleged 'marginalisation' of the Māori people today. Their own internecine strife was.

Chapter 10

What drove them to it?

'The curse causeless shall not come', we are told[16]. And the invasion and subsequent war of annihilation inflicted on New Zealand's original and peaceful peoples in the 16th and 17th centuries did not come without reason either.

Patupaiarehe descendant Monica Matamua says it was in the 1600s that a war of extermination against her people began. Morori then Māori had arrived in New Zealand and multiplied rapidly. At the same time a cooler climate led to crop failures and also reduced natural food resources just when the large existing Caucasian population, the Patupaiarehe, Turehu and Waitaha was numerous and numbers of the incoming Moriori and Māori were exploding.

Pressure on already scarce food resources increased sharply and the non-combatant, largely white resident peoples were driven back before the hungry invaders. But despite seizing their land, consuming their crops and depleting the bird life, the warrior incomers were still hungry. So they turned to eating the existing inhabitants.

But what brought such warrior cannibals to New Zealand in the first place? And what caused the dearth of natural food resources, plunge in bird populations and sharp decline in crops evidenced by the excavation of settlement sites both in the North and South islands dating from this period? For the South Island garden sites reveal a pitiful picture of kumara being desperately grown on steep hillsides and stored in rock caves to stave off starvation. In Palliser Bay near Wellington archaeological investigation of centuries-old sites there indicated the settlers were so hard put to scratch a living in cold bleak conditions they wore their teeth out within two to three decades. Editors

16 *King James Bible*, Proverbs 26:2.

of the detailed study, *Prehistoric Man in Palliser Bay*[17], B. Foss Leach and Helen M. Leach, conclude that the accumulated effects of severe climate change produced long winters, cold short summers causing kumara and potato crop failure, while sediment from heavier rainfall depleted the seafood resource. They summarise:

> The hypothesis of significant climate change in the last millennium in New Zealand has now received support from independent fields of research throughout the country. In the Wairarapa some argue that climatic deterioration was a prime cause of the virtual abandonment of the Palliser Bay settlements.

In our time, we might do well to forget global warming. As I write scientists are predicting earth will be in a mini ice age by 2030. This winter of 2015 there has been unheard of deep snow in Gisborne. Auckland suffered its coldest weekend in 63 years and Alaska's Hubbard Glacier is thickening and steadily advancing into Disenchantment Bay.

Britain's *The Daily Telegraph* reported on July 13, 2015 that Prof Valentina Zharkova of the University of Northumbria now predicts bitterly cold winters in which England's River Thames will freeze over. That last happened in the 1700s

Based on a new model of sun heat change fluctuations which, they say, gives unprecedentedly accurate predictions, Zharkhov's team of solar researchers warned fluid movements within the sun will converge to cause a dramatic temperature drop in the 2030s. Other scientists reject the prediction, believing industrial pollution or volcanic activity is still causing a warming effect.

Forced to move by climate change

In contrast to its name, the online website, *Global Warming*,

---

17 *Prehistoric Man in Palliser Ba,* editors B. Foss Leach and Helen M. Leach, Bulletin of the National Museum of New Zealand, Number 21, 1979, printed by Otago University Printing Department.

contains a useful description of 'The Little Ice Age', which followed the 'Medieval Warm Period of the 1300-1500s and ran from the 16th century well into the 18th. This freeze-up, it says, brought short, cold, wet summers with snow, long winters, crop failures, hunger and revolt. Glaciers crushed alpine villages, crops failed and famines killed millions, in the process triggering the French Revolution and other major events.

It toppled governments, precipitated the drive to find new lands and hugely changed society, the economy and agriculture. Eskimos paddled kayaks from Greenland to tour Scotland's icy coastline while Scandinavians regularly ambled over the frozen sea between Sweden and Denmark.

The freeze also affected the Southern Hemisphere. *Global Warming* cites evidence that a cold period in the time frame of the Little Ice Age occurred at several locations in the Southern Hemisphere:

> Paleo-sea-level data for the Pacific Islands suggest that sea level in the region fell, possibly in two stages, between 1270-1475AD. This was associated with a 1.5°C fall in temperature (determined from oxygen-isotope analysis) and an observed increase in El Niño frequency. Borehole reconstructions from Australia suggest that, over the last 500 years, the 17th century was the coldest in that continent, *Global Warming* says.

The fall in Pacific sea level during the cold period would expose new lands, possibly new islands would be created, and additional areas of dry land would augment the area of those already in existence. Voyaging distances would be reduced, enabling wider transfer of plants, such as taro, kumara, potato and coconut. Island populations could expand thanks to the new areas of cultivatable land now gained.

But when the warmer climate returned the reverse would take place. Well populated islands would now shrink in size and seawater would seep into low-lying gardening plots, as it is now doing in some low-lying Pacific islands such as Kiribati.

New Zealand cannibal feast. Skulls and bones: The sad remains of a cannibal orgy.

Inhabitants of low lying islands would struggle to keep the sea out and fights would break out as food supplies for what had been an expanding population ran out. There were few answers for hard-pressed islanders. One was to kill the babies, fight, kill and eat each other and reduce the population numbers. Another was to attack and overrun the residents of other better resourced islands. A third was to build canoes or rafts, set sail and hope to reach an unoccupied land elsewhere.

This last would be the resort of only a few. And it was a desperate measure by people fleeing for their lives, for the supply of new islands was fast running out. Rarotonga, which means 'Deep

South', was arguably one of the last be colonised and it was from there in the 1300s, tradition holds, that Turi set sail for New Zealand with a company who would form the nucleus of the Moriori people.

Kupe, the fabled great explorer of Māori tradition is thought to have sailed into Hokianga Harbour at the earliest in 1325AD, not earlier as previously held by historians. However, according to Waitaha paramount chief Hori Kupenga, Moriori came not by canoe but as castaways off European ships exploring the Pacific.

In 2010 writer Tom Hunt reported[18] that New Zealand academics were calling for a drastic rewrite of Pacific history because new evidence showed Polynesian arrival here to be too early by some 400 years. This stemmed from the results of 1400 radio carbon dating results from 47 Pacific island settlements[19].

The dates, tenfold greater in number than those of earlier studies, conclusively showed that Polynesians migrated from Samoa to the Society Islands (The Cooks) only around 1050AD, some four centuries later than earlier thought. The radio carbon daters concluded that it was at the earliest two centuries later (i.e. in the 1600s) that Polynesians arrived in other islands, including, last of all, New Zealand.

Cannibals before they reached these shores

The salient point to register is that internal tribal fighting, war with others, infanticide, extermination and cannibalism were already well established among Polynesians long before they reached these shores. And, as soon as their numbers grew, they resorted to them to seize territory from, plunder and finally, attack, kill and eat those who first welcomed them to New Zealand with food and shelter.

However, an exception is the Waitaha people. These folk,

---

18 *Carbon Dating the Polynesians*, article by Tom Hunt in the *Waikato Times*, December 29, 2010.

19 Published in *The Proceedings of the National Academy of Sciences in the United States.*

the mixed progeny on one hand of Mediterranean explorers, who had settled in South America before being driven out by the Maya, and Marquesas Islanders and others on their long odyssey through the Pacific, on the other, remained peaceful, according to Waitaha paramount chief, Hori Kupenga Manuka Manuka.

Over what may have been centuries they had sailed southward from island to island, establishing settlements in all unoccupied islands they encountered and inter-breeding with such islanders as they found already in residence. Hori Kupenga maintains that the Waitaha 'are responsible for fathering all the Polynesian, populations found in the Pacific from Easter Island south to New Zealand, except for those settled by the Melanesians coming from the east'.

But while some Polynesians resorted to war and bloodshed especially in their 'island hopping', he maintains the Waitaha themselves never entered into conflict. 'We were and are a peaceful people,' he insists. 'The killing, the cannibalism, the sorcery and the practice of war all came in with the influx of Melanesians into Polynesia. It wasn't us who started it'.

Undoubtedly, desperate times, such as those that prevailed at the end of the Little Ice Age on shrinking Pacific islands, can lead to desperate deeds. But they don't have to. The Patupaiarehe, Turehu and Waitaha peoples of prehistoric New Zealand endured times of hunger and stress in the many hundreds of years they lived here. They went through several adverse climate changes including some induced by massive volcanic eruptions, yet in all that time they never turned to war against each other, nor indulged in cannibalism.

Chapter 11

Ancient peacemakers

The peoples that preceded latter day European arrival in New Zealand may have had no Bible, but that did not stop some from practicing Jesus's profound statement that 'Blessed are the peacemakers for they shall be called the children of God'[20]. For there were real peacemakers, some Patupaiarehe and Waitaha and others, even Māori, amid the cruelty and carnage of intertribal war in old New Zealand.

For a start there were the women. While they might join in the haka to spur their men on to war they also often intervened urging peace or pleading for captives or tapu breakers to be spared rather than be killed and eaten.

More than that there were actual peacemakers, whose whole mission in life was to strive to keep the peace between tribes who were all too ready to go to war on the slightest pretext. These men, apparently set aside and dedicated to the role of peacemakers, much as a priest might be, toured the country as roving mediators, interceding between hostile tribes, resolving disputes and calming frayed tempers wherever possible. What's more they were received with dignity and listened to with respect.

Such venerated peace missioners were not tribal *tohunga* (priests), prophesying and praying to the war gods for victory for their particular *iwi* or *hapu*. Rather they were men who separated themselves from their own allegiances to mediate between other tribes. They appear to have flourished in the 17th and 18th centuries to mitigate the slaughter by Māori of the indigenous people of New Zealand, the Patupaiarehe and Turehu, the peaceful Waitaha people. They stepped up again in the late 18th and 19th centuries mediating

20 Matthew 5:9

This scene of Marion du Fresne's death was drawn by the French artist Charles Meryon, who visited New Zealand in the 1840s.

between Māori and Māori when the introduction of muskets inflamed desire for conquest and drove many tribes on to the war path.

Importantly, such peace negotiators were peaceful in and of themselves. They were only respected and recognised by warring chiefs because they had not participated in war themselves but passively resisted it.

From whence then did their peace-making heritage come? We need not be in doubt about that, for there is clear evidence that most, if not all of these ambassadors for peace, stemmed from the many tribes of those peace-loving peoples, the Patupaiarehe, Turehu and the Waitaha.

When muru became mercy

I would suggest their skills in negotiation were ones sharpened by long practice, for peace keeping is a learned art. Suppressing the promptings of anger, the temptation to hatred and the desire for revenge – innate in us all as sinful beings – requires careful training, persistent practice and constant vigilance. These mediators then, brought to the chiefly councils which decided on peace or war, a basket of skills shaped on the anvil of centuries of experience in keeping the peace first among themselves, then among others.

For there needs to be an ethos, a climate of kindness, peace, a practice of happiness and a culture of forgiveness and restraint for peace to succeed. As much as that was true in old New Zealand, it is also true today for each marriage, every family, country or suburban community, village, town or city today. The lesson still must be learned that to live at peace different races must practice the art of fostering harmony and nations must insist on negotiating win-win solutions to crises, not resort to war.

A hard ask, you say. For sure it is, but let us remind ourselves that for over 1,000 years it was achieved in New Zealand between the Waitaha, the Patupaiarehe, the Turehu and the many sub tribes into which these peoples devolved.

No wonder the most practiced exponents of the art of peace among these ancient peoples were called on to be peacemakers when the threat of conflict flared among the warrior Māori tribes which burgeoned from the 1600s onwards in New Zealand.

But more than merely waiting to be asked to mediate, these priests of peace proactively intervened where war was about to explode, risking life and limb to do so.

In doing so they created an ethos for peace in New Zealand today at best only half remembered, though we all enjoy its benefits to this day. Bringing peace out of intended war then was achieved first by the autochthonous mediators of the ancient past.

Then, most dramatically, it was achieved on a national scale in the 1800s by the preaching of the Christian gospel and the very nature and language of Māori changed in the light of sweeping conversion. Muru, once the word for revenge, became instead muru, the word for mercy. You see both the pre-European Māori people and the ancient first settlers in this land knew that the seeds of discord, argument, violence, hatred and revenge stem from the human heart. That is why the Patupaiarehe and Waitaha peoples practiced peace as a principle; they developed codes by which disputes were settled – sometimes by fist fights or mock battles without weapons – rather than war.

Mostly, however, it was achieved by skilled negotiation and the persistent cultivation of a cheerful, happy, peaceful disposition. Sadly that did not spare the Patupaiarehe from near annihilation.

For Māori, stemming from a warrior, cannibal culture that worshipped the gods of death and war, practiced cruelty and took offence at the slightest thing, learning the art of forgiveness became a necessity when it was realised that rival tribes were fast annihilating each other. So much so that the existence of the race was threatened.

What brought about the change? It was the good news that the Creator God who commanded, 'Thou shalt not kill', is also the Redeemer God who freely forgives men who receive Him both for crucifying Him 2,000 years ago and for all their sins since.

It was through the preaching of the gospel Māori first realised their worst mistake, that of worshipping devils of darkness rather than the God of light and love. Thanks to God's grace they then grasped by faith the truth that Christ would forgive them too. And receiving such grace changed their heart.

For, if Christ could forgive them, had forgiven them, then they could and should forgive others too. After all He Himself said so (Thus *muru* became mercy and forgiveness replaced *utu* (revenge).

But what real evidence is there of such pre-European peace-making, you ask? Plenty, according to Augustus Earle, draughtsman to His Majesty's Surveying Ship *'The Beagle'* who lived ashore for nine months in New Zealand in 1827. And Earle was under no illusions on the maverick nature of Māori society:

> There appeared to me to be no public bodies, or any functionaries employed by the people. Each chief seemed to possess absolute power over his own slaves, and there his authority terminated. Wealth made him feared by his foes, but

Monument to du Fresne and his men at Assassination cove.

> gave him no influence over his friends.
>
> All offence offered to any one of a tribe (or clan) is instantly followed by some act of retaliation by the aggrieved party; and if one tribe is too weak to contend against the one from whom they have received the injury, they call in the aid of another. But should the offence be of a very aggravated nature, and several families be injured by it, a meeting of the chiefs is called. They assemble in one of their forts, and, after a discussion, decide either for an amicable adjustment, or for an exterminating war. Thus these misguided beings are continually destroying each other for some imaginary insult.

Earle then described the ambassadors of peace that he met on his travels through old New Zealand:

> I became acquainted with a few venerable men of truly noble and praiseworthy characters such as would do honour to any age, country, or religion. They had passed their whole lives in travelling from one chieftain's residence to another, for

> the purpose of endeavouring to explain away insults, to offer apologies, and to strive by every means in their power to establish peace between those about to plunge their country into the horrors of war.
>
> I have several times met these benevolent men journeying through the country on these pacific missions; and twice during my residence here they have been the happy means of preventing bloodshed. Although the New Zealander is so fond of war, and possesses such war-like manners, yet are these peacemakers held in the highest respect, although they do not hold any sacred function – indeed, no order of priesthood exists amongst the natives.

Men who prevented bloodshed

Earle carefully distinguishes these peacemakers from the *tohungas*, whom, he describes as, *'...sacred, or, more correctly speaking, "cunning" men and women, who pretend to see into futurity, and to hold an intercourse with the Great Spirit'.*

However, their main function, as Earle saw it, apart from uttering dark incantations and curses, was to turn their prophetic pretensions to profitable account by taking payment to make *tapu* (taboo) plantations and other possessions at the chiefly whim. He comments:

> All the chiefs find these people of the greatest use in protecting their property, for they possess the power of tabooing, and when once this ceremony is performed over any person or thing, no one dares to touch either; and for a sufficiently good bribe they will impart their sacred power to any chief, who, by means of this device, thus can protect a field of potatoes or grain, at fifty miles distance from his settlement, more securely and effectually than by any fences, or number of persons he might place to guard it.

On belief in a higher power, Earle writes:

> Like all rude and ignorant people, the New Zealanders seem more to fear the wrath of their God than to love his attributes; and constant sacrifices (too often human ones) are offered up to appease his anger. They imagine that the just and glorious Deity is ever ready to destroy, and that His hand is always stretched forth to execute vengeance.

A preacher of peace

Now, without further ado, let me introduce a brave and colourful peacemaker of the 1800s, Piki Te Piki Kotaku. The great, great, grandfather of present day stalwart Patupaiarehe campaigner Monica Matamua, Piki was the last of the Ngati Hotu (Patupaiarehe line) to leave a history of his people. This has passed down to Monica Matamua. He died in 1902 at 100 years old.

Piki was an expert in the art of peace. During the Musket Wars he often mediated between tribes hell-bent on war and reportedly was highly effective in negotiation. But while the art of peace was part of Piki's natural Patupaiarehe heritage, his domestic situation must have further sharpened his practice, for over his lifetime (though not concurrently) Piki had six wives and maintaining domestic harmony must have often tried his patience. But patient and peaceful he was even in the face of provocation. Monica states:

> He was a renowned preacher of peace. He always tried to find a way to settle things peacefully whether it was in the ongoing troubles with Tuwharetoa or later with the Crown. Sadly, there were times he didn't succeed. Today there are still the legacies of peace that remain from his efforts.

One example of that is the alliance Piki forged between Ngati Hotu and Ngati Maniapoto, the tribe who fled to the King Country during the New Zealand wars of the 19th century. Monica explains:

> He was so successful in negotiating peace, and Maniapoto so agreeable, that some of that tribe came and settled at Taurewa, the last remaining tract of Ngati Hotu land on the slopes above

> Taumarunui. Here the Maniapoto people lived among us to protect the few of us that were left as the last survivors of the Tuwharetoa massacre of Ngati Hotu.

Indeed so persuasive had Piki been that on their arrival at Taurewa Maniapoto told Tuwharetoa in no uncertain terms that from then on Ngati Hotu were to be left in peace. They were definitely off the Taupo tribe's menu – or else. Thus was peace finally secured for this hugely diminished branch of the Patupaiarehe.

Since, in Monica's family at least, her people survived against all the odds and Piki himself lived to a ripe old age, it seems the words of Jesus, 'Blessed are the peacemakers,' held true in their case.

Monica explains that her great grandmother was Piki's daughter from his sixth wife, Te Rangi Kowaea. Her grandmother's name was Te Oti Mihi Te Rina. In her honour the remnant of land of the much slaughtered Ngati Hotu tribe hung on to above Taumarunui was called Te Rena. But while some Ngati Hotu remained on this lofty site in 1867, Piki himself had to flee. This was because the merciless Tuwharetoa tribe, despite having earlier made peace with Ngati Hotu, set a price on Piki's head. Tuwharetoa, evidently, was immune to the peacemaker's persuasions.

So Piki removed to Lake Rotoiti near Rotorua, leaving his six wives and many children behind him. And though he continued to plead peace between tribes living in much of the central North Island trouble pursued him. Monica says it happened this way:

> One of Piki's daughters married Te Kooti (the Māori guerilla warrior who fought first for the Crown then, after being accused of spying, against it. He founded the Ringatu, 'upraised hand' religion. Piki was with Te Kooti, not only because of the marriage, but also because he believed his prediction that the Crown was out to take land. The Crown said anyone that was with Te Kooti would have their head cut off. That is when Piki left Te Rena and retired to Rotoiti.

As to Te Kooti, while fighting alongside government forces

against the rebel HauHau in 1865, he was accused of spying. Exiled to the Chatham Islands without trial along with captured Hauhau, he experienced visions and became a religious leader. In 1868 he led the escape of 168 prisoners, seizing the schooner *Rifleman* and sailing back to the North Island. Here he began a series of raids. Pardoned in 1883 he continued spreading the Ringatu message of peace and reclaiming land from Pakeha. All of which would also make him a peacemaker of sorts.

Parihaka is perhaps the best known New Zealand example of the principle of peaeceful, passive resistance in action. What is little known is the role played by the Patupaiarehe religion of peace in the matter. Sixteen hundred police and volunteers took part in the attack on Parihaka, a settlement in western Taranaki which had become the symbol of protest against the confiscation of Māori land.

However, the invading troops met no resistance. Bands of singing, dancing children offered them food and the settlement's leader Te Whiti-o-Rongomai ordered his people not to raise a hand against the government forces. Whiti and and his fellow leaders were arrested in 1881 and exiled until March 1883.

Like Ghandi in India, Te Whiti employed non-violent non-cooperation to struggle against land confiscations. The government responded to their protests by passing laws aimed specifically at the Parihaka protesters and ultimately by imprisoning people without trial.

The question is where Te Whiti and his fellow leaders, but recently active on the war path, learned the art of peaceful protest, so foreign to their normal behaviour? The answer, according to Monica Matamua, is from Piki Te Piki Kotaku, who she says, sought to mediate between the Parihaka settlement chiefs and the government forces but, on this occasion, without success.

'With land being lost and settlers pressing for more they adopted the Patupaiarehe way of peaceful protest and resistance in the face of onslaught. In the event it failed to stop the confiscated land being taken from them and they were terribly treated by the government forces, being driven out from their homes with nowhere to go or jailed without trial for months on end,' she says.

Parihaka became of concern to the government as a possible site for the reignition of Māori opposition to Pakeha 'progress'. As the historian Hazel Riseborough wrote: 'Parihaka had become a haven for the dispossessed and disillusioned from the length and breadth of the coast, and as far away as North Auckland, the King Country, Wairarapa and the Chatham Islands.'

On the morning of 5 November 1881, some 1600 volunteer and Armed Constabulary troops invaded the settlement. More than 2000 villagers sat quietly on the marae as a group of singing children greeted the force led by Native Minister and Wanganui MP John Bryce, who had described Parihaka as 'that headquarters of fanaticism and disaffection'. Bryce had fought in the campaign against Tītokowaru. He ordered the arrest of Parihaka's leaders, the destruction of the village and the dispersal of most of its inhabitants.

Waitaha leaders were also peacemakers. The last descended Waitaha chief, *Te Upoko Ariki* (paramount chief) Hori Kupenga Manuka Manuka, says his *tupuna* (ancestor) was slain with French explorer Marion du Fresne in 1772 after seeking to maintain peace between du Fresne's party and native warriors on the other.

Hori Kupenga maintains that far from either Jean de Surville, the first historically recorded French navigator to reach these shores, or Marion du Fresne, who followed him later, 'exploring' and 'finding' New Zealand, this land's existence was already well known to them beforehand.

Long before they sailed into the Pacific, de Surville in 1769 (concurrent with James Cook) and du Fresne in 1772, the French Government knew of New Zealand and was considering establishing a colony here, he says.

What's more, he maintains his ancestor Haro as the *Upoko Ariki*, high chief over many tribes in the Far North of New Zealand, was in negotiation with the French to assist them in establishing a colony here for the purposes of peace:

> That is what has been handed down to me and it makes sense if you look at what was happening at the time of du Fresne's visit. Moriori had split into various small tribes and had attacked some of Haro's own Waitaha people. At the same time the fiercely warlike Ngapuhi Māori people were emerging as a tribal force and had begun to attack both.
>
> Haro believed that only the imposition of law by a more civilized people with order and discipline would secure peace and save the Far North from a bloodbath and thus he was working with du Fresne to establish terms for a permanent French settlement. He had been in negotiation with the French from de Surville's visit onwards.

Verification of the French intent to colonise is that, according to *Wikipaedia*, before leaving New Zealand for France on 12 July 1772, du Fresne's officers buried a bottle at Waipoa on Moturoa containing the arms of France and a formal statement taking possession of the whole country, with the name of 'France Australe'.

Further proof is that in 1838 Jean François Langlois, commander of the whaling ship *Cachalot*, set out to found a French colony at Akaroa, having negotiated to buy from local chiefs 30,000 acres of land at Bank's Peninsula.

In the event he arrived in July 1840 to find the Union Jack already flying over the land, the British Government having already secured sovereignty over New Zealand the previous May.

As for du Fresne at Doubtless Bay at first he had peaceful relations with the local tribes. Later, however, the Ngati Pou and Ngare Raumati attacked the French to obtain their guns, tools and supplies. This took place on 12 June 1772 when several hundred warriors set upon du Fresne and a crew of 26 when they were out fishing. All were killed and eaten. Then, in a follow-up raid, according to the accounts of French officers, Jean Roux and De Clesmeur, 400 armed tribesmen suddenly attacked the hospital camp but were driven off by the threat of a blunderbuss broadside.

One chief, thought to have been Hori Kupenga's great, great, grandfather, Haro Rewharewha Manuka Manuka, told Roux that the tribal chief Te Kauri had killed Marion. At this point longboats full of armed French sailors arrived with the news that du Fresne and the sailors had been killed. Surrounded by about 1,200 Māori the French retreated to Moturoa Island only to be followed by a force of 1,500 men. The French charged with 26 armed soldiers and put them to flight, the warriors fleeing back to the pa of the formerly friendly, but now clearly hostile, chief Te Kauri.

The French attacked the pa firing at the defenders, who showered them with spears. The remainder got into canoes and fled. About 250 Māori including five chiefs were killed in the battle, many French were wounded. A month later, on 7 July, Roux searched Te Kauri's deserted pa and found a sailor's cooked head on a spike, and human bones near a fire.

Hori Kupenga says of the incident:

> My ancestor was with Marion du Fresne trying to keep the peace between the French and the local Moriori tribes who were intent on war. He was slain with him when they were enticed ashore after fishing.

Chief George points out that staying as he did for nearly two months and visiting several pas and native settlements in the area du Fresne would certainly have visited the *pa* of the district's paramount chief, his ancestor:

> The story handed down to me is that Haro welcomed the prospect of a French colony and was actively discussing with du Fresne how to bring it about to secure peace in the district.

However, the Moriori tribes who had recently fought their way in to settle there under their chief, Te Kauri, got wind of the plan. Realising it would bring an end to their own way of life, which mainly comprised warfare and cannibalism, they decided to 'teach du Fresne a lesson', Chief George suggests.

A lesson it seems the French Government heeded. For Dunmore records that the events of July 1772 strengthened the view in France that New Zealand was inhabited by dangerous natives and warranted no attempt at colonisation.

In prior years Paris had lent toward Jean Jacques Rousseau's 'noble savage' view, Marion du Fresne going so far as to declare himself a 'Māoriphile'. This was an opinion Paris revised in the light of the du Fresne massacre.

However, that du Fresne and the French held New Zealand natives in such high regard so early in the piece is proof that the French knew this country and its people long before his actual arrival here.

This skull-capped or helmeted statue of a sentinel broods over a hillside in the Waikato region of New Zealand's North Island. Carved from hard limestone the figure, reminiscent of Easter Island moai, is severely weathered, possibly indicating extreme age. Is it the work of ancient Celtic stone builders, one wonders? Picture © Bryan Mitchell.

Chapter 12

Standing on the battle line

The Rev. Benjamin Ashwell.

Fresh from Africa he came as a CMS (Church Missionary Society) missionary to the Māori. And for him New Zealand's cooler climate was a blessed relief from the tropical humidity of Sierra Leone. Yet with his pith helmet askew, because it was too big for him, Benjamin Ashwell cut a comic figure when he strode into the Waikato cannibal land of the 1840s.

A small, short-necked, tubby man, he wore the over-sized helmet slumped over his head so it hid most of his face. But what he lacked in height Ashwell more than made up for in courage and kindliness.

Ashwell eventually established a mission station at Taupiri but before that spent 10 years travelling much of the North Island preaching the *Rongo-Pai* – the 'good news', the 'glad tidings', and was received by most Māori settlements.

He found the Māori had already learned about this Pakeha 'gospel of peace' and, although not gathering its deeper theology clearly understood its practical application, that of 'peace and goodwill to all men'. According to author James C Cowan[21], this dogged preacher

21 *The Story of a Peacemaker,* written as No. 18 in a series, Famous New Zealanders, in the *New Zealand Railways Magazine*, published in Issue 6, Sept. 1, 1934, retrieved from the Victoria University of Wellington's New Zealand Electronic Text Collection.

witnessed the savagery of the Musket Wars at its worst. Waikato from 1835 to 1840 was dominated by war parties. Waikato feuded with the Rotorua, King Country, Tauranga and Maketu tribes and even between local Māori battles were frequent. Cowan writes that:

> Every few months armies of Ngati Huau, Ngati Maniapoto and Waikato tribes, inhabiting the country from Matamata to Kawhia and Mokau, marched off to the Lakes and the coast, armed with muskets and tomahawks, and they often returned with slaves laden with the dismembered bodies of the slain foemen, for great cannibal feasts of victory.

For example in July 1839 at Otawhao village, near Te Awamutu, the missionary watched in horror as chiefs Mokorou and Puata led a victorious war party into the Ngati-Ruru *pa*.

They triumphantly carried the butchered limbs of over 60 enemies slain in the battle. The next day was set down for a great cannibal feast, attended by people from surrounding villages.

But as the fires burned and cooking ovens steamed, Ashwell urged all who would 'follow Christ as Saviour and Lord' to leave and, with scores in tow, 'left the fortified *pa* of the man eaters in disgust'.

Over 200 natives, wanting to become members of the *whare kura*, the 'house of instruction', followed him. Together they built a new fortified pa at Te Awamutu, where the historic church and old mission buildings still stand today.

At the Māoris' request Mr. Ashwell established daily worship, school instruction, Sunday service, and drew up laws and regulations for them. Ashwell then visited the main chiefs nearby and won from them their promise not to attack the *whare kura* believers.

By this time many Māori were weary of fighting and when Ashwell's fellow missionary John Morgan promoted growing of wheat and planting of peach and other fruit trees, agriculture became a preferred option to that of war. Water-powered flour mills were built and wheat and flour sold to Auckland. Roads and bridges were constructed.

So much so that 10 years after the Otawhao cannibal feast the Ngati-Ruru people so appreciated the blessings of peace that the old chief Mokorou could find no takers when he sought recruit a *tuau* (war party) to attack the Arawa people at Rotorua.

A few years later he renounced cannibalism altogether to become a disciple of Ashwell, who was known as *Te Ahiwera*, 'Hot Fire', to the Māori. Mokorou took the biblical name Riwai (Levi) and built a church at Whatawhata, still there to this day.

At the missionary's request Riwai parted with seven out of his eight wives, an act Ashwell hailed further proof of conversion. Cynics, however, said it was because his teeth had fallen out that Mokorou now found cannibalism intolerable.

Despite increasing peace overall, quarrels between local hapu (sub tribes) in the Waikato still flared into conflict on the slightest pretext. From his mission station at Taupiri Ashwell often considered it his duty to intervene to 'put such fires out'. More than once he acted as referee while actual bullets were fired over his head.

In one thrilling encounter, related by Cowan, the missionary brokered peace on the very firing line, standing immovable between two fuming war parties on the banks of Lake Whangape on the west side of the Waikato River.

The war parties glared at each other

Dispute had flared over usage of a large eel trap between the large Ngati Pou tribe, who lived nearby under their chief Uira and who claimed the extensive *hinaki* or woven eel traps as theirs, and Ngati Mahuta, headed by Kepa, brother of the great warrior Te Wherowhero.

To protect their eel fishery Ngati Pou built a fortified pa on the disputed spot. No sooner had they done so than Kepa arrived with 300 armed Ngati Mahuta warriors threatening an attack. Swiftly Uira sent word downstream to the missionary to come with all speed. Ashwell left his wife and the mission schoolroom and sped toward Whangape.

On Ashwell's arrival Uira was eager for peace and urged the

missionary to go to Ngati Mahuta and ask them to sit quietly. Ashwell did so and urged the Mahuta men not to fire the first shot.

Then he returned to find the Ngati Pou loading their guns, preparing for battle. He begged them to wait, exacting from them the same promise; that they would not fire first. Returning to Ngati Mahuta he found them now lathered into a frenzy and about to perform their war dance. They refused his request to stand still but instead offered:

> You draw a boundary line and you will stand on it and we will not pass you.

Rushing back to the other side Ashwell obtained the Ngati Pou's promise they too would not cross the line in the sand now hurriedly being drawn. Picture now that puny, little missionary, his pith helmet askew, standing heroically between two fierce war parties, all ferocious cannibals all not long before. The two columns, each about 300 strong, glared at each other, shouted war cries, then leapt to their feet, raised their loaded muskets and charged.

In his memoirs Ashwell wrote:

> I thought they would have swept me away they came running with such force but both parties stopped dead a few yards short of the boundary line.Each man dropped to one knee with his musket at the ready. For a lengthy quarter of an hour the two warrior bands remained there, each glaring angrily. Tense though he was the missionary stood his ground patiently between the two.

Then an amazing thing happened. One of the warriors, a mission attender, recited a verse from a psalm; it may well have been Psalm 23: 'The Lord is my Shepherd I shall not want'. The words rang out against a tense silence. There was a lengthy pause, then from the opposite warrior band the words of the second verse were heard: 'He maketh me to lie down in green pastures: he leadeth me beside the still waters'.

A feast replaced the war cries

Verse after verse was recited, first from one side, then the other. Then, according to Ashwell, followed the words well known to Anglicans as the Gloria Patri which the missionary had faithfully taught his Māori communicants:

> Glory to the Father, and to the Son, and to the Holy Spirit,
> Both now and always, and unto the ages of ages. Amen.

Tension noticeably dissipated, anger died and the warriors sat down. Peaceful speech making replaced the war cries. Soon all resorted to the Ngati Pou pa for a feast of potatoes, and eels. Who owned the *pa tuna*, or eel weir, was never settled but from that time onwards both sub tribes shared its bounty.

Sadly, Ashwell's peace-making was not always so successful. With a fellow missionary, Dr. Maunsell, he later tried to resolve a quarrel between Ngati Pou and Ngati Tipa over a piece of land on the lower Waikato. The parsons persuaded the rival war parties to draw an *autaki* (boundary line) but a young Ngati Tipa deliberately ran across it. Immediately an Ngati Pou chief wrestled him and an unlucky blow drew blood. On seeing that both sides joined the fray. Thirty two men were killed in this, thankfully the very last inter-tribal fight in the Waikato.

Chapter 13

End of the carnage

An important point was made by New Zealand High Court Judge Sir Eddie Durie speaking at the Waitangi Day church service in 2015 marking the 175th anniversary of signing the Treaty of Waitangi between the Māori chiefs and the British Crown. (The treaty is the founding constitutional document of New Zealand.)

'Let us put paid,' he said, 'to the notion that we Māori were "colonised by Christianity". Oh, no, we went out there to get it and spread it among ourselves'.

So, Europeans did not bring the gospel to New Zealand; rather, says Sir Eddie, an enterprising Northland Māori chief, Ruatara, sailed to Europe to discover what gave the British their strength and power.

Ruatara concluded it was their belief in Jesus Christ. He then searched Australia for a man to preach this gospel to Māori. That man was Samuel Marsden who at Ruatara's invitation on December 25, 1814 on a Northland beach preached 'good tidings of great joy which shall be unto all people'[22] to Māori for the first time on New Zealand soil.

He iwi tahi tātou meaning 'We are one people' was British representative William Hobson's summing up at signing the Treaty of Waitangi in 1840. Since then New Zealand, according to the online *Te Ara Encylopaedia of New Zealand*, has often acclaimed its race relations as superior to those of other countries. The Encyclopaedia notes:

> In his own name, Māori Anglican Bishop **Muru** Walters, commemorates the huge change brought about among Māori in the 1800s by the forgiveness and redemption of the gospel.

22 Luke 2:10

> In a recent address he said traditional Māori tribal culture had been driven by **muru**.
>
> The traditional meaning of **muru** was 'to act with absolute brutal ferocity and domination against all those not related to us by blood. Face to face killing, revenge killing and cannibalism, was all to maintain and assert **muru**, *mana* (prestige), power and *rangatiratanga* (chiefly rule).
>
> This **muru**, *mana, rangatiratanga*, was perceived as the only authentic, cultural way to manage and sustain the well-being of our culture.

Then came the Christian gospel, spread largely by Māori themselves. Preaching salvation through Christ brought about such a change that very word *muru* was entirely changed in meaning. Bishop Walters explains:

> When my Māori Natanahira Rarawa ancestors were transformed by following their new religious life (i.e. the gospel) … **muru** became transformed too. From meaning brutal revenge killings, **muru** became the Māori word for forgiveness, as used in translating the Lord's Prayer, for example. 'Forgive (*muru*) us our debts as we forgive (*muru*) our debtors'[23].

Sir Eddie recalls that when British missionary Octavius Hadfield arrived to minister to his Otaki tribe, Ngati Ruakawa, "we already knew, understood and could recite large passages of the gospel, learnt by heart".

Similarly when the first European missionary trudged over the hills into Poverty Bay he found several bible reading, hymn singing and praying churches had already been established among the Ngati Porou by themselves.

The 'missionaries' in this case were the uneaten residue of slaves captured by Ngapuhi on their raids down the East Coast. After

23 Matthew 6:10

Marsden's preaching and that of other missionaries these captives were freed and were taught Bible by this country's earliest mission school in the Far North. From there they took 'the glad tidings' back to their own tribes. It was the start of a huge change among the Māori.

A documentary screened in 2015 by New Zealand broadcaster *First Light*, asserted there was an explosion of Christianity among Māori in the first half of the 19th century. After a slow start so wholeheartedly was the gospel of salvation of Christ embraced between 1820 and 1850 it is estimated more than half of all Māori in New Zealand became avid Bible students.

So in just 30 years the widespread carnage and cannibalism of Māori society was brought to a sudden halt by the preaching of the gospel that 'Christ died for our sins according to the scriptures"[24]. Yet in New Zealand today, according to Government edict, Islam, Buddhism and Hinduism are ranked alongside Christianity as faiths of equal merit and importance. And the gospel of Christ is largely cold-shouldered.

But let us consider the relative effectiveness of these different faiths in combatting cannibalism. Islam has held sway in Borneo, Indonesia, for over 600 years, preaching the message that to this day maintains that Allah is merciful and that Islam brings peace to societies that submit to it.

Yet in 2011, according to Asian correspondent Richard Lloyd Parry, reporting from Singapore, thousands of tribesmen in Borneo's West Kalimantan province went on a kill and eat manhunt of Madurese people that within a week left over 200 people, including babies, decapitated and cannibalised.

Heads were displayed on poles at the roadside and warriors with bloodied spears carried human hearts and livers to eat on the way.

Before the Indonesian Army quelled the rampage at least 500 were killed and consumed. 'It's difficult to keep count', a local

24 1 Corinthians 15:4

government official complained, 'because often all we find is an odd arm or leg'. In 2009 a similar conflict left 3,000 Madurese dead with many eaten.

What's more cannibalism also infests the Muslim heartland. It is being systematically practised by rebels fighting the Assad regime in Syria and in Egypt, under President Morsi's rule, it was even taught in schools as an acceptable practice. The lessons included recipes for cooking the arms and legs of one's enemy.

According to now converted Christian, but former Muslim Brotherhood member Walid Shoebat[25], under the Morsi regime Egyptian secondary schoolchildren were taught that it was acceptable practice to kill and eat one's enemy. The Islamic studies high school syllabus drawn up by the Al-Azhar University, included recipes for grilling arms and legs. Shoebat says it was aimed specifically at 'infidels', i.e. Christians.

To add to the picture *Time Magazine* reported in December 2015 it had video proof of ISIS jihad warriors eating the heart and lungs of murdered victims. *Time* also presented evidence by Shoebat that in 2015 20 ISIL jihadists in war-torn Syria were diagnosed with *kuru*, the human form of mad cow disease medically termed transmissible spongiform encephalopathy (TSE) or Creutzfeld Jacob disease. The condition is contracted only through human cannibalism involving repeated consumption of human brains.

Since it takes as long as 20 years for this incurable disease to manifest, Time concluded cannibalizing slain victims must have been a long established practice among 'Allah's soldiers'. What's more cannibalism is a clearly allowed Islamic practice. Al Shafie, considered the founder of Islamic jurisprudence, states in his law book, *Al'Kortoby*, Vol 1, page 716:

> One may eat the flesh of a human body. It is not allowed to kill a Muslim, nor a free non-Muslim under Muslim rule (because

25 Online post January 2013 by Egyptian scholar Walid Shoebat.

he is useful to society), nor a prisoner because he belongs to other Muslims. But you may kill an enemy fighter or an adulterer and eat his body'.

So ask yourself, how could Islam ever save Dyak head hunters from their worst wickedness? Come to that, had Islam come to New Zealand instead of Christianity would not carnage and cannibalism still be being practiced in our land today?

Sadly, after the gospel of peace's huge impact for good on Māori, there came a counter attack. Many Māori returned to the old gods. Others derided the gospel saying Europeans preached Christ to steal the land from under Māori feet.

Forgiveness came as a blinding light

But why was Christianity so attractive to Māori in the first place? Sir Eddie says the preaching of the 'gospel of peace' brought in the concept of forgiveness and "broke the cycle of vicious, hateful, intertribal warfare". He asserts that introduction of muskets had 'let war get out of hand' even by ancient Māori standards.

But had it? Pre-history tells another story. Long before guns arrived Māori had systematically slaughtered and all but eradicated the peaceful, original inhabitants of New Zealand, the Patupaiarehe, the Urekehu and the Waitaha who for centuries before the Māori came had lived at peace without warring against one another.

Māori by their belief they were the progeny of fallen angels going in unto women (Gen. 6:4) (as documented in their writings and carvings), were devil-driven to commit unspeakable bloody atrocities, often, apparently, for the sheer love of doing so.

Without forgiveness, without a biblical respect for the right of all who will do so to live at peace, there can only be strife, hate, bloodshed, destruction and war. To forgive instead of to fight burst upon Māori as a blinding flash of light, as a divine revelation, which it is.

But more. Sir Eddie says redemption 'through His blood' also hugely changed Māori thinking and belief. 'In the Māori spiritual system prior to the gospel you could commit a *hara* (wrong) without knowing it. For accidentally treading on someone's grave you could be put to death.'

The gospel brought to Māori the important truth that despite having done wrong you could be redeemed through trust in Christ. For the first time they could be saved from the penalty of *utu* (payback) and *tapu* (violating the sacred), by the power of forgiveness and the redemption of putting away sin and its consequences by the washing away of sin through Christ's blood.

This was expressed in a much-quoted Bible verse at the time: 'In Whom (Christ) we have redemption through his blood, the forgiveness of sins, according to the riches of his grace'[26].

Sadly the emphasis in Māori Christianity today is more on forgiveness and redemption as practiced by themselves to each other, than it is on the quickening grace of God in forgiving and redeeming us through Christ's death, burial and resurrection. The original missionary stress, however, was on individual salvation by 'trusting in Christ' after hearing 'the word of truth, the gospel of your salvation'[27]. Today among Māori this has been replaced by a more social gospel, as it has widely elsewhere in Christendom.

But we can never overrate the huge power of forgiveness, nor the utter tragedy among people when it is absent or proscribed. Islam has no doctrine of forgiveness; result: it is hell-bent on a global war to exterminate Christians. Nor does Hinduism understand forgiveness which is why it is massacring, persecuting and driving out believers in Christ in several Indian states.

Ironically, Sir Eddie Durie, while strongly averring the saving grace of the gospel, happens also to be the Māori Land Court Judge whose decision to make a trust amalgamation of lands removed Ngati Hotu's rights to their land at Te Rena.

---

26 Ephesians 1:7

27 Ephesians 1:13

Te Upoko Ariki, Hori Kupenga Manuka Manuka, otherwise known as George Connelly.

Chapter 14

A high chief's story

I was born during the Second World War in a small Waitaha family living on the Kaipara Harbour in Northland, New Zealand. We were a small remnant of the once numerous Waitaha people who first came to this country in 550AD.

Waitaha had lived in Northland since first landing here but around 850AD many of our people sailed to the South Island to hunt moa and other birds and stayed on there.

I come from a line of high chiefs who branched out from their ancestral lands on the Poutu peninsula and elsewhere around the Kaipara Harbour to establish sub tribes in many other parts of the North Island.

Our problem was that we were a peaceful people. It was only when, first the Moriori, then later the Māori, came in and grew in number, that we came under attack. They took our villages and plantations. You see, because we were peaceful we had never seen the need to erect palisades or other fortifications to protect our villages or round-house dwellings.

Consequently we were like sitting ducks, unprepared for an onslaught by people whose culture was based on fighting first and asking questions afterwards. Sometimes those questions were only asked, if at all, after our people had been slain, cooked and eaten.

So we had to move and my forebears were driven out from their lovely home at Pouto with its wild coast, rich seafood, lush bush and fertile soils that grew kumara, potatoes and other crops, and forced to re-establish themselves many kilometres away inland.

Further depredations occurred and over time some of our people were driven so far south they crossed Cook Strait to live in the South Island. Others of my ancestors, however, stayed in the North.

They treated with the incomers and as time went on even became high chiefs over them.

However, when I was born Waitaha in the north were reduced to a low state living on only a small part of their once extensive ancestral lands around Helensville. But even there we weren't allowed to live in peace. The Government seized large tracts of land, regardless of who among the non-European New Zealand peoples rightfully owned them, then gave them to Māori to grow vegetables on them. Effectively, they stole our land.

The problem was the Māori they sent in to grow crops on our land were Ngapuhi, the worst of our historical enemies. So my great grandfather Kupenga Manuka Manuka (born 1840, died 1936 at 96) had to dodge between them as he went from one small plot of our remaining land to another to grow kumara and other crops. I was named after my great grandfather to carry on the line.

I should explain that my mother was a Waitaha lady, Rangi Pukehu, but I was named George Connelly after my Irish Māori father, George William Connelly. But neither my younger brother Sonny nor I were brought up with our father.

From babies upward we were cared for and brought up by my grandfather, Netana Kareia Manuka Manuka, at Arapaoa on the Kaipara Harbour. And as I grew up with him I found out who I really was. My grandfather told me why my great grandfather had named me after himself, as Kupenga Manuka Manuka, to carry on the high chiefly line.

At 13 I went back to live with Mum and my father. I was now old enough to look after myself. Dad gave me a plug of tobacco and said 'Now go and earn it'.

Today I know my real name is Hori Kupenga Manuka Manuka and that I am *Te Upoko Ariki* (the paramount chief). I'm the last in a long line of high chiefs of the Waitaha people who first settled in New Zealand about 550AD, long before the first Moriori or Māori did so.

My great grandfather was Hori Kupenga Manuka Manuka. He

is next to me and from him I take my name. He would not put his name over his own son but chose me to occupy the position of high chief.

That that is who I really am was proved back in the 1990s in the Māori Land Court when my mother gave testimony to who I really was and the truth of my real name. This evidence was accepted by the court, giving me title to what is now called the Manukau Block but was originally called Manuka, and to other lands.

Dangerous information

But in the 1940s and 1950s my real name was dangerous information. My true identity could have led to my death. So it was hid from me; even my mother didn't tell me. Only slowly, a little at a time, did I learn from my grandfather who I really was and why my identity had to be kept a closely guarded secret.

My brother Sonny acted as a decoy. Should the Ngapuhi, who had killed nearly all my predecessors in the *Upoko Ariki* line, come to slay me they would get my brother instead. Thankfully, that didn't happen. Nobody knew I was *Te Upoko Ariki* until much later.

Then, when I was in my 40s, I made it known. It's important to realise that prior to the coming of the British settlers, the tribes of New Zealand had no king. The highest title was *Te Upoko Ariki*. And that's what I told the present Māori King Tuheitia – you're not a king, that's an invention borrowed from the Pakeha.

In the event neither I nor my brother died or were attacked during my childhood but I believe that was largely because of the way my grandfather carefully hid me. We lived a life on the run, moving from one part of the harbour to the other. I went to so many native Māori schools, Parekura and Kaiwaka primary among them, that I never got past Standard Five.

Often I went to school by boat. I have had no college or high school education because once out of primary school I had to work to help dig, plant and harvest kumara.

That was hard work, but in my family we've never feared hard work. I have worked hard all my life and although I'm now in my mid-70s I still get out and work physically several hours a day. Planting and harvesting kumara was all done largely by hand, although grandfather had bullocks for ploughing and a konohi, a half-sled half-cart. This was our only transport.

Was there a real threat to my life? Well, you be the judge.

Six of the most recent *tupuna* (ancestors) who preceded me in this high position in the royal bloodline of the Waitaha were killed and their heads hung up outside the houses of the chiefs who slew them.

Had they killed me then that would have been the end for us. And the one *Te Upoko Ariki* who escaped death, my grandfather, they put into Carrington Mental Hospital, falsely accusing him of being mad. He died in that hospital. But my grandfather, Netana Kareia Manuka Manuka, was anything but mad. He was a *tohunga* and rich in knowing the history and ancient lore of our people.

He had four sons and he worked hard and honestly to support his family and my brother and I. However, he stood in the way of the Ngapuhi people getting our land, so they had him sectioned and put away, all so what was ours could become theirs. Fact is that not long ago it was a purely Waitaha settlement with us living on land that had been Waitaha land for centuries. There were no Māori *marae* where I grew up; they only came in later.

My grandfather owned on behalf of our people large plots of land dispersed over a wide area. But the Government seized the land and turned it into allotments to be worked by the whole community – which meant that we, as the Waitaha, became a minority and were pushed to the back of the queue.

This took place when the Māori Queen Princess Te Puia came to Helensville and, with the help of government officials got hold of much of our land, onto which she put people as some compensation for land allegedly taken from her people during the 19th century Land Wars.

In part this was accomplished by making it appear that we as Waitaha were really part of them as Māori but we're not. To achieve this Te Puia and the Ngapuhi people were taking young Waitaha children and putting them with old men so they would be seen as their *mokopuna* (grandchildren) and it would appear they were the *tangata whenua* (original people of the land), when they weren't.

George Connelly.

More than that they did this to make our royal Waitaha blood line, the line of *Te Upoko Ariki*, in which I stand, mingle with theirs to lend legitimacy to *kingitanga* (the Māori King Movement).

The Waitaha paramount chiefs were the real royalty of this land for over 1,000 years. And to wipe out this bloodline the Ngapuhi and other Māori murdered six of my predecessors in the *Upoko Ariki* line. That is why I had to be hidden. Thankfully, when I did finally emerge from secrecy the blood lust had gone along with the land – Ngapuhi and the Government had taken all of it.

However, the Māori still wanted the blood line. So overtures were made for me to marry into high ranking Māori families. But working now and standing on my own feet, I wanted none of the responsibilities of a chief, nor did I want to take my inheritance seriously.

Before he died my great grandfather told me how important it was that I had been chosen as the next *Upoko Ariki* in line after him. But I didn't believe him. As I saw it, what use was it knowing that my great grandfather, Netana Kerei, had held a Government recognised land title to the Manakau Block in Auckland and a huge swathe of land from Ahipara down to Kawhia Harbour in the Waikato if it had all been taken away?

What use was it knowing about my ancient heritage if the land and most of the older people who knew about it were gone? All I wanted to do at the time was go to college but there wasn't the money to send me.

You see because it was the Second World War, and a time of emergency when extra food was needed, the Government took big blocks of our Waitaha land as Crown land and set up an incorporation to run it. Ngapuhi and other Māori people were put in as shareholders and we were only a minority voice.

Māori Affairs built a house for my grandfather's four sons. This took place although my great grandfather's name, which is the same as mine, was, and still is, on the land deed books under our ancestral family name, Manuka. Yes, originally Manakau was called Manuka, and it all belonged to us, the Waitaha people.

During my childhood my grandfather told me the whole history of my people. How we came originally from Egypt through Peru where we lived for centuries before being forced out.

We then sailed to *Rapa Nui*, Easter Island and settled there until over population required some of us to move on. We built large reed boats, capable of carrying 100 people or more, and set off sailing southwards through the Pacific.

Over the centuries, on the long voyage down into the South Pacific we stopped off at many islands and where they were uninhabited left parties of our people on them. It was my ancestors who settled many of the Pacific islands. They were the first Polynesians.

Originally we had begun as a fair skinned, Caucasian people. We were European in appearance. I still have the square jaw typical of Caucasians. My ancestors were part of the red-haired white people who built the temples and monuments in Peru and other parts of South America.

Importantly, we were peaceful people and our tradition has it that in South America we were attacked and over time overrun by warring peoples such as the Maya and Inca.

You can see proof of this recorded in the temple paintings of Yucatan, Mexico, which depict brown-skinned warriors with plumed headdresses ritually sacrificing white people – us – on altars and also drowning them at sea. These murals even show some whites escaping on rafts.

Despite living for many centuries in South America, we left, as we had come, a fair-skinned people. To this day there are still fair-skinned predecessors of ours living on *Rapa Nui*, which today is known as Easter Island. They, like us, originate from the Northern Hemisphere.

But that changed. My people reached what are now called the Marquesas Islands and stayed there for quite a period. You can go there and still see the statues, temples and stone complexes we built. While there my ancestors inter-married with the darker-skinned people already living there. In this way we became the light-brown, coloured people we still are today, the quintessential Polynesians.

But more important than our physical characteristics is our culture and that we have retained right down to today. We have always lived in peace and refused to take up weapons. We had learned from bitter experience that once a people go out on the warpath, savagery and cruelty become a way of life.

We had our own language too. And while language changes over time today I can still speak words from it even though I converse in both Māori and English. For example, the Waitaha word for heaven is *raki*; in Māori it is *rangi*.

Throughout my childhood Grandfather was teaching me who I really was. That I came from a people who had had a wonderful, communal way of life. This came into its full flower when for many centuries in New Zealand my people lived and traded in peace with the other peoples, Patupaiarehe and Turehu who were also here.

We built large coastal canoes and, in spring took sprouting kumara plants from the North Island down to our people in the South Island, bringing back greenstone and other supplies on the return voyage.

One especially large *waka* (canoe) was the *Huruhuru Manu*, meaning 'Bird of a Feather'. Sadly, over time the Māori took over this Waitaha trading system and it was no more. Before then, whether Waitaha or Patupaiarehe, we had been all one people and our leader *Te Upoko Ariki*, who could be a chief or queen, led us out from Peru and later from Easter Island down through the islands to New Zealand.

Beside the waters

Waitaha means 'Beside the Waters" and by preference we have always lived close to the sea, lakes or rivers. In the South Island we built fish farms on the coast and also grew crops wherever we settled.

Through prayers and spiritual understanding each child was chosen for a particular task or role to fulfil and my ancestors believed that each one would be supernaturally equipped to carry out that function.

If skilled fish farmers or fishermen were needed they would be 'prayed' into being. No baby was born without being already destined for a predetermined role.

And always my *tupuna* sought to bring out the best in themselves by a selective practice of marriage. This took two forms. First, the paramount chief, *Te Upoko Ariki*, would occasionally visit each *hapu*. He would consult with the *hapu* elders then sleep with the maidens selected to be with him. In this way the best of our genetic inheritance was preserved and improved. Second, young men and young women in the *hapu* were selected by the chief and elders for marriage to each other. The aim of this practice, called *tomo*, was to join couples who would produce offspring best fitted to certain tasks. In this way each *hapu* or sub-tribe produced the farmers, fishermen, fish farmers, gardeners, carvers, house builders and canoe makers needed.

When Māori came into the land they adopted many of our Waitaha practices and culture but, sadly, not our peace loving ways. And for a time some of the Māori lived under the Waitaha umbrella.

Were we an extensive people, living on and controlling large areas of New Zealand, or were we just small sub-tribes that were really Māori but wanted to be known by another name, as historians such as Michael King have suggested?

Well again, you be the judge. My great-great-great grandfather, Ururoa Rewharewha, as *Te Upoko Ariki*, owned land over much of New Zealand, including a *maunga* (mountain) and *pa* (fortified village) in Auckland. All up he was head over 52 *hapu*, together comprising several thousand people.

These settlements stretched from the top of Northland down to the Mahia Peninsula on the East Coast, a distance of 641 kilometres.

Until recently titles to the lands the Waitaha owned were held by our chiefs. In the 1840s my direct ancestor, *Te Upoko Ariki* Mate Rewharewha, owned the area known as Hukatere, hundreds of kilometres square and stretching from the Otamatea River to Pouto. By the way, Mate was an important chief who signed the Treaty of Waitangi to bring peace to the North.

In our heyday we were the Waitaha Nation with our High Chief, *Te Upoko Ariki*, recognised as the titular head of all peoples in *Nukuroa*, which was our name then for New Zealand. It meant 'the Far Land'. You see, the ancient history of this country is very much the story of the Waitaha people.

In 850AD the Waitaha chief Te Raikau Hotu sailed from

Northland to the South Island to establish new settlements, taking a large party of people with him. My *tupuna* (ancestor) Te Raki Houha was the navigator.

But back to my life with Grandfather. We had no plough, so all the work in the huge kumara garden was done by hand with spade, hoe and shovel. The tubers were put in pits we dug and covered with fern and bracken. We worked from first light till dusk. For years I went without shoes and our staple diet was Māori bread, rotten corn and dried shark.

My brother and I soon learned to use net and spear. Thankfully, the fishing was good and birds could be caught. In those years I was close to my hard-working, pipe-smoking grandmother and to my grandfather before they took him away, that is. Like my mother he did not speak English.

When he was gone my brother and I went back to my mother. My Dad managed a 1200-acre beef and sheep farm and so we helped him farm that.

Not long after this I was given a farming apprenticeship and went to work for a European New Zealander, Max Hargreaves, who owned an 8,000-hectare station. Working for him gave me a wide experience in many aspects of farming, including horse riding and tractor driving.

He and I got on well. And I have always got on well with Pakeha. I don't think of myself as Māori or Polynesian, but as Waitaha, with closer links to the European than to them.

Apprenticeship complete, I went shearing with my half-brother Jimmy at Taihape for five seasons. We used narrow combs back then which made the going harder. Nevertheless I was a gun shearer doing 420 sheep in eight hours. However, it was Colin Bosher of our gang who set the lamb shearing record – 600 lambs in eight hours.

At 21 I married my first wife, Heather Tangaroa of Ngapuhi, but three years later she died after a short but severe illness. It was to

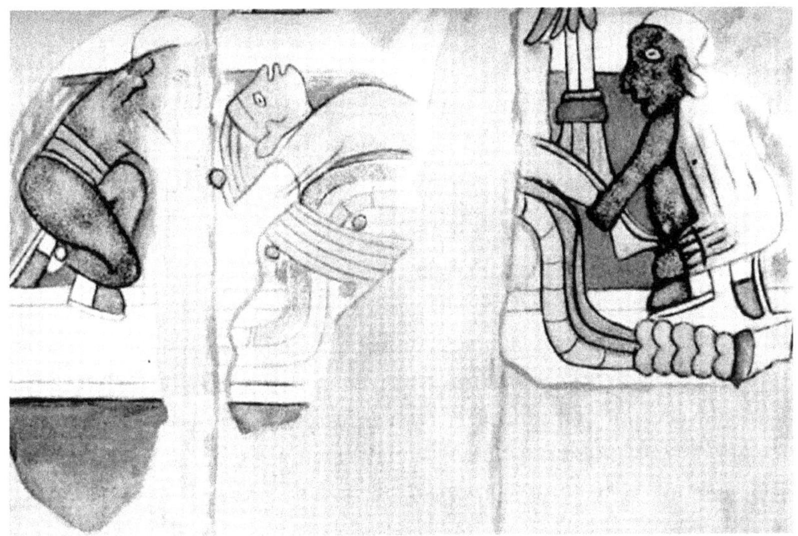

A brown-skinned Maya priest stretches out the body of a fair-skinned, yellow-haired, white person ready for ritual sacrifice. Detail from mural in the Maya temple of Yucatan, Mexico. The artists or priests who painted this mural long before the arrival of Columbus clearly knew and recorded the existence and slaughter of a people racially very different from themselves. From American Indians in the Pacific (1952) by Thor Heyerdahl, colour plates, pages 320-321.

be a long time before I settled down again. Meanwhile I worked in construction gangs at Turangi, in the tobacco fields of Motueka and in other jobs all over New Zealand. I drove buses and taxis.

Working as a road maker

Then I went to Australia and worked in the mines on underground railways. Finally, I got into road construction and asphalt laying where I was taught by the best and made this my career. For many years I felt the only way forward for me was to keep working. I thought if I stopped working I would have had it.

When I think about it, my many jobs have always had something to do with the land but perhaps the best of it has been road construction. I graded most of Auckland's motorways and laid out runways at Auckland Airport and in Nandi, Fiji. I have made roads in various other parts of the world.

I worked hard, drank with friends and moved on from one job to the next while my children from my first marriage were brought up by in-laws. Then, after I had been single for over 25 years, I met the love of my life, Robyn, my present wife. She is of the Ngati Raukara people and we've been happy together ever since.

On religion, both Robyn and I were both brought up in the Ratana Church and as a boy I went to Sunday School with a white shirt, black pants and a black bow tie. Hands were laid on me to receive the *wairua tapu* (Holy Spirit) and it was prophesied over me I should become a minister. However, as time went on I realised that Ratana was as much political as religious, if not more so. They put the four Labour MPs into Parliament.

When I found out that they were taking land but not returning it Robyn and I finished up with them. We both became born again Christians and have found much peace with God ever since. Matter of fact, all of my recent tupuna in the chiefly role were believers and read and preached from their bibles.

However, that doesn't mean that I've turned my back on my ancestors and what they believed in. Far from it. They had a peaceful way of living, a way of praying to God as they saw Him and receiving his guidance and grace and that still resonates with me.

Changes took place as the Māori conquered many tribes but even then my Upoko Ariki predecessors tried to bring about peace and stability as war and mayhem swept the country.

When I settled back in New Zealand in the 1980s it came home to me that I should take up the mantle my grandfather laid on me to be the next *Upoko Ariki*. For some reason the chiefly descent passed over my father and came to me.

My task, as I understand it, is to re-establish our large and important part in the history of this country and, secondly, to regain our ancestral land, or be adequately compensated for losing it.

I'm not a Māori

It is for the first reason I am telling my story because the true history of this country must be understood. In his popular and deemed authoritative work on New Zealand history, Michael King[28] rubbishes as 'a virulent myth' the claim Māori were not the explorers and first discoverers of New Zealand.

He describes the coming of my people to New Zealand in 550AD as the 'Waitaha myth', despite the fact that we are mentioned in Māori tradition as early inhabitants they encountered on arrival here. While acknowledging there were South Island tribes called Waitaha, he claimed these were Māori.

How can New Zealand historians ignore that I and others are still here as proof of who we are? I don't look like a Māori and I'm not a Māori. What's more I have my people's history stretching back for over 2,000 years and archaeological and other evidence proves it.

Why is it that my chiefly name, Manuka, is on the books as owning much of Manukau (a corruption of my name) and land stretching from there way beyond Helensville to the Pouto Peninsula if we didn't exist? How come I can name the line of Waitaha chiefs I descend from going back for many, many generations; going back for over 2,000 years?

We came to New Zealand long ago as a people of mixed Caucasian descent and have been here ever since. What's more, the Patupaiarehe and the Turehu were also here long before the coming of the Moriori and later the Māori.

We have been written out of history because we were a spoke in the wheel of the Government's land grab and the lands claim settlement process. Obviously, it's easier just to deal with big tribes but in the process the smaller hapu, the remaining few of the original pre-Māori people such as the Waitaha, have been left out.

---

28 Michael King, *The Penguin History of New Zealand* (2003), Penguin Books NZ Ltd, pgs. 58, 59 and 90.

These 'divide and conquer' tactics were unjust from the start. Rightful ownership of land was overridden and our people were first marginalised, then written out of the history altogether. Yet we are still here.

Here is the true history. Waitaha, Patupaiarehe and Turehu were here long, long before the Moriori, let alone the Māori. We are the original inhabitants of New Zealand.

Then, while history refuses to accept it, ships from various nations have been visiting New Zealand for many centuries; some just stayed to refit and recuperate while others brought people who settled. This process began over 1,000 years ago.

Let's face it, if the male crew of only one ship spent only a few weeks ashore and took advantage of the hospitality of the people already living here, then the resultant offspring would be enough to start a tribe of their own. But there was much more to it than that.

As is well known, sailing ships on long voyages lose many crewmen to accident, execution, flogging and disease, particularly scurvy. The record is that almost all ships sailing the Pacific forcibly recruited replacements from the Melanesian islands.

Chinese, Japanese, Spanish, Portuguese, English and French ships all reached our shores and most were wrecked. While dozens of shipwrecks have been located around our coasts, others remain to be found.

The tradition of my people says that over the centuries several large sailing ships with big crews beached here. Obviously, the larger the ship the bigger the crew needed to man her, and sometimes that meant hundreds of virtual slaves ready to jump ashore at the first opportunity.

We bore the brunt of it

And jump they did when the fierce, persistent westerly storms trapped and drove these vessels ashore along Northland's west coast. Arriving in considerable numbers these people posed a huge problem to the small settlements of my Waitaha people around the Kaipara and Hokianga harbours.

Quite simply there was not enough food to feed such companies for long and, from what I've been told, they would not fit in with the tribe and share the work load. So they were asked to leave.

Then, because they lacked the skills to live off the bush, plant their own gardens and build their own villages, they marauded our villages instead. But the worst thing was the very different culture these various Asian and Melanesian peoples brought with them. This was one of warring, bad blood, revenge, attack, and pay back and it introduced cannibalism to this land.

I firmly believe that it was from these mixed strands that the Moriori tribes formed and they fiercely attacked us and drove us out from our lands. They became the Ngapuhi, the Māori.

You see the Waitaha history is that the Māori people are really a mixture of many peoples. They have a genetic inheritance from the Chinese, Japanese, Portuguese, French, English and Spanish peoples. Also because of intermarriage and forced intercourse they also bear the genes of my people and the Patupaiarehe and the Turehu. But first and foremost they are of Melanesian extraction.

The word 'Māori' means normal or ordinary and it was brought in in the 1800s to describe the peoples predominantly living in New Zealand. All the Māori tribes come from out of Northland. They are the mixed offspring of the Ngapuhi.

Like the English, the Māori are a polyglot people, but not to be discriminated against because of that. Rather it is their culture, behaviour and attitude that has been the problem. And the original people of this land, the true *tangata whenua*, have borne the brunt of it.

On my second task, should my land claim succeed, the income from land regained will be invested in a trust not just for me, my family and the remaining North Island Waitaha, but to re-establish something of our ancestral community way of life on our traditional lands and to do so for all people.

We want to use it to contribute to community life in which all will be welcome. It's that wide inclusion of all people that the chiefs of my people stood for and achieved during the many centuries they presided over the different tribes. Their rule was not harsh or selfish; it was peaceful. There was no war, fighting or capitalism, still less cannibalism. No-one was killed. All those bad things were brought in by people of another culture, those who became the Moriori, then the Māori.

True, in the islands many descendants of my forebears became Polynesians and some were peaceful and others were not. But here in New Zealand the Waitaha always were and still are a people of peace by choice.

Seized and slain

I believe it was because historically my *tupuna* were benign and beneficial rulers and held their chiefly positions with the consent and blessing of the people, that they became prime targets on the Māori hit list as they sought to destroy the original inhabitants of New Zealand, kill their leaders and take their land.

Six of my predecessors as *Upoko Ariki* were assassinated to that end. Let me tell you something of their stories.

My great-great grandfather Mate Rewharewha, having been a signatory to the Treaty of Waitangi, stood with the British against the Māori King Tawhiao at the battle of Rangiriri in 1863. Despite that he was seized by the Armed Constabulary and held on Kawau Island. After two and a half years he escaped and returned to the Waitaha homeland at the Kaipara Harbour.

A clergyman, the Rev. Gittos, was in charge of seizing and re-assigning land around in the district at that time, and when he heard that Mate had escaped he took ship to the Kaipara Heads trying to recapture him. But before he could do so the Ngapuhi chief Kukupa, who also had his eye on the land, came to get my ancestor, seized him and five of his relatives and slew them all.

Earlier in the 1700s my *tupuna*, the Far North *Te Upoko Ariki* Haro Rewharewha Mate, was taken and killed by a Ngapuhi Māori chief when he was negotiating with French Government representative Marion du Fresne, hoping to persuade the French to annex New Zealand. This he was doing to stop the killing by Māori rampaging through the country. In the event both Mate and scores of the French crew of Du Fresne's ship were killed in the fighting.

My ancestor, the Waitaha *Upoko Ariki* Tairia Waikato Whare Herehere, paramount chief over 52 *hapu*, played a big part in the 1835 Declaration of Independence. He was one of the chiefs who signed the letter to King William IV asking him to act as protector to the 'Whenua Rangatira', the independent state declared by the *tino rangatira*, (hereditary chiefs) of the northern part of New Zealand.

This was under the umbrella of The United Tribes of New Zealand, *Te Wakaminenga o nga Hapu o Nu Tireni*. The chiefs declared that there would be no government (*kawanatanga*) except those of persons appointed by the assembly of hereditary chiefs.

King William had previously acknowledged the flag of the United Tribes of New Zealand and now recognised the Declaration of Independence. This is important history because it makes clear the vital role of the hereditary chief in making such arrangements. And I am a hereditary chief of the line of hereditary chiefs who held sway over most of New Zealand.

My ancestor Herehere went with Ngapuhi chief Hongi Hika to England to present the signed Declaration of Independence to King William but never came back. We believe he was murdered, got rid of on the return voyage, perhaps when Hongi Hika was buying hundreds of muskets in Sydney, Australia. I can certainly see my *tupuna*, as man desiring peace, trying to stop that. In the event, of course, Hongi's gun running led to the Musket Wars which destroyed people throughout New Zealand in these years.

Is it any wonder our family had to duck for cover and that as a child I had to be kept out of sight. But now the danger is past and it's time to set the record straight and for me on behalf of my people to claim back what is rightfully ours.

I'm peaceful by nature but I know how to stand up for what is right. At the Māori Land Court hearing of my case for the return of our land I refused to go into the witness box to give evidence. The judge rebuked me saying, 'You're in my courtroom now, do as you're told'. I told her, 'If it's your courtroom then take it off my land. I won't go into the witness box and come under your jurisdiction".

In the upshot I received back the particular land I was claiming despite my telling the judge she might represent the law but I had the 'lore', the ancient truthful history and tradition of our people.

But there is much more to come back. The true Manuka Block of Waitaha land stretches from Herekino right down the west coast of Northland to the Kaipara Harbour. It bears my name and that of my great grandfather and I'm sure it will come back to us.'

Chapter 15

Where the trouble began

Pouto, meaning: to cut off, is that wonderful peninsula on the north side of Kaipara Harbour where, arguably, it all began. It was a place of peace and plenty for many centuries for the ancient people of New Zealand, the Waitaha.

The present Waitaha chief Hori Kupenga Manuka Manuka says it was 'a fisherman's basket' of delights for his people. Fish and shellfish were in abundance in both the harbour and the sea.

Freshwater varieties teemed in the lake and the rich soil lent itself to growing kumara and other crops, just as it still does around Dargaville to this day.

Find this basket of natural bounty, abounding in ancient remains, by heading west from SH1 at the Dargaville turn-off. It is one of the most beautiful, fascinating and historic regions of New Zealand.

At Pouto the question to ask is: What is New Zealand's oldest *pa*? The peninsula is home to 27 old settlement sites, but which is the earliest? According to Northland farmer Logan Forrest it's the one which stands on his land near Pouto on the North Head of the Kaipara Harbour. Now Logan, with his long flowing hair and beard, is the rugged descendant of hardy farmers who took up land in the Kaipara more than a century ago. And he's very knowledgeable about this area which, in more ways than one, holds important evidence of New Zealand's ancient past.

Terraces of the ancient pa, called Tauhara, are still there to be seen on Logan's farm. And the name Tauhara itself is significant. It is shared only with one other place in New Zealand, the 3,695 foot Mt Tauhara in the Taupo volcanic caldera. Tauhara means the rejected, or unwanted, one, the 'odd man out'.

In Taupo Māori lore it is called 'The Lone Lover' because

it stands alone, the rejected male suitor for the 'female' mountain, Pihanga, to the south. Perhaps the *pa* on Logan's farm is so named because it is the remotest of the pas placed strategically to stand guard over Kaipara's rivers.

Interestingly, it is on Mount Tauhara, Taupo, that very old carvings in basalt rock are found, one of which depicts an ancient ship of Mediterranean design. The deeply incised picture of this clearly non-Polynesian vessel was revealed when a few years ago a rock slip tore away layers of hardened volcanic deposits, said to have resulted from the great 232AD Taupo eruption

But why is Tauhara the oldest Pouto pa? I ask. Logan smiles through his beard and says that some years ago the *pa* and the remains in it were examined by experts and found to be very, very old. Prof. Geoff Irwin of the University of Auckland determined by radio carbon dating of charcoal and other deposits the site was occupied as far back as 1,000 to 1,200 years ago.

This he deduced from fragments of wood and iron (yes, iron, the only trace of metal found on New Zealand's ancient sites to date) dug up from within the settlement.

But it is the age of the *pa* before it was palisaded for defensive purpose, as determined by Irwin's investigation that is the real stunner. He concluded that Tauhara Pa, had been built as a peaceful settlement sometime between 400 and 500AD.

Sadly, according to Logan, Prof. Irwin, because of academic peer pressure, later revised his estimate of the *pa*'s age back to the 1200s to fit in with the then thought arrival date of the Māori, a fate that has befell other archaeological investigations.

Interestingly, studies of *pa* sites on a wide scale in the 1980s and 1990s were conducted by the two leading New Zealand archaeologists of the time, Prof. Irwin at Pouto and Prof. Doug Sutton at Pouerua, applying for the first time a 'regional approach' by excavating and studying several sites simultaneously.

Beach wildness at Pouto. A little inland, however, birdlife flourishes in placid lagoons and the soil is highly fertile in what is ideal kumara growing land.

In both Pouto and Pouerua it was seen there had been a sharp change from undefended settlements by turning them into fortified pas. Prof. Irwin's (1985) study at Pouto was the first archaeological application of settlement pattern studies for *pa* in New Zealand archaeology.

It seems then that at Pouto the '*pa*' on Logan's farm began life as a small settlement which needed no ramparts, other than perhaps fences to enclose moa, which in Northland are believed to have been farmed for hundreds of years. From impressions left in the ground it is clear that the first inhabitants, the peaceful Waitaha people, as we learn from their principal current descendant, the *Upoko Ariki*, Hori Kupenga Manuka Manuka, lived in round, thatched dwellings. They did so, evidently, without fighting or threat of war for many centuries.

Logan points out there was a sharp change in the style of construction at the site at sometime between 900 and 1100AD when oblong, rectangular structures made their appearance. They were accompanied by palisades erected along terraces. Clearly, the Pouto *kainga* (village) was now reconfigured with new structures to make it a defensive *pa*. The aim was to keep enemies out.

Such a transition, repeated in later years at pa sites throughout the country, marks a drastic upheaval in the story of old New Zealand. It was a gut-wrenching change for peaceful settlers, who had lived weaponless for many generations, to now have to protect themselves against what they evidently perceived as an armed and aggressive enemy.

What enemy, you ask? Well it is not without significance that the date of the defensive works at Pouto and other nearby settlement area coincides with dramatic events that drastically changed early New Zealand society.

One was the emergence in Northland of a warrior, cannibal people calling themselves Moriori, later to be called Māori. Another was a series of shipwrecks on the Kauri Coast and elsewhere in Northland of sailing ships which sometimes carried massive crews. A third was that in the 1400s a fleet of Chinese ships, some carrying a crew of 1,000 or more, sailed out to explore the world.

Are these events connected? Well, you be the judge as these chapters present the facts as we best know them. Timber has been found and tested from several different shipwreck sites on the Kauri Coast and in May 2005 a massive Chinese shipwreck was confirmed. Then there is the sudden movement of peoples settled in one place for many generations, plus confirmatory truth from ancient oral history, supported by the conclusions of respected historians. Could anyone want for more?

First though let's review what we have found at Pouto. For centuries a prosperous community of Waitaha people fished, farmed and traded with others peacefully.

They lived in circular dwellings, the impressions of which on Logan's farm differ sharply from later oblong structures defended by palisaded terraces. The inevitable conclusion is that where once was peace, war had come.

And, according to Chief Hori, conflict first came with the Moriori, thought by author Max Hill to be the people who voyaged with Turi to New Zealand from Rarotonga[29]. However, Chief Hori Kupenga believes differently. He holds that the Moriori largely comprised runaway crew whom escaped from wrecked or anchored ships and who were mainly Melanesian. Later they developed into the Māori. In turn the combined Moriori-Māori peoples of the North became the Ngapuhi, today the largest Māori tribe in New Zealand.

'And it is from Ngapuhi that all the Māori tribes of New Zealand came. They spread out throughout the country from here, my people's landing place in Northland,' Chief Hori insists.

---

29 *To The Ends Of The Earth*, byMaxwell C. Hill, page 126.

Reconstructed model of a Fijian drua. Picture courtesy of the New Zealand Maritime Museum, Auckland,

Chapter 16

The Melanesian connection

Several years ago scientists found firm genetic evidence of a long suspected linkage between New Zealand Māori and certain tribes living in Taiwan. More recently, however, further studies have revealed a significant twist to the story.

This development comes on the back of the view held for some time by several researchers it was the vessels of a large Chinese fleet that brought the Māori culture from the Taiwan region to New Zealand.

The new twist is that while the mitochondrial DNA of women shows a strong ancestral link to Taiwan, the genes of Māori men reveal a strong Melanesian connection.

So much so a TV One *Sunday* report on genome research by Dr. Geoffrey Chambers, a Reader in Victoria University's School of Biological Sciences and student Adele Whyte studying genetic origins of Māori for her master's thesis, suggested that in terms of their migration to New Zealand Māori men and Māori women each come from different homelands, genetically speaking.

By comparing the DNA of people from Asia, across the Pacific Ocean and New Zealand, Whyte and Chambers claim to have revealed a 'living genetic map' of ancient Māori migration routes. They said their findings confirmed archaeological evidence that the ancestors of today's Māori originally set out from mainland south-east Asia, then hopped from island to island, starting with Taiwan and progressing through Micronesia and Melanesia to eventually arrive in New Zealand. In fact Dr. Chambers discovered Māori had just one gene marker for coping with drinking alcohol. When he looked at the same gene markers in tribes who've lived in Taiwan for some 6,000 years, he found a match.

"It turned out, that like the New Zealand Māori they had those markers too," Chambers says.

An official Victoria University press release said the research "also brings startlingly new evidence that as Māori ancestors migrated from one group of islands to the next, **men from Melanesian communities joined the boats**. This changed the genetic mix, and lead to the differences observed in the genetic make-up of today's Māori men as contrasted with their women".

The research involved two separate genetic mapping processes. The Southeast Asian homeland was confirmed by Chambers' research into the frequency of two genes that influence the body's reaction to alcohol. He found that while Taiwanese people have both gene types, Māori inherited only one. In an interview with ABC Science Online Chambers said: "We think this one was lost at the first step of migration, when people left what is now Taiwan".

In the second gene mapping process Whyte, who is of Ngati Kahungunu descent, examined sex-linked genetic markers, namely mitochondrial DNA in women, and Y-chromosomes in men. The research found that besides the alcohol genes, female Māori have other genetic markers which confirm their ancient Asian origin. To her surprise, however, the men have genetic markers that show a Melanesian ancestry.

'As a result of intermarriage along the migration trail, the signatures of the mitochondrial DNA from **women have stayed more 'island south-east Asian'**, and **the Y-chromosomes are more Melanesian**,' Whyte told ABC ScienceOnline.

Other DNA sequencing by Moroccan-born Jean Trejaut pinpointed the Amis people from east coast of Taiwan as the closest genetic match to Māori. Bunun, Amis and Yami are three southern indigenous tribes. They are recognised by Taiwan's government as fiercely independent and once practiced head-hunting. Descendants of pre-historic travelers, these people were mountain hunters and seafarers.

Language similarities also confirm the Taiwanese link. The organisation Cultural Survival reported that government representatives of Taiwan and New Zealand have established formal ties because of Chambers' genetic research.

Interestingly, Chih-Tung Huang, a member of the Amis tribe in Taiwan, experienced this link first-hand when speaking with a Māori man from New Zealand. According to Huang, "we find when we want to count numbers from 1 to 10, it is almost the same in [both] languages."

But what of the Melanesian connection? Did Māori women migrating from Taiwan just pick up another set of genes when Melanesian men joined the boats, as Adele Whyte suggests? Or are Māori predominantly from Melanesia as the Y chromosomes of Māori men suggest?

Genetics aside, the cultural similarities are striking. In Papua New Guinea, the Solomons and other parts of Melanesia, such as Fiji, cannibalism, head-hunting and human sacrifice were rife until Christian missionaries arrived.

In Fiji war canoes were launched over the bodies of several slain whose blood was poured over the decks. One Fiji chief alone is reputed to have eaten over 900 slain victims in his lifetime, keeping count by adding a stone to a cairn by his home after each human meal.

In the Melanesian islands humans were frequently sacrificed to build up the *mana* of ghosts and heads were hunted to add to the mana of both the living and the dead.

Professor J. H. Scott, 19th century Professor of Anatomy and Dean of the Medical School, University of Otago declared[30]: 'We know the Māori to be a mixed race, the result of the mingling of a Polynesian and Melanesian strain. The crania already examined

---

30 *The Osteology of the Aborigines of New Zealand and o fthe Chatham Islands*, J. H. Scott (1851-1914), published in Volume 26 of the *Transactions of the New Zealand Institute*.

leave no room for doubt on this point. The Melanesian characters are therefore more accentuated in the North than amongst the natives of the South Island."

How might that be? G. Graham[31] records how 'a strange people, probably castaways', settled on the North Island's East Coast long ago. These folk, later called 'Ngutu-au' by the Māori, 'arrived at Whare-kahika many generations ago in a canoe of remarkable construction', he states.

According to Graham, they possessed peculiarities of speech and manners. They settled at Matakawa, where they cultivated the *kumara* and remained for some time. Owing to some trouble with the local tribe of Ngati Porou, these folk launched their canoe one night and set forth to return to their distant home across the ocean. However, three remained, including Mou-te-rangi, named in another Māori tradition as one who left New Zealand to re-cross the ocean to 'Hawaiki'. He was never heard of again.

In the Bay of Plenty a tradition tells of a vessel reaching Whakatane many generations ago with a crew of very dark-skinned people. These immigrants, probably castaways from a drift voyage, are said to have settled at Omeheu, on the Rangitaiki River.

An old Māori song alludes to the voyages of olden days supposedly from Tahiti to New Zealand. It calls upon the addressed one to ascend the peaks of Hikurangi and Aorangi, which are names of two peaks at Tahiti – 'names given by your ancestors'. It proceeds: 'Turn and face Para-weranui and Tahu-makaka-nui [personified forms of south and west – i.e., face the south-west], the way by which your ancestors were brought hither by ocean monsters, when Harua-tai broke out the sea path and the ocean surges were charmed, while the path of Kahukura (the rainbow god) marked the way to land, and the fair land was concealed by the Mist Maid'.

There can be little doubt that thousands of years ago dark-

31 Volume 14 of the *Journal of the Polynesian Society, a short paper by G. Graham.*

skinned, Negro peoples 'island hopped' their way from Melanesia to people Fiji, Samoa, Tonga and beyond.

The vessels they used, according to *Wikipedia*, the free encyclopedia, would have been the drua, the double-hull sailing boat which originated in Micronesia. Druas do not tack but shunt (stern becomes bow and vice versa). Both ends of each hull are identical, but the hulls are of different sizes and the smaller one is always sailed to windward. *Wikipaedia* states: 'The Fijian double canoe (*wangga ndrua*) was the largest and finest sea-going vessel ever designed and built by natives of Oceania before contact with Europeans.'

Importantly, druas were large, up to 30 metres long, and could carry over 200 people. So, conceivably, they could have reached New Zealand at a pinch. Were they the vessels on which Ngapuhi, the tribe from which the Māori peoples sprang, first reached Northland? We may never know because today no druas exist, apart from a reconstructed model housed in the New Zealand Maritime Museum, Auckland.

However, further light is shed on Māori Melanesian origins by Hawaii Courts Officer Peter Leiataua AhChing[32] who asserts that Polynesians developed their unique culture in an area bounded by Savai' i, Upolu, Samoa and Tonga over many centuries prior to 500BC with Savai'i as the motherland (breeding ground).

Nowhere else on earth will you find ancient Polynesian remains other than within the Polynesian Triangle or maybe along the coast of the adjacent land masses like the Americas, he says. AhChing says that scientific scholars of Hawaii attribute the Polynesian bloodline to intermixing of two ancient races of forebears,one Mongoloid (i.e. from South-East Asia) and the other Negroid, i.e. from Melanesia, perhaps ultimately Africa.

Their progeny then drifted into genetic isolation and 'speciated' in the Samoa-Tonga Savai'i and Upolu area. 'They developed a unique Polynesian culture to meet their needs for survival, based on strong

32 *A Scientific Analysis on the Polynesian Origins & Culture*, Peter Leiataua AhChing, 2003.

family values, community sharing and responsibility'.

Findings of genetic studies in 2002 combined with old legends, show pure genetic Polynesians were birthed in the Samoa-Tonga realm and their forebears had migrated from the west, Melanesia. 'We Polynesians have always known as fact that Polynesians came from the west, from Savai'i of Samoa,' he says.

Importantly, he maintains that while the original Tongans were Polynesians from Samoa, they later procreated with Melanesians who moved in from nearby Fiji and Vanuatu. Melanesian cultural influence became very strong in Tonga, so the original Polynesians retreated to Samoa.

Chapter 17

Whence the Moriori?

Drive alongside the Kaipara Harbour, the largest in New Zealand and in the Southern Hemisphere, and you can still enjoy one of New Zealand's most exciting scenic routes. Kaipara means: *kai*, (food) and *para* (fish) and, teeming as it was with shellfish, fish and seabirds in times past, it is still a provider today.

Sand cliffs, wild surf and stunning beaches and beautiful bush abound here. As you drive, check the beach for remains of the old kauri forest. Fly over it and on a clear, calm day you might even see the outlines of shipwrecks beneath the water.

The road leads to the Waipoua Kauri Forest, which not only contains New Zealand's oldest and largest kauri tree, *Tane Mahuta*, but also the remains of an ancient stone city. What's more, here in the deepest and most inaccessible parts, it is said, there may still live the last remnants of a small and ancient people, the Turehu.

So maintains shipwreck explorer Noel Hilliam, founder of the must-see Dargaville Museum and an inveterate explorer of sunken ships along the coast and of inland ancient remains.

In an earlier chapter we saw clear evidence that the oldest human settlement on the Pouto peninsula was radically rebuilt as a defensive *pa* many centuries after its founding. This urgent construction took place when the peaceful Waitaha people, living in open villages of huts as they had for centuries, were suddenly driven to defend their settlements to stave off an attacking enemy. Who were these warlike incomers to the Kauri Coast? Were they an aggressive, warrior people who would come to be the Moriori?

The Moriori are now the people of Rēkohu (Chatham Islands) and Rangihaute (Pitt Island), the two largest islands in the Chatham group, 767 km south-east of mainland New Zealand, and a handful

Compare these Melanesian totem poles with the Māori carved equivalent on the next page

who still live in the Waikato. But who were they originally, where did they come from and how did they reach New Zealand? These are important questions this chapter will try to answer.

To begin with, let us note it was held by 19th century ethnographers such as Elsdon Best and other stalwarts of the Polyncsian Society that the Moriori were of Melanesian, not Polynesian extraction. Then the story changed. *Te Ara, the Encyclopaedia of New Zealand* states: 'It was once believed that Moriori were a Melanesian people, but it is now thought that they share the same Polynesian ancestry as Māori people'.

Te Ara also says: 'Current research also indicates that Moriori came to the Chatham Islands from New Zealand about 1500AD. Moriori traditions, however, hold that there were (other) people on the island before the canoe voyagers arrived.'

While online teacher resource *Pataka Education* states that the Moriori of Rēkohu (the Chatham Islands) are *T'chakat henu*, people of the land, this assertion ignores that when they first landed they found others, now believed to have been the Waitaha, already in occupation. Perhaps it was a repeat of their earlier experience in the Far North of the country, where they also encountered long established Waitaha occupants and according to some sources went to war with them. Like many tribes Moriori are reticent to speak of those displaced by their coming.

Ironically, the Moriori themselves later received the same

'silent treatment', their historical existence being denied in Māori tribal traditions. I encountered this phenomena years ago when I began investigating evidence for pre-Māori peoples in New Zealand and published an article in the *Waikato This Week* stating that Moriori were still alive and well in the Waikato. The report was greeted with shock and disbelief by some Māori, who protested that it could not be so. Yet that Moriori had been living in the Waikato long before Tainui arrived and other Māori was confirmed by Māori Studies Professor Tom Roa of Waikato University

In further proof of pre-Māori Moriori arrival, Max Hill's book, *To The Ends Of The Earth*, carried the photograph and story of Moriori chief Philip Ranga, of Raglan. Chief Philip who, with his family was very much alive and well at the time of writing this book, maintains that his people occupied most of the Waikato and land beyond for centuries before Māori arrival.

Hill believes Moriori first reached New Zealand in 1150AD and have lived here ever since. He maintains they sailed to New Zealand from Rarotonga, citing matching place names found in both countries as evidence.

Before Toi, a large white population

However, Waitaha Paramount Chief, Hori Kupenga Manuka Manuka begs to differ. He believes the Moriori are descendants of a dark skinned peoples brought to New Zealand as pressed crew aboard Chinese and European sailing ships as much as six centuries ago.

But where did the Moriori come from originally? Most scholars agree that centuries ago the Melanesians spread eastwards from Papa New Guinea, the Solomons and New Caledonia to reach Samoa, Fiji, Tahiti and other Pacific islands. This they achieved by 'hopping' from one island to another in canoes, the consensus holds.

That may well be so but in the case of their reaching New Zealand there are other possibilities. While Melanesian canoes may have successfully plied the tropical waters of the Pacific when good weather prevailed I cannot imagine them safely negotiating a southerly buster off the coasts of New Zealand.

Toi the Wood Eater is said to have arrived in the Bay of Plenty long ago with some of his people. Toi is a foundation ancestor in many Māori *whakapapa* (family histories and lines of tribal descent).

According to received Patupaiarehe history, as related by Monica Matamua in Chapter 2, Toi landed at Whakatane two centuries before Māori arrival there in the 1600s. Importantly, for our purposes, the history of Monica's people maintains that Toi was Melanesian and Māori tribal history records that on arrival he found the Bay of Plenty already occupied by a large – and white – population.

Toi beached his canoe at Whakatane but that does not mean he had sailed there from the Pacific islands. It is far more likely he arrived from the Far North of New Zealand, as the Waitaha Chief Hori Kupenga maintains.

'I understand from my people's history that the Moriori were in fact escaped crew, virtual slaves who had been seized in their Melanesian island homelands and pressed into service as crew, ' he says. Some of these ships were wrecked on the Northland shores and their surviving crew then developed as a separate people.'

Chief Hori holds that a succession of sailing ships reached the Far North including Chinese, Portuguese, French, Spanish, Dutch and English vessels. There may well have been others now unknown to recorded history.

And this is confirmed by veteran shipwreck explorer Noel

Hilliam who says that scores of such shipwrecks can be found along the Kaipara coast and elsewhere in Northland. Chief Hori believes that as pressed crew the Melanesians would have taken the first opportunity to escape and that would have come when ships reached New Zealand.

'Once ashore they would have no love for their masters, whether they were Chinese, Spanish or Portuguese,' he suggests. 'Knowing the later character of the Moriori, who in Northland became the Ngapuhi Māori tribe, I'm sure they would have taken the first opportunity to exact *utu* (revenge) on those who had hailed them forcibly aboard ship and worked them with the lash and threat of death'.

It is only disputed oral tradition that the Moriori people (progenitor of the Māori tribes, according to Chief Hori) navigated their way by canoe from the Pacific islands to New Zealand, he asserts.

Ngapuhi cultural spokesman David Rankin, who claims descent from the legendary Kupe, has publicly stated that Māori didn't navigate their way to New Zealand. 'We came on a tidal drift; *Te Tai Tokerau* (the collective name for the Māori tribes of Northland) is actually the tidal drift from the Tokelau Islands', he says.

For the record, the Māori word *tai* means either a coast or tide and, yes, a current does sweep south from the Pacific down towards New Zealand in summer months. But was it by canoe or foreign sailing ship that Mr. Rankin's Melanesian predecessors reached New Zealand?

Fact is the Tokelau Islands comprise three coral reefs 500 kilometres north of Samoa with a total area of four square miles. It is hard to see how such a small landmass could be *Hawaiki*, the legendary birthplace of the Māori and equally difficult to imagine how a fishing canoe could survive the 3,757km voyage to New Zealand.

Could *tai* then refer to a ship or ships reaching New Zealand? One unconfirmed story has it that the Waikato Tainui tribe were once Melanesians forced to serve as crew aboard a Spanish ship called *Tainui*, which, when translated would mean 'big ship', *tai* meaning tide (or, arguably ship) and *nui* meaning big.

Tai, meaning sea, tide or coast, is used to describe the coming of a people to a new land and how they got there. *Te Tai Tokerau* means 'the northern tide' and is used to describe both the people, their coming and the territory of the Ngapuhi Māori tribe of Northland.

Tai-nui also has a double meaning: 1) the 'big tide' of people coming into the Waikato 2) the big 'tide' or ship that brought them. In *The Lost Caravel* (1975) researcher Robert Langdon asserts that the Tainui Māori tribe's traditional history of arriving from the Pacific islands on a canoe named *Tainui* really refers to a bid by ship wrecked Spanish sailors in the early 1500s to build or rebuild their ship and sail to the Cape of Good Hope to return to Spain. Instead they reached Aotea Harbour, at Raglan, New Zealand where according to some accounts their storm-driven vessel was wrecked and the Spanish seamen were killed in a sudden attack upon them by Melanesian crew members.

Langdon records that the Spanish Loaisa expedition entered the Pacific in 1526. In mid-ocean the caravel *San Lesmes* separated from the fleet and was not seen by them again. Instead she struck a reef at Amanu Atoll, 800km east of Tahiti. Proof of that is that three of the four cannon thrown overboard then were recovered recently and found to be of Spanish, pre-1550 construction.

He recounts that the mainly Basque Spanish crew intermarried with Polynesians as they sailed the damaged ship among the islands, then rebuilt her and essayed to sail home. He asserts that as a consequence Spanish genes, culture, religion and technology were introduced to the Society Islands. Other Spanish ships were also wrecked in the Pacific leaving a Hispano-Polynesian cultural legacy among Māori and also in the Hawaiian, Marshall and Caroline islands.

Langdon has lent proof to Thor Heyerdahl's contention that the peoples sailing from Americas were the original Polynesians, showing they brought with them American cotton, capsicum, bananas, soapberry, tomato, manoc, maize, bottle gourds and the kumara. This agrees with Waitaha Chief Hori's assertion it was his people fleeing Peru that peopled the Pacific islands.

And the Melanesian connection? Well, *Tai* is a Melanesian word and there is ample evidence that Spanish ships sailing the Pacific routinely impressed Melanesians as crew. Beyond that there is the striking coincidence that three Spanish steamships of a later era were all named *Tainui*.

As to the alleged *Tainui* canoe, supposedly buried at Kawhia on which Tainui claims it reached these shores from the far Pacific, forget it. Author Max Hill has convincingly shown this canoe was made of New Zealand totara timber and that as an inshore fishing vessel it is far too low and narrow to survive the open sea.

Then there is the Moriori (Melanesian) use of the word *tai* to mean conquered people killed and eaten. The English translation of an old Moriori migration chant (in which tide translates *tai*) runs:

Paonga, lick up the tides of Aotea,
Paonga, lick up the tides of Aropawa,
Paonga, lick up, Paonga, devour,
The tide sounds at Pehanga-riki.

Despite the evidence suggesting that Melanesians reached here as ship slaves and then became known as Moriori, online *Te Ara Encylopaedia of New Zealand History* states that Kupe was the first 'Polynesian' to discover New Zealand (though it gives no date), sailing here from an otherwise unidentified 'Hawaiki' far out in the Pacific. Now legend has it that Kupe set out to kill an octopus (could it have been a Spanish ship?) near his homeland and pursued it all the way to Cook Strait. *Hawaiki* is found as a place name in both the Aotea Harbour (present day Raglan in the Waikato) and in the Far North of New Zealand on the banks of the Awanui River.

Hill[33] is at pains to point out that *Hawaiki* is actually the name of the region north of the Kaipara Harbour. There is also a string of other places in New Zealand named *Hawaiki*. Canoe voyages, first by

---

33 *To The Ends Of The Earth And Back Again*, by Maxwell C. Hill, page 137.

Moriori then by Māori, from the Far North of New Zealand southwards to other places in the North Island they named *Hawaiki* are the basis for many Māori tribal migration stories.

Invariably such traditions are vague about which Pacific island they supposedly sailed from and equally lacking in a detailed description of the voyage. It now seems clear that actually they all took place in New Zealand waters. In Chief Hori's view while Kupe and Toi may well have had real existence as explorers in and around New Zealand, the claim they sailed from any Pacific island to discover New Zealand is myth.

He believes that the stories such as the fable of a 'Great Fleet" of wakas sailing from the Pacific islands to New Zealand have been contrived, first to cover up Melanesian arrival in this country as escaped shipboard slaves, second to disguise the truth that this country was already well populated by other earlier peoples and, third, to falsely bolster land claims.

Ngapuhi cultural leader David Rankin makes no bones about earlier peoples. In an interview with *E-Local* magazine he stated:

> Māori are not the indigenous people of Aotearoa New Zealand. There were many other races already living here before Kupe arrived. I am his direct descendant and I know from our oral history passed down 44 generations.

More circumspect is the paper, *Poverty Bay in Pre-Māori Days*, one of Victoria University's *Behind the Veil* series of history studies. The paper states that it is not known how the mid-East coasts of the North Island were first populated, but asserts that Māori were not the original inhabitants.

Interestingly, *Behind the Veil* says that Kupe and Ngahue are thought to be the first Polynesians to visit New Zealand but reports that 'they did not stay'. The paper then asserts that in 1,200AD Toi found the East Coast 'inhabited by a race called the *Mouriuri* or *Maruiwi*'.

One does not need to be a rocket scientist to see that this is a reference to the Moriori (Mouriuri) becoming the (Maruiwi) or Māori, or that the paper's timeline for Moriori and subsequent Māori incursion is too early and too confused. Indeed the paper itself is vague about it, saying that the Maruiwi may or may not have come here even before the days of Kupe and Ngahue. It is far more likely that Moriori arrival happened much later than the accepted history supposes, i.e. when Toi and his people, Melanesians descended from those who came ashore from wrecked or other visiting ships, left what was becoming an increasingly overcrowded and violent Northland to explore less populated areas of New Zealand.

At some point they and other Melanesians in New Zealand called themselves *Moriori*. At Whakatane they intermarried with the already resident Patupaiarehe people, as Monica Matamua reports in her people's story. Time passed and then there came from the Far North other waves of Melanesian descendants who now called themselves *Maruiwi*, or *Māori*.

Fact is that Māori tribal traditions about Kupe and Toi vary hugely. None agree on where they sailed from to New Zealand and none provide a firm date. In Māori tradition *Hawaiki*, the supposed starting point, remains a place of mystery, location unknown.

In sharp contrast, both the Waitaha and Patupaiarehe traditions are definite about where their peoples sailed from, the Patupaiarehe hailing from Middle East and sailing to New Zealand from Peru and the Waitaha also sailing from Peru via Easter Island and the Marquesas to New Zealand.

According to Chief Hori, both Kupe and Toi, if they really existed and are not just creatures of myth, would have been Melanesians who built canoes of native timber in the Far North and set out from there to explore the rest of New Zealand. Hawaiki, he points out, means both the place you start from and the place you arrive at, 'which is why there are several *Hawaiki* place names in New Zealand'.

He disputes the Māori claim they were the original Polynesians to settle New Zealand. 'As they acknowledge themselves others were here long before they came. My people are the true Polynesians of the Pacific. Coming out of Peru by way of Easter Island we populated the islands down to New Zealand'. Māori lore has it that Kupe left *Hawaiki* and was led by an octopus to Cook Strait between the North and South islands of New Zealand. The stories allege both he and Toi voyaged to New Zealand shores in wakas. But did they really survive a perilous voyage of many weeks in fragile dugout canoes with woven mats for sails?

Recent re-enactments in replicas of ancient canoes cannot be considered adequate proof of such supposed voyages having taken place many centuries ago. The latter day canoes used Dacron sails, not mats and had solar powered instrumentation and electric motors while others used diesel engines. All had modern computerized communications and the availability of rescue services. So, is it unreasonable to postulate instead, since French, Dutch, Portuguese, Spanish and other ships plied New Zealand waters in the 1500s and 1600s and Chinese ships reached here in the 1400s, that some Melanesians may well have reached New Zealand aboard such vessels?

If the ships were wrecked on New Zealand's rugged coasts, as some were, then Melanesians could have been among surviving crew members. They may have been impressed crew escaping their harsh life aboard by attacking their masters at the first opportunity. Either way, it is suggested, they became the Moriori which people, according to Chief Hori, became the Māori.

'Fact is that the Moriori people were the Melanesians who first arrived in the Far North then spread south to the Waikato, to Taranaki and eventually to the Chatham Islands,' he says. 'And it was from the Moriori that the Māori people sprang. And, like the Moriori, they too dispersed throughout New Zealand.

'Of course while they are predominantly Melanesian through their Moriori heritage the Māori are also a mixture of many races that include Chinese, Spanish, Portuguese and Polynesian through my people, the Waitaha. In the beginning, however, it was my people, the Waitaha, who were the first Polynesians to reach New Zealand,' he insists.

Timetable for settlement

300-200BC: Patupaiarehe emigration fleet arrives and settles in New Zealand. Turehu also arrive.

232BC: Greek-Egyptian exploration fleet reaches New Zealand and drops off colonists.

550AD: Waitaha people reach and settle parts of Northland.

1400sAD: Chinese ships visit New Zealand, some are wrecked in Northland. Chinese masters escape to build their own village. Impressed Melanesian crewmen survive shipwreck, reach land then later maraud existing inhabitants.

Early 1500sAD: Spanish ships land at Poverty Bay and the Far North and intermingle with existing locals. French pay visit. De Gonneville's ship stays for six months in Doubtless Bay, crew intermingle with locals.

1500s-1600sAD: French, Dutch, Spanish, Portuguese and English vessels reach New Zealand and stay for various periods.

1642: Abel Tasman 'discovers' New Zealand. His fleet is attacked, crew are killed and one ship taken.

1769 Captain James Cook explores and charts New Zealand.

Late 1700s and 1800s: Latter-day British and other European settlers arrive.

All the way from Spain? Was a memory of Galician elevated storehouses like this timber one the inspiration for the elevated Māori pataka *food storehouse seen on a later page?*

Chapter 18

From Spain with love

Does Spanish blood run in the veins of New Zealand's Māori people? Did Spanish sailors live here long before either Abel Tasman or James Cook 'discovered' this land? If so is there tangible proof from the past of their sometime presence? This chapter examines evidence suggesting this is so but, as always, the reader must be the final judge.

The stories about early Spanish contact with New Zealand are intriguing. They range from a suggestion that Spanish Basques, marooned by shipwreck, introduced to the Māori marae both the cross and the raised pataka (food store) to the claim that veteran New Zealand politician and New Zealand First Party leader Winston Peters is descended from a Spanish ship's officer.

Then there is the hard core proof. A Spanish iron helmet was dredged up in Wellington harbour and a 16th century miquelet, a flintlock mechanism of undeniably early Spanish origin, was found in a coastal cave in Northland. An iron Spanish spur was found in sand dunes in the 1800s.

And in 1982 shipwreck explorer Noel Hilliam found the almost intact hull of the Portuguese ship *Cecilia Maria* lying just off a Northland beach. The ship had wrecked about 1532AD and had been built of the tropical hardwood *lagerstromeia*. Waitaha descendants say the story that has come down to them has it that the ship lost her rudder and drifted on to the beach. What happened to the crew is unknown but what is most likely is that some survived, were taken in by the Waitaha people and became part of the native population.

Later, but still long before Captain Cook reached New Zealand, a Spanish ship sailed into the Kaipara Harbour and anchored near the shore. Their intent may well have been to trade peacefully but the ship was attacked by a fierce war party said to be Māori.

How about this stone food storehouse that is a traditional feature of many parts in Galicia? Its design and purpose is strikingly similar to the traditional Māori pataka found on many maraes.

In the ensuing battle 22 of the crew were killed and eaten, the ship was plundered and burned. Only the hull below the waterline was left.

However, one man was spared. He was the captain, who was wearing armour and a helmet and was thought by the attackers to be an *atua*, a god, and therefore *tapu*, (not to be touched). His name was Pietro Contandes de Lamora and after living with the local natives for a while he moved to the Bay of Islands and settled there.

Now translate Pietro into Māori and you have Pita, Peter in English. And it's not a big step from there to the common surname Peters.

And that, I am told is why that doyen of New Zealand opposition politics, New Zealand First leader Winston Peters, can trace his ancestry back to the Spanish captain who survived the massacre of his ship's crew in the Kaipara Harbour centuries ago.

One thing's for sure, Mr. Peters has an amazing talent for staging a comeback. Twice he and his party have come back from the brink of political extinction. Does this innate ability to survive stem from his illustrious forebear, the only man to escape the massacre of an entire crew? One certainly wonders how he did it.

The name of the plundered ship and other details of its crew are not known but one other thing is. The attack and massacre were witnessed by some of the last Waitaha people still living nearby. They were alarmed by growing hostility against them from incoming strangers said to be Māori but actually at that time known to be an interbred mixture of Melanesian people, Chinese and Spanish castaways and others. Waitaha, a peaceful people, had lived at Pouto and along the Kauri coast for many centuries. But at the time of the above atrocity many had already abandoned their round hut villages and moved away inland.

Witnessing the massacre of hapless sailors was for the few who remained was the last straw. They upped and left lest a similar fate befall them. Which is why, according to the Waitaha Upoko Ariki,

A pataka from a Māori marae, as exhibited in the Te Papa National Museum of New Zealand collection. Picture courtesy of Te Papa.

Hori Kupenga Manuka Manuka, Waitaha have not lived at Pouto from that day to this.

As to the cross and the *pataka*, the mystery is how they came to be such a prominent feature of Māori culture and practice. The *pataka*, an elevated food store, elaborately styled and decorated, is not found in the Pacific islands nor in South America. Nor for that matter prior to Christianisation is the cross.

While the *pataka* is said to have been built to preserve food from rats, the evidence is that New Zealand's earliest peoples, the

Patupaiarehe, used *rua*, or pits, to store food. Rats, it seems, weren't a problem, perhaps because they were a prized food source.

So where did such an elaborate, gabled structure come from? Consider the accompanying pictures. The first set shows traditional, above ground, elevated storehouses as found commonly in old villages of Galicia, the Basque region of Spain. The second depicts a traditional Māori *pataka*. The similarity is compelling.

Galicia takes its name from the Gallaeca, the Celts who peopled that region in the last millennium BC, so there is a strong Celtic connection. DNA has shown that the traditional inhabitants, the Basques, have a higher percentage of Celtic genes than the Irish.

But how did the raised storehouses of Galicia come to be copied in New Zealand? Well, according to Robert Langdon[34] the lost Spanish ship, *San Lesmes*, was crewed largely by Basques.

The *San Lesmes* was last seen on June 1, 1526, separating from the rest of the Spanish fleet sent to reassert the King of Spain's sovereignty over the Spice Islands, and striking out across the Pacific on her own. Like all but one of the seven-strong fleet the *San Lesmes* never returned to Spain. According to Spanish records one ship was lost in the Atlantic, one ended her days in Mexico, another wrecked in the Philippines and yet another foundered off Patagonia.

As noted in a previous chapter Langdon has the *San Lesmes* running aground on the Amanu Atoll in the Tuamotos. Throwing out four cannon lightened the vessel sufficiently for her to reach the Spanish Pacific station at Hao Atoll where she was deemed beyond repair.

The crew therefore salvaged what they could of the stricken vessel and built a new ship to be called the *Tainui*, and sailed to nearby Anaa Atoll. Some Spaniards married local women and settled there; the others sailed on to Raiatea where again some settled. However, Langdon says, after some years a hard core of the crew determined

---

34 *The Lost Caravel Re-explored* (1975) by Robert Langdon.

to sail back to Spain and set out for the Cape of Good Hope but on reaching New Zealand settled there.

The *San Lesmes* then, or rather its new built replacement, the *Tainui*, may have been the second ship to have 'discovered' New Zealand after the landing and six-month sojourn here of de Gonneville (1503)[35].

Importantly, in making New Zealand their home the ship's officers and crew doubtless would have passed on to the existing native population something of their customs and ways. Hence the *pataka* and the cross.

Over 250 years later Captain Cook noted a wooden cross in a Māori *pa* (village) on the island of Motuara, Queen Charlotte Sound. He wrote in his *Journal* on 24th January 1770:

> We observed, not without some surprise, a cross exactly like that of a crucifix ; it was adorned with feathers and, upon our inquiring for what purpose it had been set up, we were told that it was a monument for a man who was dead.
>
> We had understood that their dead were not buried, but thrown into the sea; but to our inquiry how the body of the man had been disposed of, to whose memory this cross had been erected, they refused to answer.[36]

Now the cross, being a Christian symbol, seems obviously out of place in the hill fort sketched by Cook's crewman in 1769 since not until 1814 was the first Christian sermon preached in New Zealand. Yet a cluster of crosses was erected at this *pa* long before the first Christian missionary arrived.

Adding to the puzzle is that today similar crosses, strangely with one crossbar longer than other, can be found erected outside Māori meeting houses in many parts of the North Island.

---

35 See *The de Gonneville mystery* – chapter 21.

36 *The Voyages of Captain James Cook*, Volume 1, James Cook. Published by William Smith, 1846, p. 167.

Oddly, however, the *pataka* is rarely seen, the main examples now being held in museums.

To my mind the presence of Spanish officers and crew in the 1500s explains the introduction of both the pataka and crosses into native custom. Spanish Basques, being Roman Catholic, would carry crosses aplenty with them. One of their first acts on landing on a foreign shore would be to erect a cross – indeed, that is exactly what the Portuguese explorer Ferdinand Magellan did on stepping ashore at Cebu in the Philippines.

And, if one of the *Tainui*'s Spanish crew had died after the ship reached New Zealand what could be more natural than the Catholic crew would erect a cross over his grave?

Where the first cross was erected and where Māori first adopted elements of the Catholic faith remains a mystery. Perhaps the *Tainui* visited other parts of New Zealand before sailing into Aotea Harbour,

A cross erected at the side of a Māori meeting house that still stands today.

Raglan, in North Island's Waikato, where she is believed by some to have been wrecked by a storm.

On the extent of Spanish influence, inquiry should focus on two locations. The first is the Far North where the wreck of the Cecilia Maria and what are believed to be other Spanish ships have been found. The second is the North Island's East Coast.

On the East Coast the local Māori tribe, Ngati Porou, have a strong tradition of a historic Spanish presence among them. Many claim to have Spanish ancestry; some have even sought to lodge inheritance claims in Spain on the basis of it.

And here the word *Paniora* (Spaniard) seems to have passed into the Māori language. The Ngati Porou story is not only that a Spanish ship visited Poverty Bay but that Spaniards settled and lived and died among them.

Crosses already adorned this Maori hill top pa when a crewman from Captain James Cook's ship, the Endeavour, drew them during his first visit to New Zealand in 1769.

Chapter 19

An amazing discovery

Shipwreck explorer Noel Hilliam

Back in the 1400s, so native historical traditions say, a large incursion of people from afar brought unwelcome disruption to the peaceful Waitaha community at Pouto in New Zealand's Northland. This resulted from at least one, if not more, very large Chinese junks, which shipwrecked on the wild and wind-swept Kaipara seaboard. These vessels were of vast size, with multiple decks, up to nine masts, huge crews, and, arguably, a potpourri of different races and peoples aboard. So stand by for some stunning facts and a gripping story.

First though, meet Noel Hilliam, archaeologist, shipwreck explorer and diving companion of the late Kelly Tarleton. Both these men were pioneers in the truest sense. Kelly Tarleton created the star Auckland visitor attraction, Kelly Tarleton's Underwater World, while Noel founded the spectacular Dargaville Museum.

The precious collection of history and pre-history at the Dargaville Museum is a 'must see' for those who would capture the past glory of the Kaipara's kauri industry and see the 'Kauri Lady', a wooden sculpture that is crucial evidence of ancient Waitaha residence in the area. Importantly, Noel built the museum himself and stocked it with a remarkable array of exhibits, including a working gum washing plant, innumerable tools, ancient and modern, and an unrivalled collection of shipwreck artifacts, including cannon, anchors, bits of timber wreckage, wheels, tillers, masts, portholes and more.

A long-time battler for recognition of the region's ancient and non-Māori, non-Polynesian past, Noel has become a nuggety, tenacious contender for the truth that before the start of the Christian era European races settled New Zealand and that their descendants are still with us today. Dismissed by anthropologists and archaeologists alike for his stance, he is nevertheless a qualified marine archaeologist and amateur archaeologist who has explored the extensive pre-Māori stone city in the Waipaou Forest. He is also responsible for bringing to light the hugely significant 'Chronos Stone', the most compelling evidence for past ancient European civilisation in New Zealand that has been found to date.

This amazing artifact was found in a Northland stream bed after the collapse of an undercut sand cliff exposed it to the light of day. It is a stunning, eight-tonne basalt boulder laboriously carved into a complex calendar and time-keeping device. Its clock-like face is marked out in letters, symbols and numerals, some of which are identifiable as letters of the Greek alphabet.

Among his many other accomplishments, which include ocean voyaging, Noel is an accomplished pilot and owns his own plane. Taking a bird's eye view approach to marine exploration he has discovered the outlines of scores of shipwrecked vessels lying half buried in the sands off the Kauri Coast and elsewhere.

Exploring these wrecks, Noel has recovered timbers, cannon and other artifacts from Spanish, Portuguese, French, British, Australian and now Chinese wrecks.

Noel's hard-earned credentials are important for accepting his most amazing underwater discovery to date. That is the finding of the wreck of a huge Chinese junk thought to have broken up at least six centuries ago.

Stunningly, timber from the vessel's huge ribs has been radio carbon dated to the incredible age of 5,995BP (Before Present Time).

This discovery makes it all but certain that a Chinese ship, or likely a fleet of such vessels, reached this country long before the

An artist's impression of a huge, nine-masted Chinese junk such as those built in the 1400s when China explored the world. Does the wreckage of such a ship still lie buried in the sands of the Kaipara coast? Picture courtesy of Noel Hilliam.

traditional date for Māori arrival, and that at least one of these huge junks was wrecked upon our shores. It was while flying above the Kaipara coast that Noel spotted from the air the wreck of what he is now sure is a huge, medieval Chinese junk.

If he is correct in that assertion, then the wreck is eloquent testimony to the extensive Chinese ocean exploration said to have taken place both in the 15th century and also in earlier periods.

The vessel Noel found lies buried in sand several hundred metres offshore. It appears to have grounded at a 45 degree angle to the Kauri coast.

The wreckage is of a huge ship, measuring some 412ft long and more than 100ft wide. That puts it at nearly half the length of the largest American warship, the aircraft carrier, *The George Washington*, which is 1070ft long. And it is little smaller than the biblical Noah's ark, said to have had a length of 625 feet.

Sadly, only rarely is the Chinese ship's wreck site accessible. Normally it is covered by fierce waves and shifting sand. Yet during one exceptionally low tide Noel could access a rib of the ship and cut and bring to shore a hunk of encrusted timber.

Thanks to an expert in timber identification Noel learned the wood he harvested from the sea was a timber traditionally used by the Chinese for heavy construction, *yang mu*. But the timber's age came as a real shock.

A truly ancient tree

The Radiocarbon Dating Laboratory staff at the University of Waikato were so stunned by the result of 5,963 years plus or minus 40BP for a sample of this wood they sent it to two other reputable laboratories, only to find they came up with a similar result. However, the presumed 5,963-year age of timber does not mean the Chinese junk itself is necessarily that old. The tree it was taken from may have stood for thousands of years before being felled for ship construction. So how old is this huge shipwrecked junk?

Actually, the timber salvaged by Noel offers a clue to the time of the ship's wrecking. It contains a hole which is the socket for a mortise and tenon joint. Importantly, the hole contains no rust, encrustation or stains that would be present had iron or bronze nails been used. And that indicates the date of the vessel's construction. You see, Chinese history records that mortise and tenon joints began to be used in large scale ship construction in the Tang and Song dynasties (618-1,270AD).

The *China Through A Lens* online resource (retrieved from the chinaorg.cn website) explains that China's shipbuilding industry entered a period of maturity, both in quantity and quality in the Tang (618-907) and Song (960-1279) dynasties. Utilization of many shipbuilding techniques, such as the stern helm, that highly efficient propelling tool, the scull, and the sails, were further improved during this period.

The 'Chronos Stone, an ancient New Zealand sundial and calendar stone used to calculate seasons and to study the stars. Picture © Noel Hilliam.

Now you see it, now you don't. This rib of the Chinese junk underwater explorer Noel Hilliam has found on the Kaipara coast was exposed by a very low tide then covered again by sand when the next tide swept in. Picture ©Noel Hilliam.

The Sui Dynasty, though short lived, enjoyed a highly developed shipbuilding industry, with the capacity to build giant dragon boats. Assembled with mortise-and-tenon joints, the dragon boats were much stronger than those constructed with iron nails or bamboo nails. What's more China's adoption of this technology was 500 years earlier than that in European countries, *China Through A Lens* says. On some ships, vegetables were grown at sea.

During the Song Dynasty, a huge ship named Shen Zhou was made, which boasted a carrying capacity of 1,500 tonnes and a hull length of 31.5 zhang (about 100 metres). On the *Nova* website Evan Hadingham has posted an entry saying the first Chinese ocean-going trade ships were built in the Song Dynasty (906-1270) but it was the Yuan Dynasty (1271-1368) that commissioned the first imperial treasure ships and established trading posts in India, Ceylon and, importantly, Sumatra in Indonesia.

In the late 1300s and early 1400s Chinese ships also sailed to Africa, Japan, South-east Asia, Korea, the Persian Gulf and Egypt and even traded with the Philippines. There is also firm evidence they traded with and settled parts of the Americas.

The timber Noel's ship is built of definitely proves its Chinese origin. It has been identified as *yang mu*, a timber cut from trees in China for heavy construction. It is still cited as a building timber in use today. This hard wood it is incredibly strong and, as Noel found, surprisingly light when dried out.

In her wide-ranging and respected study, *The 'China Seas' in world history*, Angela Schottenhammer suggests Chinese ships may well have reached Australia in ancient times; after all that continent is only 400 miles from Indonesia. And, if the Chinese reached Australia, why not New Zealand?

Any sailing ship venturing down that far into the South Pacific might well be caught in the near-incessant south-westerly busters and forced in that direction. And a cumbersome vessel such as a large Chinese junk, ill-fitted for sailing close to the wind, might well be blown across the Tasman whether her crew liked it or not.

There is clear evidence Chinese ships reached Fiji in that in both appearance and genetic make-up the people of the island of Rotuma, 300 miles north, to this day show strong Chinese links[37]. Now, as is well known, the Chinese are above all else a trading people. They established a world trading system that reached much of the world in the early centuries of the last millennium. Voyages of exploration were undertaken with the deliberate aim of finding new lands and peoples with which to treat and trade, and to find new sources for gold, silver, other metals, precious stones and important minerals.

Wares traded by Chinese ships included porcelain, silk and jade ornaments. Could it be that learning of New Zealand's precious greenstone resource, the Chinese resolved to sail here to explore it for themselves? If true, this possibility raises the further intriguing

---

37 *To The Ends Of The Earth And Back Again* (2015) by Maxwell C. Hill, pages 132-133.

question of how the Chinese learned of this valuable mineral resource on such a far-away land. Might they have known it for thousands of years, from age-old wisdom first handed down by mankind's earliest navigators who in ancient times accurately charted the ice-free actual coastline of Antarctica?

If these very old charts were later repeated in the Piri Reis map of 1513, as a later chapter will suggest, did they also knew of and explore New Zealand thousands of years ago before what scientists are pleased to call the Little Ice Age? And did they discover greenstone and gold deposits here when they did so? Was it knowledge of these deposits that brought Chinese ships to New Zealand either in that people's first flush of international exploration from 900-1100AD or later in better known voyages of Admiral Zheng He and others in the 1400s?

These are unanswered questions although in his book Gavin Menzies[38] has claimed a great Chinese fleet reached and was wrecked on New Zealand's South Island coast. However, in the absence of concrete proof his assertions have been dismissed as speculative by cartography experts and historians alike.

However, we now have sound evidence and concrete proof that a Chinese ship, or ships, reached this country long before the traditional date for Māori arrival and that at least one of these ships was wrecked upon our shores.

This we know, not only from the shipwreck discovered by Noel Hilliam but also because of the very tangible presence of thousands of ancient Chinese-made bricks evidently used as ballast that were found long ago on the beaches of the Kaipara. Buildings in Dargaville constructed from these small bricks, each of which is stamped with a Chinese symbol, still stand to this day.

So what happened to the crew?

38 *1421: The Year China Discovered The World*, by Gavin Manzies, Bantam Press, London.

Furthermore, there are Daoist cave inscriptions in the South Island held by experts to be of undeniable and very old Chinese origin. Add to that the archaeological evidence of a centuries old Chinese village in Northland and a handed down tradition about the people who built and dwelt in it and you have a three-way proof of Chinese contact and settlement. Can it be doubted then that in different parts of the country and probably at different times the Chinese were present in New Zealand? And if they were here in the last two to 3,000 years then they had to have come by ship, which is what makes Noel Hilliam's discovery so important.

If we accept that the wreckage of a huge Chinese junk lies beneath the sands off the Kaipara coast then the question that naturally arises is: What became of the many people such a vessel carried? A ship 412 feet long and well over 100ft wide with several decks would carry a huge crew, of perhaps 2,000 to 3,000, made up of officers,

You might mistake for it driftwood but it isn't. Noel Hilliam is sure this is the remains of a top rib from the bow section of the wrecked junk. It has been radio carbon dated to be nearly 6,000 years old.

military, slaves and a workforce seized en route, animals and other cargo. Did all drown, or did some, perhaps many hundreds, survive the heavy breakers to reach shore? If they did then what became of them?

That it would have been a struggle to survive goes without saying. But maybe they were provided with food, warmth and shelter by the existing inhabitants on the Kauri Coast.

Were Chinese here before the Māori?

Such established residents would have been the Waitaha people and the Turehu. Māori history and their own tribal lore confirm, as does an impressive array of archaeological evidence, that both these ancient peoples were in residence here in Northland for many centuries before the coming of the Moriori, let alone the later advent of Māori.

What's more, they were numerous. When Noel Hilliam's predecessors bought their family farm near Dargaville in the mid-1800s the land seemed unoccupied.

'There were no Māori or Moriori in residence, neither were any Waitaha or Turehu to be seen. The land was unoccupied and the Crown sold it un-encumbered to settlers,' Noel states. But evidence it had been occupied on a large scale not long before soon emerged.

'When settlers including my great grand-parents began to plough, to break in the land, in they turned up thousands of bones. Some were just scattered on the surface. Others were buried just beneath the ground. There must have been a population of many tens of thousands of people living here not many centuries ago'. Along the coast there is firm in-ground evidence of many ancient settlements and Waitaha Paramount Chief Hori Kupenga confirms that his *tupuna* (ancestors) lived there for centuries in significant numbers.

'I certainly believe they would have been living there in the 900s and for many centuries before and after that,' he maintains.

While most likely hospitable at first, the ancients of New Zealand soon would have encouraged the newcomers to move out and establish settlements of their own, preferably at a considerable distance. Food resource while sufficient for themselves would not long support an added population of hundreds. Likely then the Chinese ship's crew would have set up camp, then built a village or villages away from their hosts.

And archaeology shows this is just what happened. The remains of a Chinese village, many centuries old, have been found in Northland and local Māori history records it existed. All this suggests the definite settlement of Chinese people in New Zealand long before Polynesian arrival. But, it must be asked, was the crew of this huge ship purely Chinese?

Chinese ships traded widely in the 1400s and even before that, and the need for constant crew replacement, saw them recruit sailors from ports in many lands. In particular the voyage from China to New Zealand was long, arduous and would have taken a heavy toll of the crew. Death accident and disease, a common occurrence on long voyages, would be augmented by scurvy, the scourge of every ship at sea for over 60 days without fresh fruit, vegetables or other sources of vitamin C.

And the journey from the great Chinese port of Guangzhou to the North Island of New Zealand arguably would be the longest such vessels ever made. One should allow the best part of a year, if not longer, for an exploratory voyage southwards from China through present-day Borneo, Indonesia and Melanesia before proceeding down the east coast of Australia and crossing the Tasman Sea to New Zealand.

Given such duration certain consequences are inevitable. That such a ship would stop frequently en route is almost certain because history records that the two Chinese emperors who commissioned large fleets of ships to sail the outside world, did so to explore new lands, find gold, silver other minerals and open up trade. A further objective was to wave the flag, show the might of China's navy and empire. Now it is a proven medical fact that without adequate sources of vitamin C scurvy can disable a man, if not kill him, within 60 days.

It may look like driftwood but it isn't. These are the timber remains of the wrecked junk protruding through the sand when uncovered by an exceptionally low tide. Picture © Noel Hilliam.

Prior to Captain Cook's discovery of tea (or *ti*) as a solution, early voyagers were hard hit by this malady. And aboard Chinese ships, as in China itself, life was cheap in ancient times. Anyone who argued was beheaded and thrown overboard.

Add in loss through illness, accident and scurvy and long before reaching New Zealand the Chinese fleet would have to round up replacements by the hundreds, if not thousands, to replenish their disease stricken and otherwise diminished crews.

New Guinea, the Solomons, New Caledonia and other Melanesian islands are located roughly half way on the route of a voyage from China to New Zealand, so such replacements very likely were drawn from natives living in these islands.

They would be especially sought after, since they had the useful advantage of experience in canoe handling and fishing at sea.

Remember these multi-masted junks (the largest known had nine masts) required huge crews to work them. It is believed a complement of between 2,000 and 3,000 was needed for the largest ships.

For a modern comparison take the United States aircraft carrier, the *George Washington* (1070ft long), on which our daughter served for four years. She carries a crew of 5,000.

It is highly probably then that Melanesians by the hundreds were seized and taken aboard this great ship to serve before the mast. Then, arguably, their ship was driven helplessly onto the Kaipara coast by a fierce westerly.

Picture then, if you will, a giant junk pounded by huge waves and driven onto sandbanks some hundreds of metres from the beach. While some of the largely enslaved crew is flogged into striking sail and casting out anchors, others try to lighten the ship by casting overboard cargo.

This flotsam might well include Chinese pigs (how otherwise did the kune-kune with its Asian genetic background get here?), ballast bricks by the thousand and anything of weight that could be spared.

While many of the motley crew may have drowned, it is reasonable to assume that hundreds swam ashore. What happened next is a matter for conjecture but let us start with the known facts.

First, a massive junk did ground and break up here; the wreck is proof of that. Second, she must have had a huge crew. Third, such a crew would include many slaves, including low-class Chinese, possibly Taiwanese, Asian men from other ports and a motley mix of shanghaied island natives (is it from this practice that term 'shanghaied' comes from?) seized from various stopover points. Fourth, there can be little doubt that hundreds of this company might well have struggled ashore and survived.

The Waitaha, being kindly folk, would try to shelter survivors but clearly the numbers would overwhelm their limited resources and the time honoured practice in such cases was to dispatch small companies of survivors to other settlements.

In later times Māori were known to kill and eat such shipwrecked mariners but the evidence suggests the Chinese ship, or ships, wrecked on the coast long before Moriori and Māori brought cannibalism to New Zealand. One thing is reasonably certain: the survival of hundreds of virtual slaves of mixed race must have disrupted the peaceful existence of the Waitaha and Turehu people, long established in the area.

Violence would have broken out. I cannot imagine pressed Melanesian and Taiwanese slaves not taking the first opportunity to revenge themselves on their Chinese masters. And their Waitaha and Turehu hosts may well have come in for a clobbering too.

There is clear evidence the Chinese built a settlement of their own, since a sketch which shows the remains of a nearby centuries-old Chinese village has been found. But were the people themselves absorbed into a new and emerging primitive culture that was both violent and cannibalistic?

Waitaha Chief Hori Kupenga maintains that their traces can be found among the Nga Puhi Māori to this day. And erstwhile Nga Puhi leader Sonny Tau, who came to prominence when he was charged with smuggling carcasses of slain *keruru* (protected native pigeons) onto an aircraft, has an undeniably strong Chinese appearance. Put a Mao forage cap on him, drop him in deepest China and he would fit in right away.

Chief Hori says that it is a racial mixing of Melanesians, Taiwanese natives, Chinese, Waitaha, Turehu, augmented later by input from Dutch, Spanish, French, Portuguese and possibly other sailors, which produced first the Moriori, then the Māori who, he says, all came out of Ngapuhi and, as they multiplied, dispersed and spread out across New Zealand.

'Both Moriori, who became the Ngapuhi, who in turn sent the different Māori tribes out through New Zealand, and Māori are mixtures of many races, he asserts.

'First they became the fierce Moriori warriors that erupted like

A mast top from the Chinese junk wreck barely lifts its head above water even at very low tide. It measures a full three feet in diameter and, if this is the top of the mast one can only imagine the huge girth at its base. The deck is thought to lie buried many metres below. Picture © Noel Hilliam.

a scourge upon our peaceful Waitaha settlements. Then they developed a new identity as the Ngapuhi people. All the Māori originate from Ngapuhi; they spread out from the Far North throughout New Zealand, pillaging and killing as they went'.

Chief Hori maintains that these attacks on their settlements caused his people first to build palisades to defend their villages and when that failed drove them to flee Pouto and the Kauri Coast for new settlements inland.

And, according to Noel Hilliam, it was they, the Moriori, who massacred and all but exterminated the Turehu, the once numerous people occupying Northland, the Turehu that once numerous people occupying Northland.

However, the Chinese and their likely Melanesian crewmen are not the only voyagers from afar that arrived in Northland. Here's why.

A lifetime of marine exploration has taught Noel Hilliam that the Kaipara coast forms an all but inescapable trap for sailing ships forced onto it by the prevailing south westerly winds.

'There are the remains of dozens, if not scores, of shipwrecks along the coast,' he states. And with his team of underwater divers Noel has discovered and explored some of them.

In 1982 he spotted a then unknown shipwreck from the air. Noel at the request of the police was flying his aircraft along the Kaipara coast searching for a missing fisherman.

At low altitude he spotted the man's body in the breakers and 'saw the outlines of a wreck unlike any I had seen before'.

Hilliam landed his plane on the beach, dived into the breakers to recover the fisherman's body, then took to the air again to observe and pinpoint the position of the wreck's hull.

'We could see this European ship so clearly, the stub of the main mast and the break where the poop deck meets the gunwale. The ship had settled into the sand and just sat there. Even the deck was still attached. It was so beautiful. Suddenly in a moment my dreams as a diver of finding an unrecorded shipwreck came true.'

A portion of a cross-member and rib was salvaged by Noel's team before the shifting sands reburied the wreck over 30 metres deep. Later research by Noel identified the ship as the *Cecilia Maria*, a Portuguese ship built of lagerstroemia, a hardwood timber grown in India and the Philippines, similar to mahogany. Specimens of the planking were recovered and laboratory tested, confirming the identity of the timber and radio carbon dating its age. However, that is when a serious controversy about the timing of the ship's grounding broke out.

Noel, from his research believed and still maintains, the ship foundered near Pouto Point in 1532. Radio carbon dating of the *lagerstroemia* wood, however, suggested the timber was but 300 years old.

What's more recognised dendrochronologist (tree ring ageing expert), Dr. Jonathan Palmer, said his findings suggested the ill-fated vessel sank in 1705, that is, after Tasman's 1642 'discovery' of New Zealand in 1642, but predating Captain Cook's voyages here by some 65 years. It was not the wreck of the Portuguese *Cecilia Maria*, he thought, but that of another, later vessel. All of which means the ship Noel found now officially ranks as New Zealand's oldest shipwreck but in the official view doesn't rewrite the accepted history of Tasman's finding of New Zealand in 1642. But then again perhaps it does. Let's see why. Now granted the teak and lagerstroemia timber samples did radio carbon test to about 300 years old. But that was back in 1982.

Since then additional information has emerged, showing that, as Noel Hilliam theorises, the ship may have been found rotten on entering the Pacific after its initial voyage from Europe. If so it may well have been repaired with tropical timbers, such as *lagerstroemia* and teak, perhaps in Goa, then a Portuguese possession, or in India, or in Java, Indonesia, or even perhaps the Philippines.

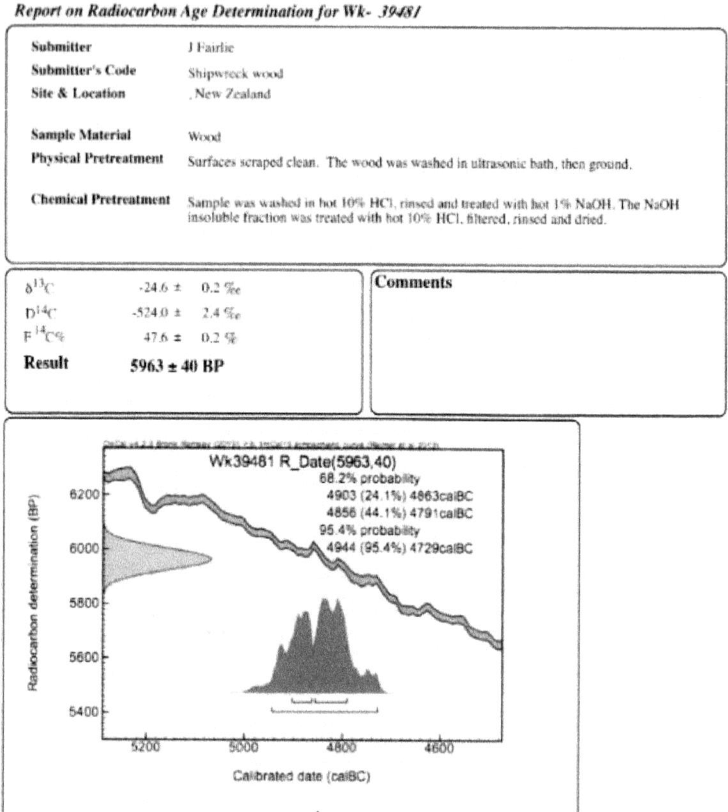

email c14@waikato.ac.nz

Radiocarbon Dating Laboratory

Thursday, 28 August 2014

Report on Radiocarbon Age Determination for Wk- 39481

Submitter	J Fairlie
Submitter's Code	Shipwreck wood
Site & Location	, New Zealand
Sample Material	Wood
Physical Pretreatment	Surfaces scraped clean. The wood was washed in ultrasonic bath, then ground.
Chemical Pretreatment	Sample was washed in hot 10% HCl, rinsed and treated with hot 1% NaOH. The NaOH insoluble fraction was treated with hot 10% HCl, filtered, rinsed and dried.

$\delta^{13}C$	-24.6 ±	0.2 ‰
$D^{14}C$	-524.0 ±	2.4 ‰
$F^{14}C\%$	47.6 ±	0.2 %
Result	**5963 ± 40 BP**	

Comments

The Waikato University Radio Carbon Dating Laboratory's report on the yang mu shipwreck timber, dating it to 5963 plus or minus 40 years.

Upon grounding and breaking up later on New Zealand's Northland coast it would be the softer and more rot-prone original European timbers that would succumb and disintegrate, leaving the tropical hardwoods to remain.

Now, it is agreed that the main timber used in constructing 15th and 16th century ships of the Portuguese Navy and mercantile marine was pine, a rot-prone and short-lived timber. Water penetration on the long voyage from Europe into the Southern Hemisphere often left pine planking dangerously soft by the time ships reached the Indian or Pacific oceans.

Consequently, ships were extensively refitted at Portuguese naval bases in Goa, India, Japan, Macau and Taiwan set up expressly for the purpose. Affected planking was replaced with tropical hardwoods. When and where such refitting took place on the vessel wrecked at Pouto Point or whether it was built of such hardwood at a tropical location in the first place may never be known.

One thing's for sure though: pine timbers would have long disintegrated and the fact is that only hardwood specimens have been recovered from the wreckage. All of which may mean the ship is much older than Dr. Palmer's preliminary testing would suggest

However, there is another way of dating the ship's tragic end, the memory and traditions of the Waitaha people who lived on the Kaipara coast when the ship was wrecked. Noel reports that according to an old Waitaha lady interviewed years ago the shipwreck occurred 'about 18 generations ago'.

Allowing 25 years per generation and working back from 1982 18 generations would bring us to around 1532 the year Noel Hilliam surmises saw the ship's sinking. 'Certainly it was before 1600,' he says.

And there is more. According to Waitaha tradition the ship did not founder in a storm but was attacked while anchored and moored in the narrow haven of Midge Bay close to the ancient Waitaha village that existed then.

The attack, it is said, came from a Māori war party that had journeyed down from the Bay of Islands to plunder Waitaha settlements. These warriors attacked the ship, slaughtered and ate the crew, then stripped the ship and set it ablaze. The story says that two accompanying Portuguese ships made good their escape, abandoning their sister ship to her fate.

Now, according to *Wikipaedia* the Portuguese Navy first visited Australia in 1522 and the book, *Australia to 1900*, by W.D.L. Ryde says the Portuguese took numbers of slaves from Melville Island to act as crew for their further exploration of the Pacific. Did some come ashore in New Zealand at this time?

In recent years Dr. Palmer has revised his estimate of the age of the recovered timbers and thereof the date of the ship's sinking to 1680 instead of 1705 as he originally thought. It would seem that dendrochronology, like radio carbon dating, is still far from being an exact and consistent dating procedure. Apparently, in some years trees do not grow the rings used to calculate their age because of adverse climatic conditions. Hence the uncertainty of dendrochronological conclusions. And on radio carbon dating, some of its findings seem arbitrary to say the least.

In her book Elizabeth Barber[39] describes the sensational 1994 find in the dry sands of the Tarim Basin of Central Asia of the well-preserved mummies of fair-skinned, red-haired people. These mummies were neither Chinese nor Mongoloid but distinctly Caucasian. So where had they come from and how long they had lain at Urumchi in the Chinese-administered remote Uyghur Autonomous Region in Chinese Turkestan?

Barber, an expert in ancient cloth making and textiles, says the anomaly of their presence in China deepened when it was found that the peculiar plain twill cloths in which the mummies were clothed matched tartans woven by ancestors of the Celts and found preserved elsewhere only in the Hallstatt and Hallein Bronze Age salt mines in the Alps above Salzburg in Upper Austria.

But the real shock came when radio carbon dating was used to date mummies found in a nearby cemetery at Qawrighu. Testing of grave carbon sent to Nanjing showed the burials dated to 4,500BC whereas archaeologists had guessed them to be no older than 100BC.

---

39 *Mummies of Urumchi*, Elizabeth Wayland Barber (1999) Macmillan, London.

Dargaville Museum president Don Elliot displays teak and lagerstromeia timber from the centuries old Portuguese shipwreck at Pouto Point. Picture courtesy of Dargaville News.

The finding of a few bronze trinkets in the graves only added to the conundrum, for there was evidence that the Bronze Age did not begin in China until around 1,500BC. To resolve the dating Beijing University tested a matching carbon sample from the graves and came up with a different date of 1880BC.

Barber reports that this date still seemed 'awfully early' to the archaeologists but 'less far afield than the earlier (Nanjing) result', so it it became the accepted one. All of which simply goes to show that radio carbon dating cannot be relied on to set realistic dates for mummies and artifacts, perhaps still less determine the real prehistory of mankind.

So where does this leave the matter of the very old *yang*

A replica of the Spanish caravel Santa Maria, a similar ship to the Cecilia Maria, the wreck of which was discovered by Noel Hilliam on New Zealand's Northland coast.

mu timber recovered from the wreck of the purported Chinese junk and what of the timing of that vessel's sinking? Very much open to interpretation is the short answer. However, some facts can help us make an educated guess.

First, *yang mu* is recorded as the age-old Chinese timber of choice for shipbuilding. The very old Qi-Ming-Yao-Shu compendium of '*Survival techniques for the common people*' indicates that during the Northern Wei period (386 -534 AD), people managed the planting and felling of trees for building in Tian-Gong-Kai-Wu, 'making things feasible by Heaven-approved work'. On ship building the compendium said:

> Use a straight fir tree for the mast; if it is not long enough, join shorter ones together to make up the length; on its surface use iron girdles 1/3 decimetre apart to surround the entire length of the tree … the ridge and fang-wall should be made of phoebe namu, camphor wood, elm, pine or ash … any timber can be used for planks. Elm, yang mu or oak should be used to make the rudder. The door securing the stick should be made with chou mu or yang mu. The prow/bow should be made of fir, kuai mu or catalpa ...

Here then is evidence that Chinese ships were being built with *yang mu* timber framing in the 386-534AD period. And, as with the Portuguese vessel sank and burnt at Poutu Point, this evidence indicates that pine or some other softer, inferior wood was used for the planking.

This gels with what Noel Hilliam's under-water exploration team discovered within the wrecks of both the *Cecilia Maria* and the unnamed Chinese junk.

Second, there is ample historical evidence to show that as early as 219BC China was building huge ships and undertaking voyages deep into the Pacific. So there are several windows of opportunity running down the centuries in which a Chinese junk could have reached New Zealand waters

Actually, it is said Chinese shipbuilding, naval war and long-range ocean voyaging underwent at least three climaxes, the first during the Qin and Han dynasties (221BC to 220AD), the second in the Tang (618-907AD) and Song (960-1279AD) dynasties with the third and final flourishing in the Ming dynasty (1368-1644AD) which produced Admiral Zheng He's famed 'seven voyages to the western sea'.

Zheng He's exploits have been brought to worldwide attention by the very popular book, *1421: The Year China Discovered the World* by Gavin Menzies[40]. Menzies in his imagination has part of Zheng He's fleet exploring New Zealand and being wrecked on the South Island's west coast near Moeraki Point in the selfsame century.

He claims the famed Moeraki Boulders, large balls of accreted rock and mud strewn across the beach below cliffs, are ballast from the huge Chinese junks. However, geologists have determined that such spheres are a natural phenomenon in several other places in the world.

Far more credible is that in antiquity China was building huge ships and sailing them to places as far apart as Egypt, India, Indonesia and Japan. Could they not have explored Australia and New Zealand back then long before the celebrated excursions of 1421?

Looking back it's stunning to consider the colossal ship building China undertook in olden times. Information on this comes from *China Through A Lens*, posted on the authoritative ChinaCulture.org website in a paper entitled 'Shipbuilding in Ancient China'. Besides the three maritime construction 'climaxes' mentioned above it says:

> Emperor Qinshihuang (221-106BC) organised a fleet capable of transporting 500,000 shi (1 shi = 170 pounds or 71.7 kg) of grain. Ancient books record this emperor led a fleet of *lou chan* (castle ships, i.e. ships with deck castles) to assault the Chu State.

So more than a century before the birth of Christ huge Chinese ships were sailing the Pacific. And only decades later the Han dynasty could launch over 2,000 castle ships for war.

Then in the period 220AD-280AD the Wu State of the Three Kingdoms once built a five-storey ship able to transport 3,000 soldiers while around 500AD river ships of 1,000 tonnes were built and man-powered paddle wheels invented to drive them.

40 Bantam Press, London.

Contradicting those who hold China's major ocean exploration took place only in the 1400s, *China Through A Lens* also mentions ancient Chinese naval maps dating to the 2nd century BC drawn up by the 'Hepu Commandery'.

It also states that, during the Song dynasty (960-1260AD) China established a permanent standing navy. By the 12th century there were 20 squadrons of big ships with some 52,000 marines. Such

A full-size model of a "middle-sized" treasure ship of the Yongle Emperor era (63.25 m long) at the Treasure Ship Shipyard site in Nanjing. It was built c. 2005 from concrete and wooden planking. Picture courtesy of Wikipaedia.

A fragment of old Chinese porcelain recovered from the site of the Kaipara junk wreck.

a large force was needed to defend South China against the Churchens of the North and also to 'escort merchant fleets entering the **South-East Pacific** and Indian oceans on their long missions to the Hindu, Islamic, African and other trading centres of the world', the article states.

And what is found in the **South-East Pacific** as you sail in that direction from China's ancient port of Shanghai? Why, only Australia and New Zealand.

Here then is a strong indication that Chinese trading interests might have reached down into Australasia in the 12th century AD setting an important possible dateline for the Chinese shipwreck at Pouto Point. But, you might ask, what would the purpose of such a lengthy voyage be?

The answer would appear to be a combination of exploring new lands for possible settlement (it is obvious the Chinese anciently founded Japan and peopled much of South-East Asia) and seeking valuable metals and minerals. In Chinese eyes one of the most highly prized finds would be that of jade and the New Zealand nephrite or greenstone with its dark hues would be especially valuable and even more sought after than gold.

Throw in the evidence of a strong Chinese presence in the South Island as attested by the finding of a 'taniwha' (mythical Māori serpent), but which is actually a Daoist symbol, inscribed in the Opihi Cave at Hanging Rock, near Temuka in the South Island, and it is possible to imagine Chinese traders and merchantmen establishing a colony in New Zealand to find and process both gold and greenstone.

Could it be then that it was thanks to the Chinese that New Zealand's exquisite greenstone carving industry had its beginning? Did Chinese experts in the ancient art of jade carving teach their expertise to some inhabitants of 12th century New Zealand, the Patupaiarehe, Waitaha and Turehu? Perhaps we will never know.

However, one thing is certain: such highly developed skills are only acquired over several lifetimes. An intricate design laboriously shaped without the help of modern machinery could take half a carver's lifetime to bring to perfection. It is hard for this writer to see how invading warrior Māori intent on slaying and eating both the moa and other birdlife and conquering existing residents to eat them also, could by themselves find either the time or patience to develop such skills.

A third and important point is that while Gavin Menzies has produced no concrete evidence of any Chinese ship reaching New Zealand, Noel Hilliam and his team have. A piece of a near-6,000-year-old timber is not to be scoffed at. Nor is the layout of the remnants of the wreck, which argue for a ship of huge proportions. Not to mention samples of the porcelain she carried.

What's more, Noel believes the Pouto Point junk wreck may not be the only one lying beneath the sands, or buried deep in inland swamps along the Northland coast.

'From all the history it is clear that the Chinese ships sailed together in considerable numbers. It could be there are several buried in these parts but we just don't know their whereabouts,' he says.

Chapter 20

Arrivals from afar

It now seems likely that long, long ago, before the Māori with their Taiwanese connection came to live among the New Zealand's original native peoples, other visitors from Asia also reached and lived upon these shores.

The existence of these folk came to light when the Melanesian Moriori people first sailed to the Chatham Islands offshore from New Zealand's South Island. The Chathams would be a Moriori homeland for centuries to come but when they first arrived they found others there who had long been in residence.

The *Te Ara Encyclopaedia of New Zealand* says this earlier race was called Hamata. So could these people be the ancient Hemudu people of China, thought by some to have reached New Zealand over 1,000 years ago? Te Ara again:

> According to the Moriori, the descendants of Rongomaiwhenua belonged to a race called Hamata. They were described as 'no ro hunu ake' (sprung from the earth). They were said to be very tall, and living on Rēkohu (in the Chatham Islands) when the first visitor, Kahu, arrived. In other theories they were descendants of Kahu's crew or a previous migration.

Proof of such early Chinese visitation to New Zealand is also found in the exquisite cave art drawing of a Daoist water dragon found in the South Island. Professor Haikai Tane, a geographer and environmentalist is an expert in traditional Dao iconography. He says the famed Ruataniwha images, featured on a New Zealand postage stamp, and thought to be Māori cave drawings, are Dao watershed icons. The pictures of a gourd, water dragon and sun bird found in the Opihi Cave near Temuka depict a Dao model of mountain-river-lake watershed.

Prof. Tane's research, which he presented to the Chinese Academy of Science, indicates that the pictures may have been drawn by descendants of the Hemudu (Hamata?) culture whom, he says, were boat nomads in the South China Sea some 4,000 years ago.

Now if the Hemudu were the Hamata and they really drew the Temuka cave art, then that takes settlement of this country far back in time. But is there more to the story than that?

Greenstone the drawcard?

Could it be these early Chinese immigrants to New Zealand, if that's what they were, took back with them to China samples of New Zealand greenstone, the prized jade of Chinese tradition?

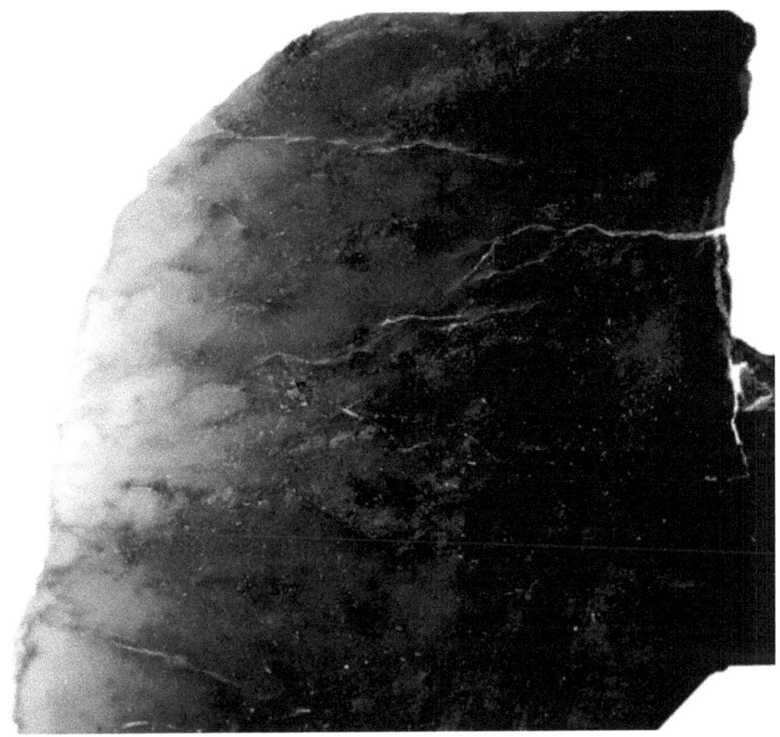

Was greenstone, the sought after New Zealand jade one reason the Chinese sailed to explore New Zealand?

If so the knowledge of this precious nephrite resource, may well have been preserved in in Chinese archives for many centuries until it was brought out and dusted off by those planning Admiral Zheng He's voyages of world exploration.

Greenstone, then in the dark green form beloved by jade carvers, could be the reason Zheng He's fleet sailed to New Zealand and, sadly, were wrecked on our shores.

A further possible clue to dating the Chinese wreck discovered by Noel Hilliam is that traditional accounts say that the Waitaha, Turehu and Patupaiarehe people were living peaceably in undefended settlements at the time of its proposed occurrence, estimated to be in the 1400s.

As already stated, Māori history and an impressive array of archaeological evidence show these ancient and original settlers of New Zealand had lived here in Northland for many centuries before the coming of the Moriori, let alone that people's later development into the Māori people. Hilliam has himself found caves of what he believes are Turehu skeletons and skulls.

'DNA samples from these burial remains were tested and show that their closest genetic link is with Welsh people who lived 3500 years ago,' he says.

Along the coast there is firm in-ground evidence of many ancient settlements and the Waitaha Upoko Ariki, Hori Kupenga Manuka Manuka (George Connelly) confirms that his tupuna (ancestors) lived there for centuries in significant numbers.

It was Moriori and Māori attacks on the Waitaha and Turehu settlements that caused these peaceful peoples to build palisades and fortified pa to defend themselves and eventually to flee Pouto and the Kauri Coast for new settlements inland.

And, according to Noel Hilliam, it was they, the Moriori, who massacred and all but exterminated the Turehu that once numerous people occupying Northland.

Chapter 21

The de Gonneville mystery

Is there more than meets the eye to the accepted history of French attempts to colonise New Zealand ahead of the British Government's annexation in 1840? Actually, there are good grounds to believe that the French connection with Nu-Terre, as it was called back in the 18th century, was both earlier and more extensive than is commonly believed.

The very fact this country was called Nu-Terre (New Land) by both the British and natives in the Treaty of Waitangi negotiations is a dead give-away. The history New Zealand schools and universities teach is one-sided; it deals largely with the British view of events and ignores almost entirely the native side of the story making the truth of what happened undisclosed, if not forbidden, history.

If the French records and preserved native traditions are fully considered then a very different picture emerges, one in which much

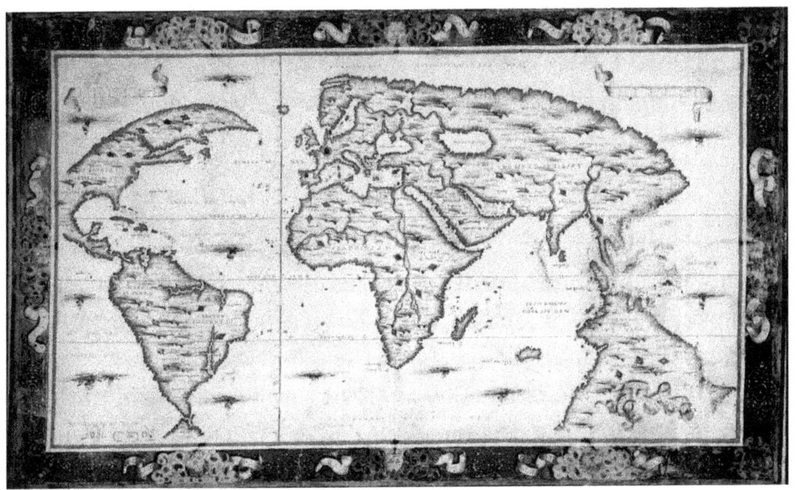

A 16th century Dieppe map showing Jave-le-Grand, as Australia was once known and just possibly the two islands of New Zealand to the east of it.

De Gonneville, picture courtesy of Wikipaedia.

suggests that the French were far more intimately involved with this country far earlier than our historical records allow. So much so that that it is highly probable it was a Frenchman in the 1500s, and not Abel Tasman in 1642, who was the first latter-day European mariner to reach these shores.

According to one preserved tradition of the Waitaha people, New Zealand was first discovered by the French explorer Binot Paulmier de Gonneville way back in the 16th century long before any other Europeans have reached the South Pacific

In this daring voyager's own testimony he says he and his crew reached a large land far to the east of the Cape of Good Hope in 1504 and stayed there for six months possibly pre-dating Tasman's visit in 1642 by 138 years.

The big question was this 'large land' reached by de Gonneville really New Zealand or some other country? And herein lies the mystery.

You see conventional history has concluded that de Gonneville did not come to New Zealand at all but reached Brazil which lies to the west of the Cape of Good Hope. The scholastic consensus this was so was reached after some 200 years of dispute in which, mostly, it had been believed that de Gonneville had reached the 'Great Southern Land' enigmatically portrayed on some early medieval maps without clear outline or accurate location.

Actually, it was the smuggled out French reports of de Gonneville's alleged 'discovery' of the 'Great Southern Continent' that inspired several cartographers to denote such a land mass on their maps which prompted later European explorers to search for it and, ultimately, to 'discover' Australia and New Zealand. Arguably, had such British mariners as John Byron and then Samuel Wallis, who separately but in the same ship, the Dolphin, circumnavigated the world in the 1760s, believed de Gonneville had reached Brazil, and not a major Southern Hemisphere landmass, then they would not have ardently searched the South Pacific seas for the conjectured 'Great Southern Landmass'.

Fact is, a whole series of European explorers set forth to comb the Pacific Ocean searching to find and further explore the long reported and partly mapped 'Great Southern Land' in the 1500s and 1600s.

They included the Portuguese navigator Pedro Fernandes de Quieros (1565–1614), who led a 1605-1606 expedition which crossed the Pacific in search of Terra Australis and utimately Marion du Fresne who anchored his ships, *Marquis de Castries* and *Mascarin*, in the Bay of Islands from May to July 1772.

Also in on the quest was French admiral and explorer Louis-Antoine, Comte de Bougainville (1729 –1811) who found Tahiti, the Tuamotos, negotiated the Great Barrier Reef and sailed through the Solomon Islands, claiming the island of Bougainville for France. Would his contemporary, Captain Cook, have combed the southern seas for the 'Unknown Southern Continent', as it was called, had he thought de Gonneville had not found 'a large land' in those latitudes?

Yet, turning their back on de Gonneville's testimony that the landmass he discover lay **east** not **west** of the Cape of Good Hope, and the indisputable evidence that for 200 years European map makers and navigators clearly believed such a land existed and sent out expeditions to find it, later historians at the turn of the 19th century decided collectively that the land de Gonneville found was Brazil.

This although in the record of his voyage de Gonneville twice declared this 'large land' lay six weeks' sailing to the eastward of the Cape.

Now, granted any sailor blown off course, as de Gonneville says he was, might well lose track of his precise position but one thing he would never do is mistake east for west. And therein lies the heart of the mystery.

A single glance at any world map shows that south of the Cape of Good Hope there is clear water in every direction. To the left or west the nearest landmass is South America; sail to the right or east and eventually you strike Australia and New Zealand.

In the light of that, to maintain de Gonneville sailed west when he says he was driven east by wind and current, seems to defy logic. Unless he lied and there is no reason to believe that he did, then, undoubtedly, he sailed east from the Cape, not west. Fact is that European sailors had had the compass since the 12th century and a simple glance at the binnacle would have shown de Gonneville the direction he was headed in.

Accordingly, I have to believe that the real 'discovery' of New Zealand by this courageous French mariner so early in the piece has been dismissed from history for what appear to be later political and revisionist reasons.

The story of his voyage is this. According to *Wikipaedia* in 1503 de Gonneville, challenging the Portuguese policy of *mare clausum* (literally, Closed Sea), sailed from Honfleur, Normandy, with his crew and the help of two Portuguese pilots, heading for the East Indies which according to the wisdom of the time lay north-north west from the Cape of Good Hope.

However, when de Gonneville reached the Cape his ship, *L'Espoir* (The Hope), was hit by a savage storm and driven far off course. De Gonneville then sailed east and, driven eastward by wind and current, reached the 'large and unknown land' he describes in his report as having been discovered after six weeks' sailing from the time of the storm.

In 1505 he returned to France claiming that he had discovered the 'great Austral land', which he also called the 'Indies Meridionale'. According to de Gonneville, he stayed six months in this idyllic place 'where the inhabitants did not have to work because of the riches of natural abundance'.

The French navigator stated emphatically that the new land was six weeks' sail east of the Cape and that he anchored in a broad river. Evidently it was well sheltered for he stayed there six months, refitting and re-victualling his ship. This would make his likely destination Doubtless Bay in New Zealand's Northland which is both well protected and is entered by large rivers.

Support for this contention is that Doubtless Bay is the very destination that two later French navigators, de Surville and Marion du Fresne, both made their safe haven when they voyaged to New Zealand more than a century later. The question to be asked is: How did they know this haven was there? Did they learn of its precise location from directions left behind by de Gonneville? Or did the excellent charts of this country drawn later by the Portuguese come into their possession?

Latter day historians argue that the land de Gonneville reached was not Australia or New Zealand, nor, as has been proposed by some, Madagascar, but part of the coast of Brazil on and around Santa Catarina Island. *Wikipaedia* asserts that the inhabitants he encountered in this strange land were Carijo Indians and that one, named Ica-Mirim (rendered by the French as 'Esso-mericq' was taken back to France and eventually married de Gonneville's daughter.

But were the natives de Gonneville found South American Indians? Ica-Mirim sounds more like *Ika Miri* or *Hika Miri* in Māori, meaning either 'caressed fish' or 'fire threader'. The name is a far cry from 'Esso-mericq'.

Then there is *Namoa*, the slave who accompanied Ica-Mirim on the voyage. *Namoa* sounds Polynesian and *nama* in Māori means ‘debt’. Arguably, *Namoa* may mean the ‘indebted one’, that is, a slave.

Originally, De Gonneville was sailing for the East Indies, a course which would have taken him north-east from the Cape of Good Hope toward India, Indonesia and the Philippines. To be then blown directly east would put him on course for Australia or New Zealand.

There is also the matter of wind and current to consider. The fast Agulhas Current reaches the foot of Africa. Then, as it moves south, retroflects sharply to the east. Ships caught by it are driven south-eastwards whether they like it or not.

This current combined with easterly winds could well have taken de Gonneville south to intercept the prevailing West Wind Drift Current which also sets to the east. Driven southwards and eastwards *L’Espoir* would likely encounter the winds of the Roaring Forties, said to be the most powerful easterly winds in the world. These winds are used by competitors in the Whitbread Round-the World yacht race to effect the fastest passage to Auckland, New Zealand, their next port of call after leaving Capetown.

Did de Gonneville know of these powerful winds that circle Antarctica or was he the first to discover them? Perhaps we will never know but history records that in 1611 Dutch mariner Hendrik Brouwer discovered that sailing from Europe to Batavia, the then Dutch colony in what is now Indonesia, was much quicker if the Roaring Forties were used to take a ship westwards past Australia before picking up the South East Trade Winds to sail north-eastwards to the East Indies.

Until his discovery the Dutch had used a route copied from Arab and Portuguese sailors who followed the coast of Africa, Mauritius and Ceylon.

The Brouwer route involved sailing south from the Cape of Good Hope (which is at 34 degrees latitude south) into the Roaring Forties (at 40-50 degrees latitude south) then sailing east before turning north to Java using the South Indian Ocean Current. The Brouwer route became compulsory for Dutch vessels in 1617.

The problem with the route, however, was there was no easy

way at the time to determine longitude, making Dutch landfalls on the west coast of Australia all but inevitable with some being wrecked on shoals. It also meant that the vessels of European explorers could just as easily wash up in New Zealand.

To date, the de Gonneville voyage has been assessed by historians only in terms of European knowledge and surmise. No one until now has considered what native New Zealanders knew about the matter. However, we have already seen that Waitaha Chief Hori Kupenga asserts from his ancestral tradition that the French knew of the land of New Zealand long before de Surville or du Fresne anchored in Doubtless Bay in the 1700s and these two captains sailed to that haven not by accident but by pre-arrangement.

George maintains that de Surville came here in 1769 to confirm the willingness of the then local paramount chief, George's ancestor, Haro Rewharewha Manuka Manuka, to allow the French to colonise *Nu Tirene*, or *Nu-Terre*, as it was known before signing the Treaty of Waitangi.

And it is clear that on his 1772 visit du Fresne came specifically to carry out that intent. Only his sudden death at the hands of Māori and that of his officers and some of his crew, stopped the enterprise for which he had come prepared with flags, declarations and a body of marines to effect French colonisation.

These two French visits then, and the history supplied by Chief George, strongly suggest there had been earlier French visitation to New Zealand, most likely starting with de Gonneville's stay and augmented in later years by other French voyages to Doubtless Bay.

However, these visits may well have been kept secret for fear of alerting Spain and Portugal, the self-declared maritime masters of the Pacific, to the existence of this significant land, seen as so ripe for colonial plucking.

It may also explain why a large landmass, said to resemble Australia, with New Zealand tucked into that country's right hand corner, appears on some of the Dieppe maps drawn up in France in the

Marc-Joseph Marion du Fresne.

1500s. This crudely drawn land mass is entitled Jave-le-Grande (the Great Java), an understandable name if it was discovered by a French navigator blown off course to the east when following the Brouwer route toward Java in Indonesia.

Chief George maintains that his Waitaha tradition holds there was French contact with his ancestors, then the paramount chiefs over much of the Far North in New Zealand, long before de Surville and du Fresne reached these shores. This again points to de Gonneville possibly being the first to open such negotiations and to the unreported arrival here of French ships subsequent to his visit.

According to Chief George by the early 1500s incoming Morori were already bullying and attacking the Far North's peaceful Waitaha people and their chiefs were seeking a solution to what was a growing problem. Now, if New Zealand was the place where de Gonneville laid over, repairing and re-victualling his ship in 1504, then he received peaceful and willing cooperation from the natives he encountered.

That was not the case with many other European ships who later reached these shores. Clashes between ship's crew and Māori were the rule rather than the exception and several vessels were attacked and some wrecked and burned. One can only presume that de Gonneville encountered the peaceful Waitaha rather than the warlike Moriori or Māori on his 1504 visit.

Neither de Surville in 1769 nor du Fresne in 1772 enjoyed a peaceful stay. De Surville, barely able with his weak, scurvy-ridden crew to bring his ship to anchor in Doubtless Bay soon ran afoul of local Māori and was forced to flee, kidnapping Ranginui, one of their chiefs. And it got worse. According to one account de Surville drowned in heavy seas off the Peru coast in April 1770 while seeking help for his dying crew. However, a different version is recorded by Alan Villiers in his book, *Captain Cook – The Seaman's Seaman*. He insists that de Surville was captured by Bay of Islands Māori and eaten.

Du Fresne, as already noted, came in 1772, with the clear aim of colonising *Nu-Terre* for France but was slaughtered by Māori with his officers and crew while fishing to augment the ship's food supplies. Between de Gonneville's visit in 1504, if New Zealand was indeed the happy land he visited, and when du Fresne arrived 168 years later, evidently much had changed. Instead of the welcoming, peaceful and happy people de Gonneville said he encountered, there were warlike Māori who had learned to attack and seize vessels.

According to Chief George the Waitaha lived peaceful, happy and undisturbed lives until the coming of the Moriori, who, he says became the Māori.

Then they came under attack first from the fierce Moriori and then later by the emerging and equally warlike, opportunistic Māori tribes the Moriori developed into. Some visiting ships had been attacked and destroyed, their crews eaten by these people. Thus it was a very different *Nu-Terre* that the latter French navigators came to.

To recap, tersely summing up de Gonneville's voyage, *Wikipaedia* says the land he claimed he had landed 'east of the Cape of Good Hope' after being blown off course was long thought to have been Australia 'but now it has shown to be Brazil'.

But how could it have been Brazil when, as the online encyclopaedia itself admits, that country is north-west, not east, of the Cape? Any world atlas shows it is Australia and New Zealand that clearly lies to the east, not South America.

Some researchers have conjectured that de Gonneville reached Australia but the likelihood is that the prevailing wind and current would have pushed him east-south-east towards New Zealand. Others have suggested that de Gonneville lied about the true direction of the land he discovered but there is no evidence to support that.

Discoverer of Terra Australis?

It was widely believed in 17th and 18th century France that de Gonneville was the first finder of *Terra Australis*; he became a legendary hero because of it. The French Government and Admiralty believed the navigator's report that land he had found lay east of the Cape. The later historians, however, begged to differ arguing that de Gonneville had not supplied an accurate latitude and longitude 'fix' for the new land.

It is possible that de Gonneville falsified his account of the voyage to hide the true location of the new land he discovered. But it is far more likely that centuries later, when competition between

European powers to seize new lands in the Southern Hemisphere was at its height, France engaged in a policy of misdirection to those without, pointing those reading of de Gonneville's voyage westwards to Brazil to conceal the true identity of land he had discovered and to which France held 'first right of discovery'.

The facts are that on his return voyage to France when almost within sight of his native land de Gonneville's ship was attacked by an English corsair, seized, stripped of cargo, papers and anything else of value and destroyed. Items such as plants, birds, animal remains, tools and clothing which would have proved whether he had had sojourned in Brazil or in New Zealand were lost.

Worst of all de Gonneville's log and written account of the voyage vanished too. Later researchers cannot identify the English privateer, nor is there any British record of taking the French ship. Robbed of his ship, cargo, log, papers, journal and charts de Gonneville limped back to France a broken man and reported as best he could from memory to the voyage's merchant backers and to the French Admiralty.

In 1663 interest in his venture was revived when a French cleric, de Courtonne, published an account, entitled *Memoirs Concerning The Establishment of a Christian Mission in the Austral Land*, in which he claimed to be the great-grandson of the 'Indian' brought back to France by de Gonneville in 1505.

At the time French pride was wounded by Dutch and English voyages of discovery in the South Pacific. To bolster Gallic prestige de Gonneville's forgotten tales were dusted off and presented as the basis for a French 'right of first discovery' to exploit these lands. This led to the French expeditions to the Pacific of Bouvet, Bougainville and Kerguelen and to French colonisation of Tahiti, and the Falklands Islands.

However, New Zealand, or *Nu-Terre*, as the French called it was the greatest prize. France intended to annex and settle the country with native consent and but for the du Fresne massacre, would have done so in 1772.

If de Gonneville reached New Zealand in 1504 and alerted France to its potential as a major South Seas colony then other French voyages to further explore *Nu-Terre* would have taken place between then and de Surville's arrival in 1767.

Gorge Connelly's ancestral history has it that his predecessors as *Te Upoko Ariki* (paramount chiefs) in Northland had long been in negotiation with the French to persuade them to annex New Zealand to bring peace and law and order before they, as the Waitaha, were destroyed by the increasingly savage conflict then sweeping the land.

'We were a basically peaceful people and were under severe attack from the rapidly growing numbers of Moriori and Māori who had brought a total war culture into the country. My ancestors had learned from early visits by French ships of a different world and a far better way of running society where rule of law restrained evil and violence. They wanted the French to bring that to New Zealand,' he says.

And even after the setback of the du Fresne massacre French determination to seriously settle New Zealand persisted. So much so that to prevent it Britain speeded up its own decision to annex New Zealand.

The 1835 Declaration of Independence drawn up by chiefs at the instigation of missionaries, drafted by British Resident James Busby and signed by 34 northern chiefs, stemmed from fear that France would declare sovereignty over the land first.

Another impetus to the Declaration was that several Northern Māori chiefs, including a Waitaha chief, had visited New South Wales and England and seen how government worked there which provoked discussion about unifying the tribes in New Zealand to form their own government. It was deemed necessary by both tribal leaders, missionaries and British representatives that some form of government should quell the lawlessness of British settlers, end war between rival native tribes and provide a recognised flag for New Zealand shipping.

Māori chiefs owned and sailed New Zealand trading ships during this period and the seizure by Sydney customs officials of the Hokianga-built *Sir George Murray*, because she had no British recognised flag, had caused great resentment.

Serious French intent to settle and annex New Zealand was demonstrated when Frenchman Charles de Thierry claimed to have bought 40,000 acres of land in the Hokianga to establish a colony there.

He styled himself 'Charles, Baron de Thierry, Sovereign Chief of New Zealand and King of Nuku Hiva (i.e. the Marquesas Islands)'. And it was more than a mere jest when others laughingly said they too aspired to be 'King of the Cannibal Isles'. What's more not even the hoisting of the flag of the United Tribes of New Zealand and signing the 1835 Declaration of Independence recognised by King William IV of the United Kingdom dampened French determination to have the *Tricolor* fly over New Zealand.

On 2 August 1838, at Little Port Cooper, Captain Jean Langlois, a French whaler from Le Havre, negotiated with several Māori chiefs to establish a French colony at Akaroa in the South Island. After this somewhat dubious land purchase he established the Nanto-Bordelaise Company in France to finance and carry out the project. In 1839 King Louis Philippe agreed to lend his support.

The French representative for the settlement, Captain Charles Francois Lavaud, sailed for New Zealand in April 1840. A month later the *Comte de Paris* set off for Akaroa carrying 53 emigrants but arrived too late, the Treaty of Waitangi having been signed a bare two months earlier, ceding sovereignty over New Zealand to Britain.

On the Crown's behalf William Hobson officially asserted British sovereignty over the South Island in June of that year. The upshot was that the French settlement remained on the clear understanding that the Union Jack, not the *Tricolor*, flew over Akaroa.

A further point to support the contention that de Gonneville may well have reached New Zealand in 1504 is that when Abel Tasman's little fleet arrived in 1642, 138 years later, the boat crew he sent ashore to collect water was attacked and killed by Māori wielding mere as weapons.

And as Tasman retreated out of what he later named Murderer's Bay (now Golden Bay) he was again attacked, this time by 11 waka. This native war fleet menaced his ship, the *Zeehaehn*, which opened fire. The point to note is this hostility was in marked contrast to the peaceful and happy reception accorded de Gonneville during his six months' stay 138 years before, if we accept that the great French navigator did reach New Zealand.

So what had changed? First, drawing from his ancestral tribal lore Chief George points out that between de Gonneville's probable landing in 1503 and Tasman's arrival in 1642, Māori from the North Island had pushed into the South Island attacking the peaceful Waitaha people and others in those parts. It was a campaign of slaughter and extermination.

'My people would not have attacked a visiting ship nor its crew. We would have welcomed them and helped them. But Māori already on the warpath would undoubtedly attack, seeing the taking of the ship as an opportunity for conquest,' he opines.

But, you might ask, where and when had Māori become so familiar with European sailing vessels they felt confident enough to take them on? For their attack on Tasman's ships indicates familiarity with such visiting vessels and their crew and learned behaviour about how to attack them, implying previous experience. And why is it that from Tasman onwards many visiting ships were attacked, their crews eaten by Māori?

This when without exception all early European exploration vessels reaching these shores came in peace. Desperate for clean water and crew sick and dying from scurvy their captains came seeking succour not war. They came in peace seeking to trade.

When first sighting such a strange vessel, a ship of white sails manned by white men, natives throughout the islands treated the visitors with respect, believing they were *atua*, gods. That was precisely the reception at first accorded to Captain Cook. That the natives of Golden Bay immediately attacked Tasman's boat's crew without provocation and assaulted his ships, to my mind, strongly suggests they had encountered and been aboard earlier European vessels.

It also suggests that Tasman was not the first latter-day European to reach New Zealand as conventional history holds, but that de Gonneville really reached here in 1504 and that his discovery of this land was followed up by French, Dutch and perhaps other European ship visits in subsequent years before Tasman's arrival, albeit these voyages remain part of undisclosed, if not hidden and forbidden, history.

At the very least then a serious question mark must be placed over whether Tasman was the first latter day European to 'discover' New Zealand.

Chapter 22

An obsession with maps

My friend Max Hill is the first to admit he has an unusual way of looking at things. Sometimes he sees them as upside down; on other occasions back to front. What's more he has a keen eye for the unusual or out of place.

A now retired Waikato farmer, Max has also had an unusual hobby for one of his calling. For 30 years he has studied maps, old maps in particular. And his obsession with them has led to two remarkable discoveries that not only upset present notions of New Zealand pre-history but also put a time bomb under the conventional history of exploration of the Pacific.

His first 'find', that led him to write his first book, *To The Ends Of The Earth*[41], was the discovery that outlines of the coasts of Australia and New Zealand appear on Martin Waldseemuller's world map published in 1507AD. In it Australia is drawn as though connected to South-East Asia, although the continent's distinctive shape is recognizable for all that. And above and to the right two disproportionate and ill-shaped islands are drawn in the right location for New Zealand.

How, wondered Max, could this be, given that the map was drawn in 1507, long before Tasman and Cook reached the Antipodes? When he researched the origin of Waldseemuller's map and that of others, such as that drafted by Henricus Martellus (1489), the mystery deepened.

For Max found all of the European penned maps that sparked the dash to explore both the Americas and the lands 'Down Under' were copies from much older world charts drawn up by the ancient Greek-Egyptian cartographer Claudius Ptolemy who died in the 1st

41 *To The Ends Of The Earth.*

Detail from the 1507 world map of Martin Waldseemuller. Derived from the wolrd maps drawn by Claudius Ptolemy some 1500 years earlier, this map clearly shows Australia (in two parts) and islands to the east of it that may well be New Zealand.

century AD. And he reported that in drawing his maps Ptolemy had worked from much older ocean charts once held in the Great Library of Alexandria.

So now the question became who in ancient times had voyaged around New Zealand and Australia to chart the coasts and take this information back to Egypt for Ptolemy to include in his wonderful 'earth in the round' global maps?

That quest led to much wider research in which Max with Gary Cook and Noel Hilliam put little known facts together to come up with the theory that ancient Greeks set off from Egypt in 232BC to sail around the world to prove Greek mathematician Eratosthenes' claim that the world was round.

That such an expedition of several ships reached the South Pacific is supported by the rock solid evidence of cave inscriptions dating and describing the voyage, naming its leaders, Admiral Rata and Navigator Maui, as found in Iran Jaya, on Pitcairn Island and in Santiago, Chile.

Then in his second book, *To The Ends Of The Earth And Back Again*[42], Max sprang a further, history shaking surprise. On page 252 he exhibited the photograph of a map of Australia drawn long before history has latter day European explorers reaching its coast. The map accurately traces the continent's coastline and depicts its rivers and lakes. Found by Australian historian and lawyer Eric Whitehouse the map, first published in 1470AD, is held in the Public Library, Florence, Italy.

And now something even more amazing about old maps has come to light. It seems that even Ptolemy's world charts penned around the turn of the 1st century AD were based on earlier and far more accurate maps of the world dating back thousands of years before his lifetime.

This is surmised from the clear statement of 16th century Ottoman Empire Admiral Piri Reis that his enigmatic world map of 1513 and a series of atlases, including the notable Kitahi Bahriye, were drawn from a collection of 20 very much older maps.

Controversially, his map is held to show part of Antarctica without its present ice cover. This in 1513 when proven existence of this vast southern continent would not be officially determined until 1819AD. Reis (real name: Ahmet Muhiddin), when on active duty in the fleet of Suleiman the Magnificent, charted lands he visited, but also demonstrated a keen passion for acquiring maps, particularly old ones. The Admiral admits in notes on the 1513 map he compiled and copied the data from many source maps, some of which dated to the 4th century BC or earlier.

---

42 *To The Ends Of The Earth And Back Again*, by Maxwell C. Hill, published April 2015 by Ancient History Publications, printed by the Copy Press, Nelson.

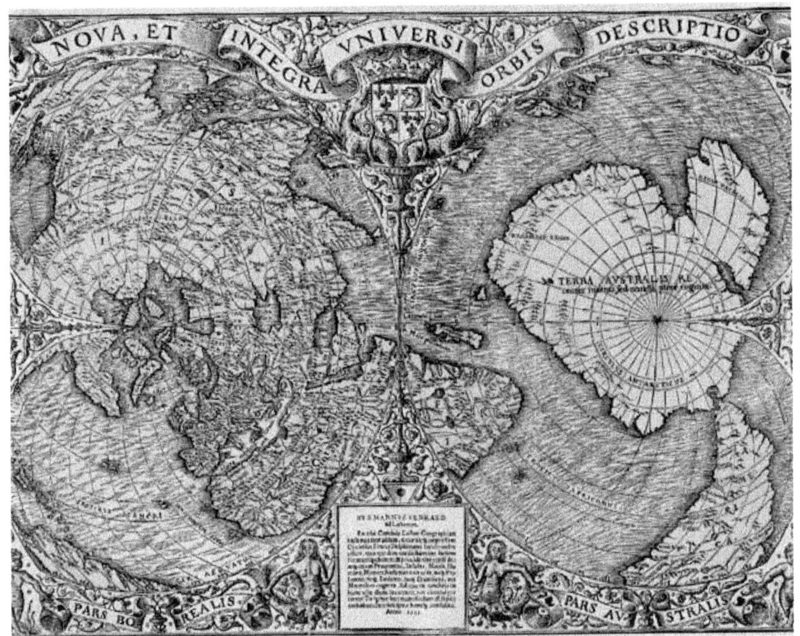

The Oronteus Finnaeus Antarctic map of 1531

He writes that eight maps derived from the time of 'Alexander, Lord of the Two Horns', i.e. from the days of Alexander the Great. Other charts used in the Piri Reis compilations included some acquired from a Spanish sailor he had captured, a man who had accompanied Christopher Columbus on his voyages to the New World.

To save his life and secure his freedom the sailor handed over charts he said Columbus had used to locate the islands of the Caribbean and the Americas. It appears then, that Columbus, like Cook in 'finding' New Zealand, made his 'discoveries' using maps drawn up thanks to the work of others who had charted these new lands long, long before he got there. The moral, if there is one, is that it's always easier to find 'unknown lands', when you have a map pointing you to their precise location.

Of course, controversy clouds these claims. While the Piri Reis map undoubtedly exists – drawn on gazelle skin it is in the Library of the Topkapı Palace in Istanbul – the claim it is based on much earlier charts of great antiquity is hotly disputed.

Whole books have been written to assert the map was cobbled together from maps of Piri Reis's day, that its precise placing of South America and Africa in correct relative longitude did not anticipate later navigational developments and even that its depiction of Antarctica's 'Queen Maud Land' was instead that of South America.

What's more Prof. Charles Hapgood has been lambasted for suggesting in his erudite and persuasive book, *Maps of the Ancient Sea Kings*[43], that an ancient, much more knowledgeable and much more technically advanced civilisation than any known to conventional history prior to the 20th century must have charted some lands found on the Reis maps.

This assertion defies prevailing evolutionary opinion which holds that mankind evolved slowly from ape-man to caveman, then to hunter gatherers and farmers, such process taking millions of years.

But the evidence of ancient technical prowess in building the Great Pyramids, raising the colossal stones at Baalbek – a feat still impossible today – and constructing the thousands of huge and ancient stone temples and pyramids in the Middle East, Africa, Europe, the Americas, India, South-East Asia and even in the South Pacific belies that.

Add to that science's refusal to accept Genesis and other ancient literature as accurate historical record and it is clearly almost impossible for most people today, brainwashed by scientific 'theory' as they are, to accept that many thousands of years ago people were far more intelligent and multi-skilled than they are today; that in fact, far from advancing, mankind has gone backwards for thousands of years, forgetting and losing earlier gained knowledge. The Dark Ages are a clear case in point.

---

43 *Maps of the Ancient Sea Kings*, Charles Hapgood, published 1997 Adventures Unlimited Press.

Historians dedicated to demolishing anything that even hints at 'diffusionism' – the doctrine that an early civilisation spread throughout the world in ancient times, imparting technological knowledge as it went – will find what follows anathema, but it might just be true for all that.

According to Keith Hunt in the online treatise *Secrets of the Lost Races*, support for Reis's claim he used maps from Alexander the Great's time to compile his own is found in that the Piri Reis map centres on the intersection of the Tropic of Cancer with the meridian of Alexandria, 30 E. longitude. Fact is Ptolemy and all other Greek mapmakers used this meridian as their baseline.

Now, granted, the Reis map's projection is said to be distorted by a 4.5 per cent over-statement of the earth's circumference. But this again points to its Alexandrian origin since it was the Greek-Egyptian astronomer and mathematician Eratosthenes who made that over calculation. Importantly, when the map was re-projected to remove the Eratosthenes mistake, longitude errors were reduced to next to nothing.

According to Hapgood, this means that the Alexandrian map makers, when drawing up charts using Eratosthenes' calculated circumference of the earth, must have worked from much earlier source maps that were without error.

He concludes that the world geography Piri Reis featured in his map originated from a people who lived long before the Greeks and who in their far distant time charted all the continents and islands of the world.

It is to this source he attributes the accurate placing, according to longitude and latitude, on the Piri Reis map (once corrected) of the African and South American coasts, the Canary Islands, the Azores and the Isle of Pines, Andros Island, San Salvador and Jamaica, some of which, according to accepted history, were only 'discovered in 1513.

French geographer Phillipe Bauche's map, published in 1737,

is also said to have been copied from far earlier maps. His chart also shows Antarctica long before the continent was 'discovered'.

Amazingly, it also shows Antarctica with no ice and with a waterway that divides Antarctica into two islands. Did Bauche have access to very old charts that accurately depict under the ice features? If not how could he, who never visited the Southern Hemisphere, have shown what is believed to be an accurate outline of the Antarctic land mass beneath the ice and depicted a waterway dividing the continent into separate land masses? It is a stunning fact that in 1958, when the first Antarctic seismic survey was done, such a waterway was discovered under the existing mile deep ice.

Importantly, Bauche's map not only places the Canary Islands correctly but also accurately portrays the extensive underwater plateau around them, something considered impossible to chart, given the technology of his day. A 1531 map of Antarctica by French mathematician and cartographer Oronteus Finaeus (Oronce Fine) when redrawn on the modern equidistant azimuthal polar projection, compares closely with the modern map of Antarctica on the same projection, according to *The Christian Science Monitor*.

Maps of the Ancient Sea Kings contain letters Hapgood says he received from Harold Z. Ohlmeyer Lt. Colonel, USAF Commander and Lorenzo W. Burroughs, Captain, USAF Chief, Cartographic Section, 8th USAF Reconnaissance Technical Squadron, concluding that both the Reis and Finaeus maps accurately depicted Antarctica when it was relatively free of ice. Ohlmeyer reportedly said:

> The claim that the lower part of the map portrays the Princess Martha Coast of Queen Maud Land, Antarctic, and the Palmer Peninsular, is reasonable. We find that this is the most logical and in all probability the correct interpretation of the map. The geographical detail shown in the lower part of the map agrees very remarkably with the results of the seismic profile made across the top of the ice-cap by the Swedish-British Antarctic Expedition of 1949. This indicates the coastline had been mapped before it was covered by the ice-cap. The ice-cap in

> this region is now about a mile thick. We have no idea how the data on this map can be reconciled with the supposed state of geographical knowledge in 1513.

Hapgood's own conclusion was:

> The (Piri Reis) map bears irrefutable testimony to a scientific achievement far surpassing the abilities of the navigators and map makers of the Renaissance, the Middle Ages, the Arab world or any of the ancient geographers. It is the product of an unknown people antedating recognised history'.

An unknown people, he asserts. But were they unknown? I believe not. I would submit that not only was the origin of these skilled and highly knowledgeable people known from their beginning but also that their descent and dispersion around the globe can still be traced today.

What's more, I believe their descendants can be identified as still living among us today right here in New Zealand. This we explore in the next chapter.

Chapter 23

The 'unknown' mappers

'An unknown people antedating recognised history'. This is Charles Hapgood's description of the ancient mappers who charted an ice-free Antarctica and, he maintains, accurately recorded the geography of the world.

But were they unknown? Not if you study the world's most authoritative record of the times in which these great explorers flourished, for in that account names are put to the founding ancestors of tribes said to comprise the ancient nations of the earth.

The Book of Genesis, said to have been written by Moses at God's direction some 4,000 years ago, records the creation of earth and heaven, the making of man, plants birds, fish and animals, and their destruction bar a handful in Noah's Flood. It states that after this global deluge mankind began again as the progeny of Noah's three sons and their wives.

Importantly, in Genesis chapter 10 we find all the nations of the post-Flood earth named under their patriarchal heads and accurately placed in their homelands where, mostly, they still live or can be traced to today.

What's more, Genesis provides compelling evidence these people mapped the whole earth some 5,000 to 6,000 years ago and why and how they dispersed across the face of it. And there is scientific evidence to support Genesis's statement that the descendants of Noah's sons were 'scattered abroad… upon the face of all the earth.[44]' Most amazingly of all, chapter 10 names all of these nations and states their fathers. No other historical record does so.

So how did all this happen? Well, imagine, if you will, being

44 Genesis 11:8, 4

locked inside a large boat with animals large and small for nearly a year as the earth is inundated by tossing flood waters. Then, as howling winds dissipate the waters, slowly land appears. But it is an entirely different world. It has been reshaped. While some mountains may be recognizable, the rivers and almost all known landmarks have disappeared.

As Noah's family looked out from the ark's lofty landing place in the mountains of Ararat the view would have been of a vast and slowly draining lake or swamp. Thankfully, the water was fresh, for, Genesis implies, the earth was still undivided and the sea was still in one place. It had not yet had the thousands of years needed to create the salty sea we known today.

Consequently grass, herbs and multiple other forms of vegetation sprang up quickly. The released animals had no problem in finding food. Neither, evidently, did Mr. and Mrs. Noah or their three sons and their wives for Noah 'began to be an husbandman', that is a farmer. And while Genesis says he planted a vineyard and got drunk, methinks he must have planted other crops first.

So Noah and his descendants had food, shelter – archaeological explorers claim to have found their 'village', replete with marker stones and rock inscriptions – and they soon became a vast extended family. 'These are the three sons of Noah and of them was the whole earth overspread'[45].

God commanded them to 'be fruitful and multiply and replenish the earth'[46] and to 'bring forth abundantly in the earth and multiply therein'[47]. And they must have done this 'exceedingly' if the many names of their descendants and nations in Genesis 10 is anything to go by.

As strangers in a new and different world they clung together

45 Genesis 9:19

46 Genesis 9:1

47 Genesis 9:7

and moved as a people seeking a place to settle. They were 'all of one language and one speech'[48] and they journeyed westwards to the plain of Shinar, the land of Mesopotamia in present-day Iraq.

Here they stopped and, defying the divine command, refused to go further. They made brick and built a city and a tower, '... lest we be scattered abroad on the face of the whole earth'. But scattered they were. In response to their rebellion '... the Lord scattered them abroad from thence upon the face of all the earth and they left off to build the city'[49].

Genesis not only sheds great light on man's global travels, it also discloses the origin of the detailed and superbly accurate world maps that predate recognised human history. You see, neither DNA research nor anthropology can adequately explain where the original nations came from, or where they went, as they moved around the globe. But in Genesis is found the beginning of all the present peoples of the earth going back to Noah's Flood. Earlier Adam and Eve's children had multiplied into millions in the ante-diluvian age but then, as Genesis has it, they were all drowned.

As scholar Finis Jennings Dake says: 'All races, colours, and types of men came into being after the Flood'. Science today scoffs at the Flood. But this cataclysm, which drowned the old world and introduced our present world is reported as true by ancient cultural traditions right around the world.

Of these the closest to the Genesis account is the written Babylonian Epic of Gilgamesh which tells the story of Unapishtim (Noah) who built a huge boat at the behest of the god Ea. Significantly, Ea is the Mesopotamian god of creation, order and of the waters and flood. Unapishtim gathers humans and animals aboard the boat which sails through a huge storm to survive a Flood that devastates the earth.

Greeks also knew of the Flood. In Plato's *Timaeus*, the book's hero says that Zeus (the Greek 'Most High God') was angered because

48 Genesis 11:1

49 Genesis 9:8

ancient humans made wars constantly and decided to punish humanity by a flood. Prometheus the Titan knew of this and told the secret to 'Deucalion' (the Greek name for Noah) urging him to build an ark to save his family.

When the water receded, supposedly after nine days and nine nights, the ark landed, not on the mountains of Ararat as Genesis has it, but as better suits Greek prestige, at 'Mount Parnassus in Greece'.

Today even some Christians doubt the Flood was worldwide. But, if it wasn't, then how does one account for the charming Flood myth of Tiddalik the Frog, which Aborigines in Australia, on the opposite side of the world, have retold for many generations?

Tiddalik, this legend says, awoke one morning with a huge thirst, and drank until all fresh water was greedily consumed. Creatures and plant life everywhere died due to lack of moisture. Other animals conspired against Tiddalik and the wise old wombat devised a plan to make him to release the water he held.

To execute it Nabunum the eel made Tiddalik laugh when he tied himself in comical shapes. And as Tiddalik laughed, the water rushed out of him to replenish the lakes, swamps and rivers. The Tiddalik tale is not only an important 'Dreamtime' story, but like many legends contains a germ of truth – that there was a worldwide Flood preserved in human memory.

Halfway between Mesopotamia and Australia lies India and in the old Hindu texts called Puranas we find mention of the Deluge. The Satapatha Brahmana tells how the 'Matsya Avatar of Vishnu' warns the first man, Manu, of the coming Flood and tells him to build a giant boat.

From India to China, where the Chinese *Shujing*, or 'Book of History' (c. 500BC) records that Emperor Yao faced 'flood waters that reached unto heaven'. However, the famed hero, Da Yu controls the Flood and founds the first Chinese dynasty. The *Shanhaijing*, 'Classic of the Mountain and Seas', reports that Da Yu struggled for 10 years before controlling a deluge whose 'floodwaters overflowed heaven'.

And down to New Zealand at the 'ends of the earth'. Here the Flood story is also preserved in ancient folklore. Ngati Porou, the East Coast, North Island, Māori tribe, tell the legend of Paikea who drowned his chiefly rivals then summoned a great storm of waves which only he survived (Reedy 1997:83-85).

The 19th century Governor of New Zealand, Sir George Grey, in his book, *Polynesian Mythology*, recounts how Tawhiki's ancestors released 'the floods of heaven', in which the earth was overwhelmed and all human beings perished.[50]

According to one source, over 600 legends of the Flood are found in folk traditions of people right around the world. Can they all be wrong? What's more in every case the deluge story has a hero who alone, or with his family, survives and is the founder of a race of peoples.

So did the first inhabitants of New Zealand the Patupaiarehe have direct descent from Noah's sons? Can their line be traced back to those named in Genesis 10? If not then from whence did the Māori of New Zealand obtain the account of a lone Flood survivor whose descendants filled the earth?

So who were the ancient earth measurers? Again Genesis 10 provides the answers. According to Hunt, three of Noah's decendants arec named for their expertise in surveying and map making. He believes all three lived during a 300-year span after Noah's Flood in which the earth was mapped. And the truth that this was so is found in the meaning of their names.

Consider the two sons of Eber in Genesis 10:25-26. Peleg's name means a division or measurement. The biblical statement, 'in his days the earth was divided' could be rendered, 'in his days the earth was measured'. Then there is Peleg's brother Joktan's son, Almodad. His name means 'measurer'. The *Paraphrase of Jonathan* says he invented geometry and 'measured the earth to its extremities', one

50 *Polynesian Mythology* by Sir George Grey (1963) Reed, pg. 165, in a footnote.

of which of course would be New Zealand. Last in the trio is Noah's grandson Mizraim whose name is said to mean 'to delineate, draw up a plan and make a representation'.

Egypt was the centre of ancient map making it seems. Both the Piri Rels map and the 1510 Reinal Circular Projection use Egypt as the focal point and it was there that the great cartographer Claudius Ptolemy drew his maps, working from earlier copies.

The archetype of all the legendary Flood heroes must be Noah himself and, if you'll pardon the pun, Genesis 10 makes no bones about attributing to him all the posterity of mankind in the earth today. It is from Noah's three sons, Ham, Shem and Japheth, that descent of all the earth's ancient races are traced in the biblical account. But can this record in Genesis 10 be trusted as an accurate historical account?

This partly petrified structure embedded in the foothills of Mt Ararat measures 500ft and lines up with the dimensions of Noah's Ark as recorded in Genesis 6. Arguably it is one of the best pointers to there really having been a Great Flood.

Internationally recognised authority on Middle East archaeology, Professor W. F. Albright, insists it can. He describes the Genesis 10 record of the origin of the nations as a comprehensively accurate, genealogical account stating:

> It stands alone absolutely alone in ancient literature without a remote parallel even among the Greeks. 'The Table of the Nations' remains an astonishingly accurate document. It shows such remarkable 'modern' understanding of the ethnic and linguistic situation in the modern world, in spite of all its complexity, that scholars never fail but to be impressed with the author's knowledge of the subject.

Introducing this 'Table of the Nations' Genesis 10:1 says: 'Now these are the generations of the sons of Noah, Shem, Ham and Japheth: and unto them were sons born after the flood'.

Then in verses 2 to 4 are named the seven sons of the sons of Japheth and verse 5 records: 'By these were the isles of the Gentiles divided in their lands; everyone after his tongue, after their families, in their nations'.

Such a bold assertion throws down the gauntlet to sceptics. Can they name the founders of nations, distinguish them by language and tongue, trace their descent and determine their ancient homelands? Judging by this excerpt from a learned academic prehistorian they cannot:

> The history of pre-Celtic Europe remains very uncertain. According to one theory, the common root of the Celtic languages, a language known as Proto-Celtic, arose in the late Bronze Age Urnfield culture of Central Europe (c. 1200BC). In addition, according to a **theory** proposed in the 19th century, the first people to adopt cultural characteristics **regarded** as Celtic were the people of the Iron Age Hallstatt culture in central Europe (c. 800-450BC), named for the rich grave finds in Hallstatt, Austria. … This Celtic culture was **supposed** to

> have expanded by diffusion or migration to the British Isles. (Emphasis mine)[51].

Compare that vagary with the 'certainty of the word of truth'[52] found in Genesis 10 which begins in verse 1: 'Now these are the generations of the sons of Noah, Shem, Ham and Japheth, and unto them were sons born after the flood'. It continues in verse 5:

> By these were the isles of the Gentiles divided in their land: every one after his tongue, after their families in their nations.

Now the English word 'isles' translates the Hebrew word iy, variously meaning, habitable plot, desirable spot, dry land, coastline, island or a country. The context decides which meaning is appropriate and, in Genesis chapters 10-11 the context is that of a people all of one speech and an earth of one land mass[53] before the land and the people were divided up.

Therefore the meaning in Genesis 10:5 is that each of Japheth's sons' sons were allotted a divided portion of **dry land**. It's important to understand that, according to Genesis, that the single landmass of the earth remained undivided until the 'days of Peleg'[54] which occurred several generations later.

Reading on, we learn that the progeny of Ham's sons, Mizraim (the first name of Egypt), Cush who fathered Nimrod (the despot and rebel), Phut and Canaan, spread abroad through much of the Middle East and beyond. Again verse 20 firmly states, as fact not theory, that:

> These are the sons of Ham, after their families after their tongues, in their countries, and in their nations.

From the Genesis record it is easy to see that Syria (ancient Assyria) came from Asshur (a son of Shem), that Babylon came from Babel and that the Phoenician city of **Sidon** is named after **Sidon**,

51 *History of the Celts*, online article retrieved from *Wikipaedia* .

52 Proverbs 22:21

53 Genesis 11:1 and 10:25

54 Genesis 10:25

Canaan's first born. And **Sidon**, which still exists today, was the heart of the Phoenician homeland. And it is from this ancient trading, sea-faring nation, I submit, that Monica Matamua's people, the *Patupaiarehe*, are descended.

Then are listed the sons of the sons of Shem, the Semitic peoples. And here the record homes in on Eber, father of the Hebrews, and his descendants. One is mentioned in particular: Peleg, 'for in his days was the earth divided'. The genealogy ends with the familiar format:

> These are the sons of Shem, after their families, after their tongues, in their lands, after their nations.[55]

The entire family tree of present mankind is summed up in the statement:

> These are the families of the sons of Noah, after their generations, in their nations: and by these were the nations divided after the Flood.[56]

But can we really trace from this amazing table of nations the origin of ancient peoples such as the earliest inhabitants of New Zealand?

Well, according to archaeological researcher Keith Hunt[57], yes we can. He comments:

> It is very apparent from the generation lists of the sons of Noah that the post-Flood peoples spread rapidly across the surface of the earth. In just the second generation the grandchildren of the patriarch (Noah) had settled in lands from Iran to Spain, from northern Europe to Ethiopia.
>
> The following generation and their offspring were of course even more widespread. It also becomes obvious that in order

55 Genesis 10:31

56 Genesis 10:32

57 Online study, *Secrets of the Lost Races No 3*, retrieved from the website, *Restitution of All Things*.

> for the Genesis 10 genealogy list to have been composed there must have been an advanced degree of communication among all these people.
>
> Someone living during the colonising of these distant lands had the ability to correspond with all the descendants over a relatively long period of time – otherwise the composition of such a detailed listing as 'The Table of the Nations' would have been impossible.

Here Hunt makes an important point. It is that a few thousand years ago a mass of different peoples dispersed out over the earth but remained in communication with one other.

Enter the Celts

And this has huge implications for our understanding of real prehistory, the origin of stunningly accurate ancient maps, and the dispersal of white, fair or red-haired and green-eyed European and Mediterranean peoples to Europe, the Americas and even right down to New Zealand.

We will further explore these connections in the next chapter. Meanwhile this is Hunt's summary of who Noah's descendants had become and how far abroad they had settled the earth by their fifth generation:[58]

> The first and second generations of Noah's sons left their mark in Egypt, Palestine, Asia Minor, Assyria, Phoenicia, Armenia, the Persian Gulf region and lands in between. The third generation (c. 3230-2780BC) moved into Europe, Spain, southern Arabia, Lower Egypt, Upper Egypt, the Black Sea region, and Babylonia.
>
> The fourth generation (c. 3096-2674BC) made swift moves into the area presently called the Yemen ... subsequently known as the home of the Queen of Sheba. When the fifth generation

58 According to Genesis 10

(3001-2507BC) arrived on the scene, the record tells of the descendants of Eber, meaning 'pilgrim, migrant', the father of a widely scattered people called Habiru, (or Hebrew).

And from then on the biblical history concentrates on the 'Chosen People'. The fact remains, however, that Genesis 10 is the only ancient document extant showing the ancestors from which all the ancient races – whose descendants are still with us today – come.

Take the example of the white or fair skinned, green eyed and red-haired Celtic people now found across much of the world from Ireland and Scotland and much of Europe, including Portugal, in the north to the Americas and to Polynesia and New Zealand in the south.

According to eminent scholar, Dr. E.W. Bullinger, these people, commonly known as the Celts, stem from Gomer, the son of Japheth. In his notes in the *Companion Bible*, Dr. Bullinger says:

Gomer. In Assyrian *Gimirra* (the Kimmerians of Herodotus), progenitor of the Celts'. Herodotus the 5th century BC Greek historian said these Kimmerians or Cimmerians inhabited the Caucasus between the so-named mountains and the Black Sea for more than 1,000 years before being driven into Anatolia, present-day Turkey.

Dake[59] identifies Canaan as the progenitor, through his son Sidon, of the Phoenicians of Tyre and Sidon in Lebanon. These cities were Canaanite strongholds from the most ancient times and they still exist today. Linkage to the red-haired, fair-skinned and freckled peoples we now know as Celtic is supported also by the fact that a high proportion of today's Lebanese population have these same features. As so do the Portuguese, Peruvians, other South American peoples and the original inhabitants of New Zealand, the Turehu and Patupaiarehe.

It must also be said that the same physical characteristics, predominately that of lifelong brilliant red or golden hair, appear in ancient mummies found in Egypt, China and South America.

59 *Dake's Annotated Reference Bible* by Finis Jennings Dake © 1963.

And the huge *Moai* heads that brood over Easter Island also bear testimony to this same race of people, known throughout Polynesia as the *Urekehu*, because they bear red top-knots, indicating their fiery hair. We trace them further in the next chapter.

Chapter 24

'Red heads' or ancient Celts?

A present day girl of the Chachapoya people, who are called 'Gringuita' by modern Peruvians.

But is there further proof that Sidon's descendants can be identified as the Phoenicians who emerged a generation or three after the Flood and its associated Ice Age? Yes, there is.

Clear evidence from DNA comparisons shows that Monica Matamua, of the Patupaiarehe people, can trace her ancestry back to the Middle East and back to the Phoenicians. The DNA record also tracks her people's long migrations through Borneo and South America to New Zealand.

Genetics also underlie claims by cultural scientist and documentary filmmaker Hans Giffhorn that the Chachapoya mountain people who had lived in eastern Peru for many centuries before the Spanish arrival, and whose many descendants still live there now, are closely related to the Celts.

Because of their appearance – white, red or blond-haired and some with freckles – the Chachapoya remain a mystery for anthropologists. But in his book[60], Giffhorn asserts that early in the 2nd century BC Carthaginians, fearing annihilation at the hands of the Romans, fled seeking a new home far from their enemies.

With Celts, probably from Mallorca, they reached South America and became the white-skinned red or fair haired megalithic stone builders whose monuments are found throughout that continent. Such a voyage would not be impossible in ancient times, he opines, for Phoenicians had reached the Gulf of Guinea and, according to Greek historian Herodotus, circumnavigated Africa around 500BC.

Importantly, he says it is well known that when sailing ships venture too far off the West African coast – as Giffhorn thinks the Carthaginians did for fear of the Romans – currents and winds drive them almost inevitably toward South America.

According to Giffhorn it was at first by chance, when he was a documentary filmmaker in search of a species of extinct hummingbird, that he encountered the descendants of the Chachapoya in Peru, and after many discussions with archaeologists and other historians there, learned the history of this nation. Today, Peruvians call the Chachapoya descendants '*Gringuitos*'.

The Chachapoya culture – characterised by its massive stone buildings and beautiful thatched, round stone houses – with no evidence of input from preceding cultures living in South America – appeared from nowhere somewhere between 100AD and 400AD. That is to say, that both north and south of the Amazon, there suddenly emerged a previously unexplained culture. Ceramics give evidence for this, as do evidences of cremation unknown in Latin America, but known in Europe. These people built round, stone huts and practiced trepanning, and evidence of this has also been found in New Zealand.

---

60 *Was America Discovered in Antiquity? Carthaginians, Celts and the Mystery of the Chachapoya* ("Wurde Amerika in der Antike Entdeckt? Karthager, Kelten und das Rätsel der Chachapoya").

Later they would build the same round homes on the Pacific islands and in New Zealand. Exploration of the 'Stone City' in the Waipoua Forest of New Zealand's Northland found many circular heaps of stones that once were round houses. And where there was no stone, thatched round houses were fashioned from timber, as confirmed by archaeological digs on the sandy promontory of Pouto, as detailed in an earlier chapter.

Giffhorn postulates that in the 2nd century BC, a large fleet carrying hundreds of Carthaginians and Celts drifted to the area around the mouth of the Amazon. Over subsequent centuries they migrated far

Traditional round houses as found today on the Pacific island of Ouvea (above) are a matcher for the Peruvian Chachapoya dwellings (below). Picture courtesy of Peter Marsh.

up the Amazon, to the subsequent settlement area of the Chachapoya.

Nowhere along the way were they able to settle for long, because – as the first Spaniards were told – the migrants always came into conflict with belligerent, hostile Amazonian peoples. And that fits exactly with Monica Matamua's account of her people's migration. 'Always my ancestors had to move on because they encountered peoples who were determined to fight,' she says.

And then there are the very similar pictographs, petroglyphs, signs and words are found spread around the globe wherever there is evidence of red-haired, white-skinned peoples and their impressive stone buildings.

Hawaiian writer Peter Marsh[61] opines this ancient civilisation may have suffered a catastrophic event in its Northern Hemisphere homeland. Perhaps a tsunami, precipitated by isostatic rebalancing[62] as the final meltdown of the last Ice Age (a.k.a. Flood) occurred thousands of years ago.

Pulses of meltwater as ice dams broke and 1-2km thick ice shelves collapsing into the sea would have caused rapid flooding with the possibility of tsunamis. Scientists believe that sea levels could have risen 20 metres in 100 years. After this terrible event, many survivors feared the ocean and moved up rivers into central Asia, the highlands of Luzon, Taiwan and New Guinea.

The Chinese civilization, Marsh asserts, is a product of this coastal culture travelling up the Hwanghe River and mixing with more northerly, people of inner China. Fleeing rising melt water possibly explains why discovery of red-haired mummies at Urumchi in the dry sands of the Tarim Basin of Central Asia, part of China, caused a major sensation in 1994.

As stated earlier, the mummies radio carbon dated variously to

---

61 Peter Marsh, *Studies on the peopleing of the Pacificl,* retrieved from the website *Polynesian Pathways*.

62 Isostatic rebalancing occurs when deep ice layers melt and the land beneath 'springs up' when this weight of ice is removed.

2,200BC according to one test and to 4,500BC in another. Author and researcher Elizabeth Wayland Barber reports that the well preserved remains were of fair-skinned, red-haired people adorned in well-made clothing[63].

Importantly, they were neither Chinese nor Mongoloid but distinctly Caucasian. The Tibetans and Thais also moved inland to higher ground, according to Marsh. A Polynesian legend states that they were swept away on a large tree, to make landfall on the Queen Charlotte Islands of Canada.

Marsh argues persuasively that a fair-skinned, red-haired race settled in Hawaii having sailed there from Alaska, not from Micronesia and Melanesia, over 2,200 years ago. He upholds Thor Heyerdahl's scientifically derided but nevertheless convincing thesis that the Pacific was populated by peoples from America who rafted this great ocean borne by prevailing winds and currents.

The island called 'Sun People White'

Interestingly, he recounts the Alaskan Tinglit legend of a major Flood catastrophe several thousand years ago which dispersed many peoples from an Asian homeland. The Flood also occurs in a Hawaiian legend which says that the first man and woman were descended from the great-great ancestor Huka-ohialaka and describes Nu'u (Noah?), his wife and their sons and their wives, as the discoverers of Hawaii. Two events are confused here, but what a testimony to the seminal truth of the Genesis flood account this is:

> They arrived at Ka Houpo-o-Kane before it was disrupted by a great flood that occurred during the reign of Kahiko-Luamea. This great flood carried away a floating log of wood named Konikonihia. On this log was a precious human cargo and it came to rest on the land of Kalonakikeke (Alaska).
>
> Many generations later, Nuu, travelled from Alaska with his wife, Lilinoe, their three sons and their three wives in a canoe

63 *The Mummies of Urumchi*, Elizabeth Wayland Barber (1999) Macmillan, London.

called Ka-Waa-Halau-Alii-O-Ka-Moku (the royal canoe of the continent), and it rested upon Mauna Kea (white mountain), on the island of Hawaii. They were the first Hawaiians.

Ka Haupo-o-Kane is said by Marsh to be the Queen Charlotte Islands of Canada from whence the later 'Flood' swept survivors on to Alaska. Centuries later, according to Marsh, these ancestors sailed from Hawaii in a catamaran, the *Hokulea*, to Tahiti and from there later discovered other islands in the South Pacific.

Marsh maintains that island names such as Rarotonga (Sun in the South) and Tonga Tapu (South Forbidden) only make sense if named by people who came from the North, i.e. Hawaii, or from South America.

Significantly Marsh says that the 'sacred' island of Ra'iatea, was named after the people already living there. The name means 'Sun people white' and was noted by Captain Wallis, who visited the island in 1767, to have a high proportion of pale skinned people, many with red hair, living on it.

Pale skinned, red haired people also lived on both Easter Island and Tahiti. And when Portuguese mariner Mendana reached an island in the Tuamotus in 1595 he reported that its chief had "a mass of red and rather curly hair, reaching half way down his back." Captain Roggeveen visiting Easter Island in 1722, recorded that the first chief to come aboard was "an entirely white man."

Early visitors to Easter Island noted that some islanders were not only very fair and tall, but had soft, reddish hair, with greenish, blue eyes. On many islands in southern Polynesia, these people were often found to be holding positions of high rank, but as the years went by, less and less sightings were reported.

But were they Celtic? Marsh reports that in 1972 Professor Jean Dausset studied the Caucasian blue/green eyed, red heads of Easter Island and found them to have an ancient strain of Caucasian blood, which can also be found in the Basques of Spain, characterised by A29 and B12.

The analyses revealed that 39% of Basques and 37% of the Easter Islanders were carriers of the HLA gene B12. These were the highest and second highest proportions tested throughout the world. No other people in the world had remotely comparable figures."

From the above tests the Easter Islanders appear to be of almost as pure an ancient Caucasian racial stock as the Basques! This links the Easter Islanders firmly to the Spanish Celts who survived the last ice age (a.k.a. the Flood) by holding out in northwest Spain until things warmed up before going to Ireland. And it is from Easter Island that the ancestors of both the Patupaiarehe and Waitaha peoples set sail southward through the Pacific to eventually reach New Zealand.

However, if that linkage to the white-skinned red heads who first populated the Pacific and settled New Zealand is not Celtic enough for you, then learn that, according to Michael O'Laughlin, of the online website *Irish Central*, that the closest DNA match with the Irish in all Europe is that with the Basques.

Geneticist E. Gomez-Casado found that Basque genes of Spain were part of an ancient Caucasian gene pool that included the blonde haired Berbers of Morocco, the Tuareg, Egyptians, Minoans, Palestinians, Israelis, Lebanese, Kurds and Turks, running as far east as Iran.

The red haired Phoenicians and Celts, two great seafaring nations that commanded the Atlantic and Mediterranean oceans, were also from this gene pool. Importantly, Marsh asserts extreme antiquity for the Phoenician and Celtic peopling of the Pacific and particularly of New Zealand.

He says their presence prior to 2,000 years ago is confirmed by Phoenician and Egyptian writing from the Bronze Age and possibly earlier, which has been found in places such as Pitcairn Island, Tonga, New Zealand and Australia. Furthermore he claims the Trireme spike as seen on Phoenician ships has been adopted in Samoan canoe design.

Again, these ancient European venturers into the Pacific were not only accomplished seamen and master navigators and geographers

One of the Tattoed Rocks at Raglan, North Island, New Zealand. Are these inscriptions written in pictographic Hebrew, the oldest language known to man?

but also superb masons and writers.

A worldwide survey has led Canadian amateur archaeologists William and Mae Marie Coxon[64] to conclude that many centuries before Christ the peoples they dub 'The Stone Writers', left their rock inscriptions and signs on every continent.

What's more they found the same symbols and devices were used in the Middle East (201 sequences), the Far East (171), and the Americas (131). By comparing Nile Valley petroglyphs with Egyptian history the Coxons deduce that Stone Writers were on earth 1500 years before the rise of Egyptian civilisation.

They insist that far from being the hunter gatherers that evolutionists picture at this period these ancients were intelligent and systematic; their repeated symbols had meaning and purpose.

Above all they were explorers, sailing the oceans, charting the coastlines and penetrating far inland along rivers and lakes, leaving guide signs for others to follow them. The Coxons write:

64 Reported by Rene Noonbergen in *Secrets of the Lost Races.*

The Stone Writers were probably the very same explorers and geographers who charted the world after the Flood.

Support for this contention comes from English archaeologist S. F. Hood[65] who found correlations between tablet symbols unearthed at the prehistoric Tartaria site in Rumania with others found in Crete, Iraq, Egypt and the Balkans.

He concludes that a single system of signs and glyphs originating from the Middle East was spread widely throughout the earth less than 6,000 years ago and that it was constructed in a short time span.

Signs apart, there is also language evidence of ancient wide spread dispersal of people from the Middle East right down to Australia and New Zealand. American Irish etymologist John Philip Cohane[66] has spent decades studying the origin of words and found that six root words are found in the place names in every language around the world. He believes that long before the Egyptian, Greek, Carthaginian and Phoenician eras, two major worldwide migrations by the post-Flood descendants of Noah took place, each outward from the Middle East.

These dispersions he traced from his discovery that each emigrating group took with it a previously established group of root words. The first dispersal, said by the writer of Genesis to have been caused by God's confusion of the hitherto single language[67], apparently covered the entire world in a short time. Cohane explains:

> If one puts a charted overlay containing only the first group of names on top of a map of the world and then puts on top of that another overlay containing only the second group of names, the most logical conclusion is that, in prehistoric times, instead of one, there were two dispersions from the

65 Co-author with J. Boardman of *Early Iron Age tombs at Knossos.*

66 John Philip Cohane, *The Key: A Startling Enquiry into the Riddle of Man's Past.*

67 Genesis 11:7-8

Mediterranean, the first truly worldwide, the second petering out along the eastern coast of the Americas in one direction (and) in Japan the Philippines, **Australia** and **New Zealand** in the other.

Did you get that? The language lines marking dispersal from the Middle East and the difference in language trace an ancient emigration of Caucasian people right through to New Zealand.

Cohane also points out that all the key geographical names in both dispersal groups have prominent origin points in Semitic legends and mythology as well as Semitic place names.

To my mind, this is supportive of there being two great migrations of post-Flood peoples around the world, the first to explore the hugely altered landscape after the Flood, the second to map it yet again after the division of the continents and islands from the original single landmass in the subsequent Ice Age[68]. And if these explorers sailed to and around Antarctica why wouldn't they also have reached and, arguably, stayed in New Zealand?

Cohane also claims that the Phoenicians adopted their alphabet, one of the world's first, from a prior culture which, he says, is that of the original universal human language which, he believes, was Hebrew.

And this gels with the findings of New Zealand-born onetime Harvard professor and epigraphic expert Barry Fell who found that petroglyphs in caves in Iran Jaya, Pitcairn Island and Santiago in South America all recorded an epic 232AD Greek-Egyptian expedition to the other side of the world and traced back the alphabet these venturers used to the ancient 'Mauri' language, i.e. one from the Mediterranean and the Middle East and similar to, if not derived from Hebrew.

Such alphabet letters were also employed, he asserted, in the incisions found on the Tattoed Rocks still to be seen today at Raglan

68 Genesis 10:25

in New Zealand's North Island.

All of which means that is now hard, if not impossible, to deny that that ancient Caucasians descended from Noah's sons and who have the same DNA markers as the Irish and the Basques of Spain, at one time populated the Pacific islands and were also the first people to settle in New Zealand.

Marsh[69] asserts that the white, red-haired voyagers who first explored and settled the Pacific islands worshipped strange stone idols and Ra the sun god. They also practiced an ancient birdman religion still found amongst the floating reed bed people of the Indus. They made reed rafts and they had a strange writing system akin to the ancient Harappa script.

They made Peruvian style, interlocking stone walls, and they had circular burial tombs called Tullpa, similar to the Chullpa tombs of Peru, and they used the Egyptian and South American knotted cord, Quipu, also used by Māori and called kupu in that language, for working out sums and memorising information.

The red haired Paracas mummies and numerous legends of Peru all indicate that red heads were once a significant part of the population in Peru and that they can be found still living there today. The brownish/red haired, green eyed, Araucano ('Gold People') of Chile are only one of several ancient peoples who survived the onslaught of the Incas.

Events that unfolded in Peru leading to the exodus of red heads into the Pacific can be read in the ancient Rongo Rongo text of Easter Island, Marsh maintains. This writing was successfully deciphered in 1892 by Dr. A Carroll and describes the ancient history of Peru.

It names the many tribes of Peru and their relationships with each other, their allies, their enemies and the wars fought that led up to the final exodus of the Puruha (note the *ur* in the name) and Cha-

69 Peter Marsh, *Studies on the peopling of the Pacific*, retrieved from the website *Polynesian Pathways*.

Rapa (note the *Ra*) or Chachapoya people into the Pacific. Carroll's decipherment contains detailed information that would not have been available to him, unless he was reading it from an ancient source.

Marsh comments that, unfortunately, because this text did not say what the scientists wanted to hear, his valuable work and the meaning of the Rongo Rongo text was ignored. Thus it became forbidden history. Interestingly it mentions that wars against settled people who had arrived in ships from down the Pacific coast caused the exodus of some of the Charapa/Chachapoya people from South America into the Pacific.

Put all these strands of evidence together and it emerges that there may have been not one but several migrations of ancient Caucasian peoples into the Pacific and thence to New Zealand.

As Thor Heyerdahl found on Easter Island, the earliest settlers had fled there from Peru and built the great stone structures that remote island is famous for. They laboriously carved the moai, the great stone head statues, all of which faced east (to South America) and originally all bore red 'hats' or topknots indicating their red hair.

Importantly, these 'red heads' were the stone builders and rulers over the Melanesian prototype Polynesians who later came to Easter Island or *Rapa Nui* (Big Place of the White Sun People).

What's more, these 'Long Ears' kept themselves to themselves; they did not intermarry with proto-Polynesian 'short ears'. So much so that, as March reports, when the 'Short Ears' rebelled and slaughtered the whites only one 'Long Ear' male, and, presumably, at least one female, was left to preserve the 'red head' posterity.

As population pressure increased some of the 'Sun White People' sailed southwards, leaving behind clear evidence of their presence in the names of the islands they settled. Thus Ra'iatea means 'Sun People White' and Rarotonga 'Sun in the South'.

That much said, it becomes important, in terms of the diffusion of different peoples in the Pacific to distinguish between 'white skins', 'red skins' and 'dark brown', or 'black skins'. Not for any racist reason but simply to trace where such peoples came from, where they went, who they intermarried with and what culture they brought with them..

The 'white skins' then were the ancient Phoenicians who sojourned in Peru before establishing themselves at *Rapa Nui*, then sailed south to establish island colonies all the way down to New Zealand where they became known as the Patupaiarehe. Apparently, for more than a thousand years they remained largely separate, retaining mostly their unmixed, Caucasian, genetic inheritance until forcibly intermarried with or otherwise absorbed into Māori tribes in recent centuries.

Descendants such as Monica Matamua, as her DNA test proves, have few Polynesian or Māori mitochondrial genes; those she does have are predominantly Celtic and European. The Maui-Rata voyagers of 232BC who sailed from Egypt through Irian Jaya, to New Zealand and then on up through the Pacific to South America may well be another branch of this genetic inheritance.

The 'red skins' are the brave voyagers who made it first from Asia – it is thought from Taiwan – to Canada and Alaska and from there to Hawaii. By 600AD these bronze-skinned Hawaiians (brown perhaps because of their North American Indian connection) were overpopulating their island, so they mounted an ocean expedition to find new land.

Marsh asserts that one group landed on a '*Distant Land*' they named '*Tawhiti*' (for which read Tahiti) and found nearby on *Ra-ia-tea* (*Sun-People-White*) a group of white people who worshipped the sun.

On their return and sailing to windward, so as not to miss Hawaii, they found another group of low islands, they called *Tua-motu* (*back and off to the side-islands*).

Further explorations led them to *Ra-ro-tonga* (*Sun in the South*), *Ra-vae-vae* and *Ra-pa* (*Sun village*) and eventually to *Ra-pa-nui* (*Sun Village Big*) where they met more white sun worshippers.

The next development was crucial. Marsh writes:

> Exploration now led them (the Hawaiians) to *Whiti* (*Crossover* – of a cultural kind), where they found a different breed of people with dark skin and frizzy hair. *Tonga-tapu* was the boundary for battles between these culturally very different peoples and was called *South-Forbidden* as a warning to venturesome seafarers to avoid these dark-skinned cannibal warriors.

The trouble began at Tahiti

It seems that while the Hawaiians got on happily with the white sun worshippers, they found themselves in immediate conflict with the Melanesians who by this time had reached and settled in Tonga and Fiji.

And it was there, at *Whiti*, or *Ta-whiti*, that the cruelest battle lines were drawn, marking the start of ongoing war throughout much of the Pacific between basically peaceful white and bronze-skinned peoples on the one hand and the black-skinned people of Melanesian origin who worshipped war and practiced cannibalism on the other.

Both Patupaiarehe and Waitaha traditions relate that the prospect of such unsought conflict caused them to sail on, the Patupaiarehe to New Zealand and the Waitaha to the Marquesas where they intermarried with brown-skinned natives already in residence before, centuries later, themselves sailing to New Zealand. The Waitaha, according to Hori Kupenga Manuka Manuka, intermarried with and settled peoples on many Pacific islands on their protracted journey down to New Zealand.

'But the trouble began at Tahiti,' he says. 'There were people there of a very different culture. They worshipped the gods of war and practiced cannibalism. Eventually they too came to New Zealand and were known as the Moriori and later the Māori. Their culture was all about war, killing and eating the conquered. My people, the Waitaha, were peaceful,' he explains.

The red-headed 'top knots' of the Moai statues on Easter Island. Are they the work of red-headed Celtic peoples fleeing violent onslaught against them in South America to find refuge on this, the world's loneliest landmass? The traces of a red-haired, fair complexioned and green-eyed people can be found all the way from the Hebrides in Scotland through Spain and France to the Middle East, South America, in the Pacific islands and also right here in New Zealand.

To complete the classification, the 'brown skins' are the Polynesian descendants representing a mixture of the 'red head' genes, the 'brown' Hawaiian strain, mixed with Melanesian blood.

Marsh speculates that as Peru's Quechua language is 30 per cent Austronesian, it is highly likely that the white skinned, red heads from Peru spoke a similar language to the Hawaiians and therefore, despite the adoption by ancient Peruvians of the Egyptian sun worshipping religion, they both realised that they had a common connection in the distant past and were happy to assimilate with each other. The genetics were another matter. Marsh remarks:

> Unfortunately the pale skinned red heads were mostly rhesus negative, which proved fatal for all but the first born babies with a rhesus positive father – of which all the Hawaiians were. Not only this, but blonde/red hair and blue eyes are both recessive genes, therefore as time progressed fewer and fewer pale skinned red heads survived. Their affection for these people is seen in the tradition of brides hiding from the sun before their wedding day, so that their skin is as pale as possible.

He argues that because of this recessive gene intermingling between the white skins, red skins and later the brown and black skins progressively phased out the white-skinned fair-headed characteristics and a coffee-coloured mix became predominant.

Except in New Zealand, that is, where, because of thousands of years of relative isolation, the white-skinned, green-eyed, red-haired Celtic Patupaiarehe people kept their distinct physical characteristics up to and into recent times.

Monica Matamua's appearance and genetic history are undeniable proof of that.

Sharp-nosed and stern the face of King Badezir glares down from its rocky parapet above Gavea Harbour, Rio de Janeiro.

Chapter 25

The *Urekehu* Odyssey

There is more than one strand to the story of the fair-skinned, red or blond-haired tall people who first settled New Zealand and came to be called the Patupaiarehe. In fact there may be several strands.

We have followed the path the Phoenicians took to South America, from Peru to Easter Island and from thence down the Pacific to New Zealand. We have seen stunning proof that 'white people' did reach Peru long ago and are still there. To this day the Chachapoya stand out as fair, Caucasian and very different to the bronze-skinned descendants of the Inca who form the majority of Peru's population.

But there is more. There are the *Urekehu* and the best introduction to them is found in Thor Heyerdahl's ground-breaking book, *Early Man and the Ocean*. He had this to say:

> Amongst the chiefly families of New Zealand, Easter Island and the Chatham Islands there is a genetically different group who are: tall, pale skinned, bearded, long-headed, with a Semitic nose, narrow lips and occasionally reddish brown hair with a wavy texture. The Polynesian name for families carrying this racial type is *Urukehu* and they are said to be descended from an earlier population of blond and fair skinned people.

Still living today on the shores of Lake Titicaca in Peru, bordering Bolivia and Peru is a tribe named Uros. These people claim descent from the demi-god Viracocha, said to have been a tall white bearded man, whose sons built the city of Tiahuanaco on the lake's shores.

As will be further explained, the syllable 'ur' forms an important clue to the destiny of such people. 'Ur' is found in Uruguay, Urekehu and Ur, the ancient capital of Chaldees mentioned in Genesis,

A bearded man peers out from a high, weathered cliff face towering in Whangape Harbour, Northland, New Zealand. He has a crown with a pyramid on top, eyes, Semitic nose, mouth and goatee beard. Another Phoenician king perhaps?

the Uros, and is a component of the names of a string of ancient towns and settlements along the South American coast. The Uros also call themselves 'Children of the Sun'.

According to Patrick Marsh[70], they live on reed mats floating in the lake and their gardens float alongside their residences. They practice swamp agriculture also employed to this day in the Tigris and Indus river lands near the ancient city of Ur.

The Uros make wonderfully crafted rafts, from the reeds of Lake Titicaca, the same species found growing in an Easter Island crater lake and still used by the Rapa Nui islanders to make rafts. Importantly, the 'god' who brought the Totora reed from Lake Titicaca to Easter Island was called 'Ure'.

The Uros consider themselves descendants of the ancient Uros recognized as the first major ethnic group to have settled in the Andes, specifically the Lake Titicaca watershed.

Having long undergone attack from the Inca and Aymara peoples they are now largely confined to Lake Titicaca and to the islands that float upon it.

And now for another connection. On pages 304 and 306 are two images carved on two different but huge cliff faces are shown. One adorns a cliff face overlooking a deep water anchorage in Whangape Harbour, Northland, New Zealand. The other is found in Gavea Harbour, near Rio de Janeiro in Brazil.

Your challenge, should you accept it, is to compare them and answer the question: Are they similar in age and purpose? If so who sculpted them? Take a second look and keep reading to find out. The huge monument pictured with the sharp nose is a major tourist attraction and stands at the entrance to Gavea Harbour, near Rio de Janeiro, Brazil, overlooking a deep water anchorage. It is a depiction of a royal Phoenician personage. This is supported by the Phoenician writing inscribed on the side of the image's head which states that

70 Patrick Marsh, online article series, *Polynesian Pathways*.

image is that of an ancient king of Tyre and Sidon.

Now on the second image, can you see a high-browed face of a goatee-bearded man incised in massive proportions into a cliff face above the waters of Whangape Harbour, Northland, New Zealand?

And would you believe that this carved face, in some ways similar to that at Gavea Harbour, might very possibly also be that of a Phoenician king?

That is deduced from the fact that clearly he has a 'crown' in the rock-carved circle above his head which in turn is surmounted by a small shaped, rock pyramid. All these features have been hewn out of solid basalt rock – a huge undertaking because the image as a whole is nearly 100ft tall. Note also the eyes, nose, mouth and a prominent goatee beard.

Importantly, like the rock face image at Gavea Harbour, the Whangape Harbour carving overlooks a safe and sheltered deep water anchorage for ships. Could it be that Phoenician and other ships of antiquity dropped anchor here after their long voyage to reach New Zealand, perhaps from Brazil?

Back in Gavea Harbour near Rio de Janeiro the inscription on the side of the image of 'King Bazedir' presents an enigma and a riddle to scholars and archaeologists.

Some affirm it is genuine; others deny its authenticity. However, Christian da C. Karam, archaeologist, of Port Ellegre, Brazil, reports in his online study about ancient South American archaeology that the image, in his view, is undoubtedly what it purports to be. He writes that the inscription on the rock states:

'Here Badazir, King of Tyre, Jethbaal's oldest son'.

Karam says hundreds of other rock inscriptions, marker stones, carved rock images, inland ports, ancient ship yards and even the remains of wooden vessels with bronze nails attest to Phoenician presence in Brazil.

The inscription in ancient Phoenician, which identifies the scultped face as that of King Bazedir, is clearly seen in the side of the massive rock face.

However, scientists have dismissed these claims, asserting that the Gavea rock face and inscription result from natural weathering. In doing so they blithely ignore the undeniable additional archaeological evidence of shipyards, buried boats and ancient copper mines in Brazil.

Researcher Austin Whittall writes that Pedra de Gávea ('Topsail Rock', in Portuguese) is right beside the beach and rises 842m (2760 ft.) above sea level. The strange marks on its sheer rock face are said to be man-made inscriptions and are just some of many alleged pre-Hispanic inscriptions found in Brazil.

Rendered in English letters, and read right to left, the inscription is:

LAABHTEJRABRIZDABNAISNEOFRUZT.

In 1920 self-educated archaeologist and historian, Bernardo Azevedo Silva Ramos (1858-1931), president of the Instituto Geografico de Manaos, compiled several hundred 'Phoenician inscriptions' from the Amazon and elsewhere in South America.

His book published with government support[71] dealt with Gavea's inscriptions. Their translation, according to Silva Ramos, is:

LAABHTEJ – RAB – RIZDAB – NAISINEOF – RUZT.

Knowing that the Phoenicians wrote from right to left (like modern Hebrew), Ramos inverted the phrase to read:

ZUR -NISIAN – BADZIR – RAB – JETHBAAL

which he then translated as:

Tyro Phoenicia, Badezir, Firstborn Jethbaal.

This cryptic phrase has historical backing. It is recorded that Badezir ruled Phoenicia from 855 to 850BC, and he was the son of Jethbaal, who ruled from 887 to 856BC.

The name exists, in a list of '*Kings that reigned at Tyre*' published by Roman-Jewish historian Josephus. As his source Josephus cites a Phoenician author of the second century BC, Menander of Ephesus who apparently wrote:

> ...Pheles who took the kingdom and reigned but eight months though he lived fifty years he was slain by Ithobalus the priest of Astarte who reigned thirty two years and lived sixty eight years he was succeeded by his son Badezorus who lived forty five years and reigned six years he was succeeded by Matgenus his son.

By the way, the Old Testament's Queen Jezebel is the daughter of Jethbaal. She married the King of Israel, Ahab, and led him astray from Jehovah inducing him to tolerate the cult of Baal[72].

---

71 *Inscricoes e Tradicoes da America Prehistorica – Especialmente do Brasil*, in two volumes (R. de Janeiro, 1930-39).

72 1 Kings 16:31

Well, so much for the Phoenician king whose face allegedly adorns this high peak at Rio de Janiero. Now what about the not dissimilar face found in Whangape Harbour in New Zealand's Northland? The face is very possibly also that of a Phoenician king, since we have established a strong link between the Phoenicians and the Patupaiarehe, arguably the first settlers of New Zealand. Carved in a rocky outcrop protruding from a steep hill hill rising above Whangape Harbour (as seen On the Following page), it is also huge, more than 100ft. high and gazes towards the the sun.

A relief of King Badezir.

New Zealand archaeological researcher Martin Doutre believes the face itself was carved in a way that deliberately leaves it fluted or channeled causing a high degree of shadow play across the face between the time of the Summer Solstice and the Winter Solstice, and throughout each day of the year. He comments:

> The winter sun would leave long shadows on the face and an adept reader of the interplay between light and shadow would be able to fairly accurately determine both the time of year and the time of day. The pyramidal marker stone atop the head would have served the function as an observatory position for solar observation.

Reportedly, although I haven't confirmed it, a similar face of an old, bearded man at Tokatoka, Ruawai, overlooks the Wairoa River as it enters Kaipara Harbour and is mentioned in Waitaha oral traditions. If so, both these huge carvings of 'old men' lie close to and overlook deep, navigable channels to the sea. To this day ships could anchor right beneath their gaze.

It has been suggested that these huge carvings represent Tangaroa, the Māori god of the sea and ocean migrations. Martin Doutre, for example, says, that it seems reasonable to assume that mariners heading to the open sea would say prayers to Tangaroa and, upon a safe return, express their thanks. But with respect I would disagree and assert that both the Gavea Harbour and Whangape Harbour cliff face sculptures depict ancient kings.

Doutre reports that Tangaroa is described in oral traditions of Polynesia as white complexioned with sandy coloured hair … whose offspring were 'the fair skinned moon-maidens' and the greenstone folk (the 'fish of Tangaroa'). So arguably the face at Whangape might represent *Tangaroa*. However, the carving may well predate Māori and Polynesian arrival in New Zealand and thus represent a far older dignity.

Indeed, it seems more likely that the face carved in rock at Whangape may represent Viracocha, that ancient leader of the white-skinned, red-headed peoples we have identified as Phoenician and whose descendants became the Patupaiarehe and Waitaha.

This personage, venerated as a demi-god is the *Kon-Tiki* of ancient South America, whose white, red-haired and bearded face, is depicted in carvings and statues not only in South America but also on Easter Island, other Pacific Islands such as the Marquesas and Austral Islands and, also now, I dare to suggest, in New Zealand too.

Phoenician inscriptions have been found in Tyre on tombstones which are now kept in London. They mention an expedition of a Phoenician navigator to a region far beyond the Strait of Moloch (today's Gibraltar) where 'the sea penetrated into the land ... a place where there was an abundance of food and lots of wood'.

In 1860 French archaeologists excavating a site at Sidon found many ancient wooden artifacts wrought in timber that could have come only from Brazil, according to archaeological tests.

These revealed that the timber in question was the famous Brazilian *quebracho* or *quebra machado* (the 'axe breaker'), a

Shell-obsidian inlaid eyes on a red-haired Easter Island statue, next to a Hittite statue with the same inlaid eyes, dating back some 4,000 years. Centre right is a Mesopotamian dragon in bronze, adjacent to a near matching New Zealand Māori taniwha, held to be a talisman of great powwer and a spiritual guardian. Pictures courtesy of Patrick Marsh; bone carving image supplied by www.boneart.co.nz.

timber renowned for its hardness. Karam says that all the cuneiform inscriptions discovered in the Amazon region, in the Ararí area, and in French Guyana and Surinam, such as hieroglyphs and rock characters, demonstrate clearly their origin from Aramaic, Syriac and even Sanskrit scripts.

In Brazil's National History Museum many photographs show huge inscriptions widely spread from the Solimões River up to where its name changes to Amazon River (that is, from *Ararí* to the *Madeira* River). By the way, does the name *Solimões* commemorate ancient Israel's King Solomon, whose close ally was the Phoenician king of Tyre, Hiram?

Marsh asserts that the Gavea carving and inscription of King Badezir and other discoveries suggest there was a Phoenician port right there, close to Rio de Janiero, developed so trading ships could catch the westerlies to sail back across the Atlantic. He points out that due to the ancient Phoenician trading presence, South America's western coast abounds in place names containing the syllable *Ur*, including *Ur*atai, *Ur*uguay, *Ur*ubamba, *Ur*uacu, *Ur*uana, *Ur*ubu, *Ur*ubupunga, *Ur*ucuca, *Ur*utagua), forming a trail that leads right up to very old tin, gold and silver mines in the Andes.

Tin was prized thousands of years ago because it was needed to make bronze. Interestingly, an island near the mouth of the Amazon River is named Urutai and Marsh claims that Mediterranean DNA connections and cultural traits still found among Amazonian tribesmen to this day suggest the river was used by Bronze Age traders to penetrate the interior.

Language then forms a link between the ancient biblical Ur that was home to Abraham and Uruguay and a string of towns, ports and ancient settlements in South America. It also connects the *Uros* tribe of Peru and Bolivia with both the Phoenicians and the *Urekehu*, the name by which the ancient white, red-haired voyagers were known throughout Polynesia and in New Zealand.

But is there bone hard, rock solid proof you ask? Well, try the picture on the previous page for size. The ancients of Ur treasured a mythical dragon that is almost identical to the taniwha design much used in New Zealand greenstone and bone carving. Their near neighbours the Hittites made statues with white shell eyes inlaid with obsidian, reminiscent of the carvings of figures on Māori meeting houses. But such designs may not have been original to Māori, deriving instead from those early New Zealand pioneers, the Patupaiarehe and Turehu

Both *Ur* and the ancient *Urekehu* or Patupaiarehe people seem to have much in common with the carvers of Rapa Nui who inlaid the eyes of their huge *moai* statues. And, clearly from the evidence above the dragon/taniwha design in New Zealand far predates much later Māori arrival. To carve such a talisman in precious greenstone could occupy much of a single craftsman's lifetime. The art of carving in such exquisite detail, like net making, was learned by the latecomer Moriori and Māori settlers from the Patupaiarehe who long preceded them in New Zealand and who, over many centuries, had developed such crafts into a fine art.

Easter Island, a definite stop over on the Urekehu trail, seems to have undergone several different cultural inputs during its near 1500-year history. Among them is the Harrapan culture from India, recent research reveals. The cult of bird worship as practiced on Rapa Nui, during the annual seabird egg race is still found among 'birdmen' living on the swamps of the Indus River. And this region was once home to the Harrapan script, from which the Easter Island Rongo Rongo writing is derived.

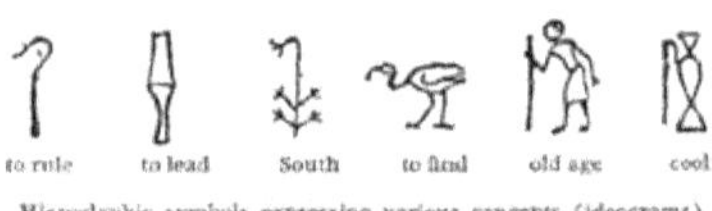

Hieroglyphic symbols expressing various concepts (ideograms)

EASTER ISLAND

I II III IV V VI VII VIII

This connection came to light after discovery of Indus Valley seals dating to around 500BC. Subsequently researchers noticed a close correlation between the script on the Easter Island tablets and these Indus scripts.

Nineteenth century New Zealand historian Elsdon Best reported a Māori tradition that the forebears of their people had travelled from a hot dry land called 'Iria'. Above is a sample from the *History of Writing* illustrating the similarity between the Indus Script and the Easter Island (Rapa Nui) tablet writing called 'Rongorongo[i]'. Columns I, III, V and VII belong to the Indus Script. An online article entitled *Rongorongo and the Indus Script*[73], says that current scholars have downplayed the significance of these similarities for two reasons.

First, the Indus Script was written 2,000 or more years before the Easter Island tablets and second, Easter Island is on the opposite side of the globe from the Indus Valley and separated by two oceans.

However, distance and time are not insurmountable barriers for human beings. Look at the Egyptians who maintained a writing system for thousands of years and also sailed far abroad. When the modern

73 See more at www.boloji.com

world writes history it denies these pioneers of several thousand years their rightful place in maritime exploration. Also ignored is the vast trade and exchange between peoples in both the Indian and Pacific Oceans.

Perhaps a closer look at the similarities between the Indus and Rapa Nui writing systems could be a starting point for historians investigating this issue to consider. Marsh reports that recent genetics research suggests several arrivals of Eastern Mediterranean genes into Central and South America in remote prehistoric times. There is also an Indian input into Venezuela about 500BC. One product of this mix are the Cuna Indians with Eastern Mediterranean and Dravidian genetic and cultural traits. They also have a script related to Harrapan and Rongo Rongo script.

All these three scripts are read in the same unique manner, in which the script is turned upside down for each successive line. This is termed *boustrophedon* script. Marsh insists that it is more than coincidence that reed rafts, the birdman cult and boustrophedon script keep re-occurring together. These traits have been learned from one another, reinvented and then isolated in cultures living in remote areas creating a slightly distorted time capsule of a culture that once existed thousands of years ago on the other side of the world.

In 1892 the Easter Island scripts were deciphered but this important achievement, with Heyerdahl's ground-breaking discoveries, have been set aside and today experts continue to argue over their possible meaning. However, the 19th century translation, according to the Harrapan script interpretation, gives a detailed history of tribal conflict in South America, leading up to the exodus to Easter Island of the *Ra* people! They even mention which tribes were from the ancient land of *Tulapin* (turtle) thought to now be a sunken continent.

Thor Heyerdahl concluded that on Easter Island there were two main phases of habitation. The well-made stone walls of the first occupation appear to be connected to the *Ra* people (from Ur), i.e. the *Urekehu.*

These people did not arrive in Easter Island until about 300AD, he believed, and came there from having lived for many years in South America before being persecuted and driven out. The cruder stonework of Polynesian arrivals on Easter Island came much later. In his book *Early Man and the Ocean*[74], Heyerdahl also has this to say:

> On Easter Island, detailed traditions insist that the island's earliest ancestors came from the vast desert land to the East and reached their island after sailing for 60 days toward the setting sun. These are the same directions given to the Portuguese mariner Mendala in Peru when asking Peruvians about finding islands in the Pacific.

Which would make both the ancient Peruvians, as led by Viracocha, and the first settlers of Easter Island the same people, the Urekehu. Their long journey can now be traced all the way from Ur of the Chaldees through Sidonia, present day Lebanon, to Borneo, South America, and down through the Pacific islands to that Far Away Land, New Zealand,

---

74 *Early Man and the Ocean*, by Thor Heyerdahl (1979) Doubleday.

Chapter 26

Corn's amaizing story

Eyebrows have been critically raised at Monica Matamua's assertion in her story that her Patupaiarehe ancestors brought maize and potatoes to New Zealand over 2,000 years ago. Her claim boldly contradicts the orthodox academic wisdom that 'maize was probably first introduced into New Zealand in 1772 and that it has been grown by Māori and others ever since'[75].

But there is no proof that is so, nor evidence to disprove the Patupaiarehe tradition they brought maize to this country before Christ was born. The conventional tenet is that maize was first domesticated

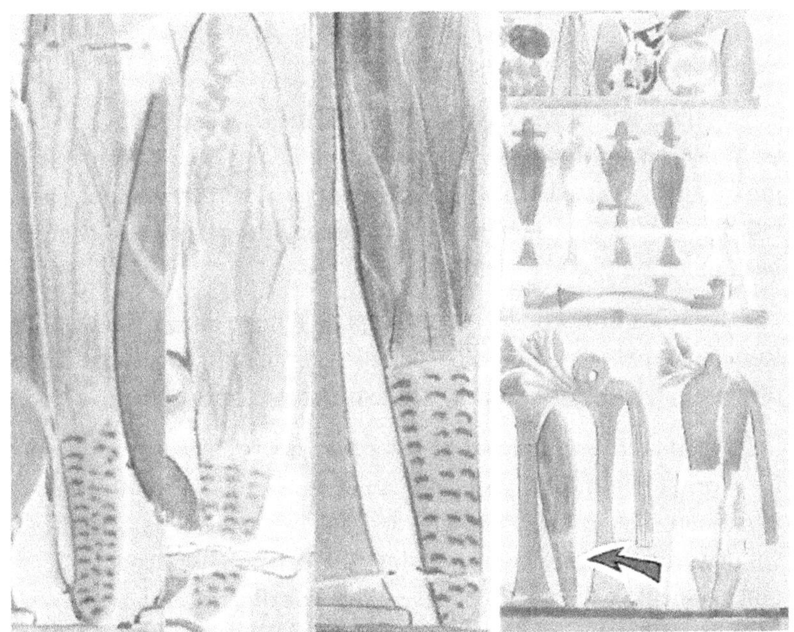

One picture says it all: A mural painted in Queen Hatshepsut's mortuary temple in the 1400sBC vividly depicts the true colours of sweetcorn.

75 *Te Ara Encyclopaedia of New Zealand.*

in South America and only comparatively recently spread to the rest of the world.

The *New World Encyclopaedia* perpetuates this unproven assumption saying maize was 'native to the New World', being domesticated in Mesoamerica by 3500 BCE, and then spread throughout the American continents. It spread to the rest of the world after European contact with the Americas in the late fifteenth century and early sixteenth century'.

But there is ample evidence to show maize made its way from South America to the Northern Hemisphere many thousands of years ago, making it inevitable it would be a staple food of choice aboard long distance sailing ships of antiquity.

What better grain to easily store aboard ship, cook and grow quickly in a summer season ashore? And if it was a staple aboard ships in ancient times then it is an odds-on probability it was brought to New Zealand by Monica's ancestors.

Fact is, that while corn cobs found preserved in a Mexican cave have been dated to 4,700BC, incised engravings show maize being grown and harvested in ancient Egypt nearly 1500 years before Christ. Other evidence shows it was grown in India, Europe and elsewhere far back in antiquity.

It is a little known fact that maize fed the lower classes of the Roman Empire for 300 years, yet all this remains largely hidden, if not forbidden, history because academics have ignored the evidence.

Actually, the incredible story of how maize spread around the world thousands of years ago is the key to unlock several ancient mysteries that puzzle scholars and historians to this day. These enigmas may include how and why Egyptian, Greek, Phoenician and other ancient voyagers reached the other side of the world, the location of 'Punt', the fabulous land to which Egyptian Queen Hatshepsut sent a maritime trading expedition in 1470BC, the type of corn Joseph used to save a starving Egypt several centuries before, and the true location of the fabulous 'Ophir' from which Solomon obtained gold to build his temple in Jerusalem.

But one puzzle remains unsolved: just how maize was domesticated. Early botanists were sure it originated from pod corn, a plant in which small grains are enclosed individually in husks. Later it was thought the South American wild grass teosinte (*Euchlaena Mexicana*) was the progenitor. However, in 1939 Mangelsdorf and Reeves found that teosinte, while a close relative is a recent hybrid of maize and Tripsacum, a third near relative. Today the jury is still out.

What should no longer be in doubt is that maize farming underpinned growth of large-scale early civilisations not only in Egypt but also in South America on the other side of the world. It changed the face of the ancient world and was both cargo and cause of some of longest global voyages undertaken in antiquity.

Research now shows that hundreds of species of plants and animals were shipped from one side of the world to the other producing huge agricultural expansion and establishing large trading empires in their wake.

Maize and other food providing plants can be said to be the very key to understanding how and why such voyages were made. But don't take my word for it. The authors of the major treatise, *World Trade Biological Exchanges Before 1492*[76], present over 600 pages of plants ancient mariners took back and forth across the major oceans of the world and in particular from the New World to the Old, all long before Christ. Such plants include maize, potatoes, peanuts, tobacco, cocaine, hashish, sunflowers, gourds, chilies, cotton and grain amaranth.

Other works have addressed the diffusion of a plethora of animals and birds shipped or otherwise transported from one hemisphere to the other, so long ago that they have developed into other species.

---

76 John L. Sorensen and Carl L. Johanesen, *World Trade Biological Exchanges Before 1492* (2004-2009), Bloomington IN iUniverse.

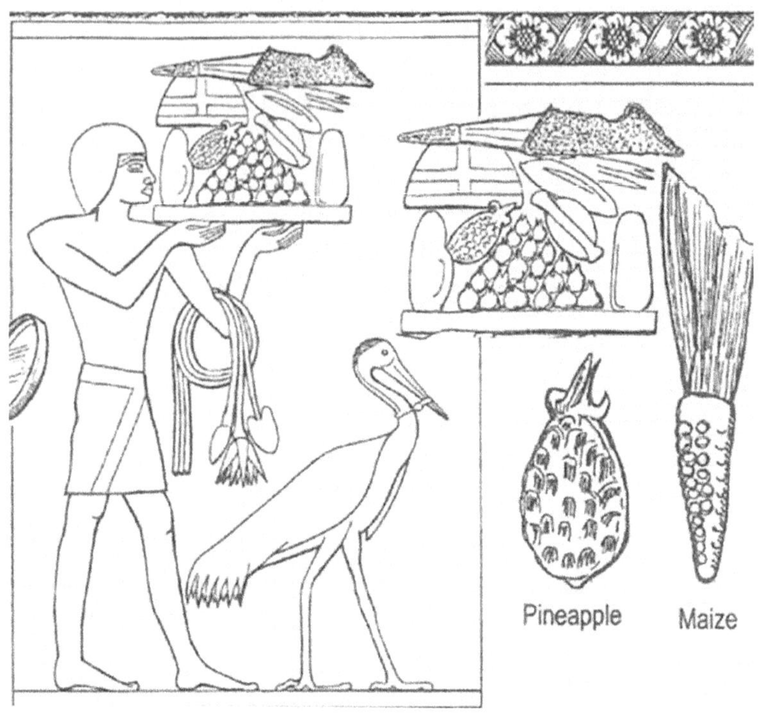

Diagram of the Queen Hatshepsut temple mural of the Punt fruits, showing corn cobs, pineapples and oblong squash – all New World plants.

The leopard brought from Africa to Egypt and then taken to the New World may have become the jaguar of South America. And peacocks, said to have originated from the Indian subcontinent and Java, reached Athens by 450BC and perhaps even earlier were introduced to almost every part of South America, Africa and parts of Europe. While academics insist plants, animals and humans developed only slowly in their place of origin, the vast, complex and ancient record of *diffusionism* (that dreaded 'D' word that is the bane of orthodox, evolutionary-minded professors[77]) tells a different story.

77 *Diffusionism* is the sensible understanding that civilisations of old shipped plants, animals, technology and themselves to other parts of the world. It is rejected by mainstream academia who adhere to the *isolationist* paradigm which refutes widespread contact between ancient peoples, saying instead that the New World and Australasia was only reached by Europeans in the last 300-400 years.

Thousands of years ago, from elsewhere in the world, lions, tigers and monkeys were imported into Egypt, giraffes into China and elephants into Europe. Today it's difficult to know what came from where and when.

Returning to maize, Sorenson and Johannesen's book features a photo of a Java stone bas-relief carving of maize cobs dating to 500 years before Columbus supposedly discovered America. Another photo is of a Han Dynasty Chinese ceramic bird made by being moulded over a corn cob over 2,000 years ago. (In the firing the cob burnt to ash but left its imprint on the inside of the clay bird). The artifact is housed in Xinxiang Archaeological Museum.

Stone-carved images of maize cobs said to date from 1100AD show the plant was widely grown in India. And in Britain images of maize cobs have been found dating to Roman times. They were found in Roman villas at Londinium and can still be seen in the British Museum.

But let us go further back, to the late 1400s BC when Egyptian Pharaoh Queen Hatshepsut built a fabulous palace temple at Deir al-Bahri, called the 'Splendour of Splendours', to commemorate the triumphs of her reign. Murals inside the temple show golden, yellow corn cobs depicted with green husk leaves. The maize cobs stand upright between food jars, breads, onions, figs, baskets of fruit and oblong vegetables, clearly squash, which like maize, is another New World plant.

Evidence of this is recorded in a 1909 photograph, copied and restored in colour by Howard Carter, the famed Egyptologist who discovered the tomb of Tutankhamen, and who remarked that the pictured cobs were of the right size and proportion for sweetcorn[78]. Researcher and author Gunnar Thompson[79] asserts that Hatshepsut's famed palace enshrined the legacy of the huge trading empire she

78 The photograph of Queen Hatshepsut's corn cobs is also found in *The Archeology of Ancient Egypt* by Stevenson W. Smith, pages 133 and 135 (1958, reprint 1999) New Haven, Yale University Press.

79 *Secret Voyages* by Gunnar Thompson (2006), publisher, Misty Isles.

established during her reign. He devotes a chapter to Hatshepsut and argues convincingly that at her direction maize was brought back to Egypt from South America by an expedition to 'Punt' led by the Nubian Admiral Neshi.

But where was 'Punt'? In the ancient Egyptian inscriptions there is reference to 'Punt'. However, there may have been more than one 'Punt', possibly several of them. Undoubtedly Egypt traded with various parts of Africa from its earlier days and various locations, including the Arabian Peninsula, Somalia and Eritrea may have been the 'Land of Punt'.

Several places in Africa, including Libya, could be said to be 'Lands of Punt' because 'Punt' is actually the Egyptian rendering of the name Put or Phut named in the Book of Genesis as the son of Cush and the great grandson of Noah. And Phut has a real connection to Egypt because while Phut founded Libya his brother Mizraim founded Egypt. The Mizraim name is found in the phrase 'the two Mazors', meaning the two lands of Egypt, and is commemorated to this day in the Misr Bank of Cairo, for example. Importantly, since Phut and his descendants got around a fair bit, there would be several African locations that in ancient times could be called 'Punt'.

There is also reference to 'The Land of the God' and the 'Paradise overseas'. Probably these destinations were differently named to distinguish them both from each other and from 'Punt'. Yet this likelihood has been studiously ignored by the history pundits who consider them all 'the land of Punt' and seek to locate it in Africa.

Yet if maize and pineapples were brought to Egypt, the only place they could have come from is South America. And much the same could be said for gold for which the pharaohs had an insatiable desire. History has it that Egyptians were deep sea voyaging as far back as 2,500BC when Pharaoh Sahure of the Fifth Dynasty obtained gold from Ta Netjer, the "Land of the God", although gold from 'Punt' is recorded as having been in Egypt in the time of king Khufu of the Fourth Dynasty of Egypt. Subsequently, there were more expeditions to the far off lands in the Sixth, Eleventh, Twelfth and Eighteenth dynasties of Egypt.

As ancient murals show, baboons and ivory were celebrated imports brought back by Egypt's 'Punt' expeditions and there is no doubt these came from Africa. However, according to Thompson, other valued cargo brought home by Egyptian ocean voyagers included monkeys, exotic woods, bags of grain, cinnamon (only found in the Spice Islands), incense trees and the 'enigmatic green-gold metal called Emu'. Of interest, ancient gold and copper mines have been found in Mexico and Peru and Thompson holds that South America was a destination known and traded with to by earlier Pharaohs who reigned several centuries before Hatshepsut.

The historical background is important. Hatshepsut was determined to make Egypt a world trading nation. Her predecessors had relied on chariot raids on Syria and Palestine to fill the royal coffers. Hatshepsut ordered a halt to such military attacks and as a

This mural in Queen Hatshepsut's mortuary temple shows fruits of the Punt expedition: maize cobs, pineapples and oblong squash, all of South American origin. Picture courtesy of www.denyignorance/abovetopsecret.com

regional peacemaker plumped for friendly trading relationships instead. To sell this idea to her people she had this aim incised in stone as 'God's will' for Egypt, saying she had been commanded to make peace and trade by the Supreme Being, Amun-Re. Under her orders 83 ocean-going ships were built in the Koptos shipyards on the Nile near Thebes.

This huge maritime endeavor to sail the Mediterranean – and beyond to South America, I submit – began only after the Mt. Thera volcanic explosion in the Aegean Sea destroyed the civilisation of the Minoans who had been the maritime masters of the Mediterranean until then. Later Phoenicians, Greeks and Romans would wage war to rule these waves but under Hatshepsut Egypt moved quickly to dominate this sea trade before others could. Not that Egypt did not trade anciently and hugely with the Arabian Peninsula and Africa, for it was from the Dark Continent Egypt's supplies of ivory, ostrich feathers and eggs, elephants and other animals came. This trade flourished especially in the years Egyptian fleets were excluded from the Mediterranean.

Accepted history asserts Egypt's 'Punt' voyagers set sail from the Red Sea. However, if South America, 'The Land of the God', was the destination it makes far more sense they sailed from the Nile Delta across the Mediterranean to the 'Pillars of Hercules', now Gibraltar. After all Egyptian ships were already plying the whole Mediterranean while also sailing from the Red Sea to locations in Africa. But clearly maize, squash and pineapples could not have come from Egypt's African trading partners; they are South American plants that could only have come from that continent.

Thompson argues that from Gibraltar the fleet had only to 'follow the track of the setting sun', the 'Path of the God', to sail westwards across the Atlantic Ocean to Mexico in Meso-America. Following this route the voyage would be hugely shorter than sailing through the Red Sea to India, through the Indonesian archipelago then right across the Pacific to reach South America's western coast.

But it is not the shorter distance but the goods brought back that provide convincing evidence that Queen Hatshepsut's 'Punt' lay in South America and not in Africa as commonly thought. Thompson reports that 'after several years away', the Hatshepsut 'Punt' expedition returned with incense trees (their roots in baskets), leopard skins[80], monkeys, exotic woods, cinnamon and an enigmatic metal called 'green gold', now identified as a copper-gold alloy. He identifies the incense trees, prominently featured in Hatshepsut's temple murals and called *antyu*, as the Mexican *copal* bush, anciently used in South America to produce the copious quantities of incense used in temple ceremonies.

The Hatshepsut temple murals also depict date palms among the plants the Queen's expedition brought from the 'oversea Paradise' of 'Punt' to make glad the hearts of her people. Did they too come from South America? If they did then it would contradict the widely held view that date palms are indigenous to Egypt and Arabia.

The *Encyclopaedia Britannica* thinks they originated in Egypt and Arabia, saying that Spanish missionaries were the first to carry date palms to the New World in the 18th century. But if that is true what can be made of the clear statement of English author Samuel Purchas in 1525 that 'Mexican natives wrap their lumps of unrefined *copal* incense in date leaves' for preservation?

If date palms didn't come from South America to Egypt, did they diffuse in the opposite direction; that is from Egypt to Meso-America? Thompson says a credible explanation must be found because for thousands of years before Christopher Columbus arrived South American natives enjoyed a cornucopia of Old World fruits that included apples, almonds, oranges, grapes, cinnamon, pomegranates, bottle gourds, dates and bananas. He postulates that as early as 3000BC voyagers took plants and animals from the Old World Mexico and

80 Leopard skins were required dress for priests of Anubis. Jaguars are thought by some to have sprung from leopards brought to South America from Africa, perhaps by the Olmecs, whose carved stone images clearly portray their African Negroid origin.

Peru while searching for metals. What's more he produces a plethora of ancient Egyptian artifacts found in Central America to support his contention.

They include very old stone carved statues of the main Egyptian deities, Isis and Osiris, found by an archeological dig at Cajuta, El Salvador, Mexico[81], images of hand-held incense burners depicted in both Egyptian and ancient Mexican rock incisions[82], carved depictions of the Egyptian religious symbol, the ankh, of the deified jackal, Anubis, wheeled toys as also found in Egypt and ceramic ink wells and depictions of writing that match those found in Egypt[83].

Another conundrum is the pineapple. While the wild plant, a bromeliad, hails from southern Brazil and Paraguay, little is known about the origin of the cultivated fruit which natives spread to the Caribbean, Central America and Mexico, where it was cultivated by the Mayas and the Aztecs. Columbus found it in 1493 on Guadeloupe. The Spanish introduced it into the Philippines. But how, pray, did it come to adorn the walls of a 15th century BC temple in Egypt?

Possible support for the pineapple's arrival in the Northern Hemisphere is found in the Greek myth of the *Labours of Hercules* in which the hero fetches 'golden apples' from an island far across the seas. Historians are as baffled about what these 'apples' might be as they are about the island they came from.

However, maybe ancient Egyptians sailed to and established trading settlements in South America. The abundance of Egyptian artifacts found in Mexico and Peru support this contention. And, of necessity, there must have been return voyages for New World products such as maize, pineapples and incense trees to reach Egypt as evidence suggests they did. One scientist asserts that traces of cocaine, marijuana

---

81 *Historia de la Nacion Mexicana* by Manuel Cuevas (1940).

82 Incense was offered in Egyptian, South American and Jewish temple worship.

83 Chroniclers of the Spanish conquest of the Americas in 1521 recorded that the government of the vanquished Aztec Empire used no less than 1,000,000 sheets of paper in its last year in office.

and tobacco have been in ancient Egyptian mummies, though others have sought to disprove this by suggesting later contamination.

However, it is hard to deny that African seafarers reached South America as early as 1500BC, leaving the behind oldest iron tools found in the Americas as evidence of their arrival. The colossal and very Negroid stone heads of La Venta, Tres Zapotes and San Lorenzo attest to the early arrival of this African-sourced Olmec civilisation in the Americas. Is it coincidence that the 'pronounced Nubian lip' on these statues is also found on the sculptured faces of Egyptian royalty, said to have had a definite African connection?

So, if we have Negroid Africans establishing an advanced civilisation in South America when Egyptians were trading deep into Africa, is it surprising there is an Egyptian-South American connection?

And is it not likely those ancient voyagers to New Zealand, brought sweetcorn and other maize varieties to New Zealand, having sojourned as they did, variously in Egypt, the Mediterranean and South America? Maize has had an amazing journey around the world, from one side to the other and back again. Could it be that New Zealand was one of its early ports of call?

Chapter 27

So what should we do?

We have reached the end of this journey back into time and the question now is: what should we do with the information we have learned?

Well, putting it bluntly we need to get 'stuck into the real history of this country,' as correspondent Kevan G. Marks succinctly urged in a letter to the *Northern Advocate*[84]. Doing so should lead to a whole new and more truthful understanding of who we all are as New Zealanders.

To highlight that need consider that beautiful spot, the Cherry Grove at Taumarunui. A tree-lined drive leads to well-manicured public gardens with the confluence of the Whanganui and the Ongarue rivers as a superb backdrop. Enhancing the site is a brick-columned gateway and arch erected in 1932.

What is not commemorated is that in 1832, 20 years before the first latter-day European set foot in Taumarunui, a three thousand-strong war party of the Maniapoto tribe descended on this peaceful Patupaiarehe settlement, rounded up 600 of the Ngati Hotu (Patupaiarehe) residents and at Cherry Grove systematically killed and washed them in the Ongarue before cooking and eating them. Surely this is an important historical event that should be commemorated. Yet it is not.

Nor is the salient fact that Tamatea Pokai Whenua, hailed in tradition as the first major Māori explorer of much of New Zealand's North Island (c.1350AD)[85] is said to have lived 10 generations ago[86].

84 'Truth unwelcome', a letter published in the *Northern Advocate, Monday January 4, 2016.*

85 *Te Ara Encyclopaedia of New Zealand* 1996.

86 Book, *Taihape 1910-2010*, foreword by former New Zealand Prime Minister Jim

When we do the math: 10 generations x 30 years (the average pre-European native generation) the sum comes to 300. We find then that Tamatea lived some 300 years ago. That means that his exploration took place in the 1600s not the 1300s. That in turn means that Māori did not arrive in force in the middle and lower North Island until the 1700s, not the 1100s or 1200s as existing history claims.

And this late date for Māori incursion and invasion from the Far North of the rest of the North Island accords with both Monica Matamua's assertion and that of George Connelly that Māori arrival in much of the country took place in the 1600s. In turn this makes pretentious Te Ara's claim that:

> Tamatea-Pokai-Whenua was born in Hawaiki in the period before the Great Migration. He was the son of Rongokako and a descendant of the legendary Maui. He came to New Zealand in the *Takitimu* canoe but left it at Turanga (Gisborne) and travelled overland, keeping close to the coast, until he reached Ahuriri. There, according to the legend, his pet crocodile, Tapu-Te-Ranga, escaped. From Ahuriri he continued towards the Ruahines, but his son, Kahungunu, was unwilling to cross them and returned to settle on the Heretaunga Plains. Tamatea continued his journey until he reached a high mountain, where another of his pets, the serpent, Pohokura (or Pukeokahu), escaped.

Escaping serpent and crocodile apart, not much else of Tamatea's story makes sense. There was no 'Great Migration', the Great Canoe Fleet being a myth. Hawaiki is the name of several places in Northland, not islands overseas and, most likely, Tamatea simply sailed south from the north of the country to begin Māori exploration and conquest of middle North Island lands already occupied by the ancient tribes of New Zealand. We really need to get the true story of New Zealand's past straight.

Bolger.

This book has presented ample evidence that the 'first New Zealanders' were neither Māori nor latter-day European arrivals. They were Caucasian, of European Celtic origin, or the progeny of the same people intermarried with Pacific islanders on their way down to New Zealand.

It also shows that human occupation of this country can now be seen as stretching far back into prehistoric time. Almost certainly the first mappers of the world sailed to New Zealand to chart its shores; evidence suggestive of that has come down to us in the form of ancient maps copies of which are available in books at your public library today. They are derived in part from charts the first mappers of the world produced.

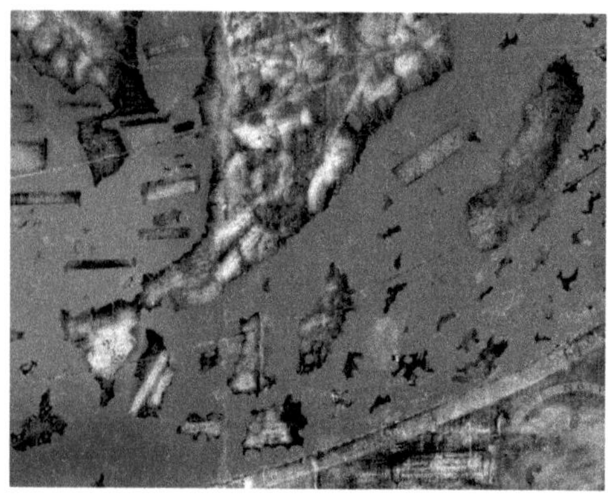

The Martellus 1491 world map clearly showing Australia and New Zealand. Picture courtesy of Yale News.

Consider, again for example, this segment of the Martellus world map of 1491 at left. China and Indonesia are crudely drawn as attached and Australia seen split in two halves at the foot of this 'continent'. And to the right, or east, of Australia can be seen two large islands which can only be a very badly drawn New Zealand. Clearly this map was drawn very long ago from earlier works. And the authors of those original charts must have sailed around New Zealand and Australia to chart their coastlines long, long before the Māori reached here.

Fact is that latter day European explorers of the Pacific, such as de Gonneville, Tasman and Cook, all made their 'discoveries' using these already existent charts clearly showing Australia and New Zealand

Thankfully, research is continually pushing back the likely time the first human beings walked on New Zealand's green and pleasant land. A few years ago it was thought incredible that the mixed-race Mediterranean crews of Rata and Maui could have reached here late in 232BC on their attempted round the world cruise, as asserted by the late Professor Barry Fell. But recently the dates have been pushed further back by others. Australian archeo-astronomer Alan Seath has publicly stated that Auckland's hill top volcanic pa in their stone marked configurations form alignments that date back about 3,500 years.

Going further back an adzed tree stump found deep beneath layers of volcanic deposit in Auckland, strongly suggests it was cut by human hand well before the nearby volcanoes first erupted. That might push human occupancy of New Zealand back beyond 4,000 years ago. Also research into pollen deposits indicates there may have been forest burning by human beings in both North and South islands, to stimulate fern root growth, stretching back as far as 4,000BP.

And, as the scientific debate about whether New Zealand human settlement began from 1,200AD onwards (the short term chronology) or long before, continues, one clear and early line has been drawn in the sand. New Zealand archeologists have decided collectively, albeit by a narrow majority, that that presence of the rat *Rattus exulans* in New Zealand over 2,000 years ago also indicates human arrival here dating back that far. However, they stress, human arrival does not necessarily imply human settlement, despite the clear evidence from Monica Matamua that her people did settle here in biblical times.

The same archaeological paper (*The timing of the human discovery and colonization of New Zealand*, Douglas Sutton, John R. Flenley et al [2007]) that concludes there was human and rat arrival in New Zealand over 2,000 years ago, also reports that human DNA studies of the Y chromosome (inherited down the male side) of New Zealand Māori suggest there is a very strong proportion of Melanesian genes among the Polynesian ones in their make-up (Underhill et al., 2001). This coupled with DNA research on *R. exulans* by Matisoo-Smith et al (1998) showing that *Rattus exulans* underwent multiple introductions to New Zealand, including one from Fiji, prompted Sutton and Flenley to say:

> One could be tempted to speculate there might have been a small initial human colonisation from Melanesia (Fiji), followed by a larger later one from Polynesia, but there is no direct evidence for this at present.

Sutton and Flenley conclude that 'the idea that people had been in New Zealand for some time before AD 1200, should be pursued as a hypothesis for further investigation'.

So slowly and hesitantly the New Zealand academic community is admitting that human presence in New Zealand may well date back thousands of years. However, while acknowledging a possible Melanesian origin for the Māori, it is still far from admitting that European and Mediterranean peoples settled here long before arrival of the Māori, even though evidence for this continues to amass.

Among such evidence is the solid fact of an eight-tonne boulder. Laboriously carved in intricate detail into a massive stone calendar and sundial, this stunning artifact is simply ignored by archaeologists because it is such an impossibly large oopart (an out-of-place-artifact) that does not fit their timetable for human settlement of New Zealand.

However, the author has made a detailed study of ancient time keeping practices to resolve the puzzle of this important artifact, which has been dubbed the 'Chronos Stone'. The research which resulted from this investigation was published in Max Hill's second book[87]. Entitled '*An attempt to solve the Chronos Stone puzzle*', it concludes that this instrument is most likely the only surviving example of a unique development in ancient sundial and calendar stone technology.

87 *To The Ends Of The Earth And Back Again*, by Max Hill, The Copy Press, 2015.

Found in an undisclosed, remote location, the 'Chronos Stone' actually may rank in importance alongside the finding of a 3,000-year-old electric battery in the ruins of Babylon or the recovery from the Mediterranean shipwreck of the more than 2,000-year-old *Antikythera* geared astrolabe mechanism that in its day revolutionised Greek shipping and is believed to have been an important aid in the Greek-Egyptian 'Māui and Rata' 232BC attempt to sail around the world.

These were the Greek-Egyptian voyagers who explored New Zealand and settled a colony here, Hill and other prehistory researchers believe. And, if there were people living here in New Zealand a thousand years or so before even these Egyptian-Greek-Mediterranean adventurers arrived, as the latest research now suggests, then there must be a huge pre-history of this country yet to be explored and acknowledged.

Thankfully, DNA research is already shedding light on this quest. One exciting discovery said to have occurred is the finding that DNA analysis of specimens from the ancient Turehu people of New Zealand, discloses that they bore genes replicating those found in Welsh people who lived in Britain 3,500 years ago.

In conclusion, the original New Zealanders clearly had strong connections with both the Northern Hemisphere and with South America. Some technology, skills and cultural practices can be traced all the way back to Europe, others to Egypt. The traditional New Zealand native storehouse, the *pataka* apparently owes its origin to the Celtic culture of Basque region of Spain[88].

On Egypt, there is the *tewhatewha*, an ancient New Zealand ceremonial weapon, still used today, that can be traced back to the land of the ancient Pharaohs. Historical photographs show latter-day Māori warriors bearing this weapon while 15th century BC ancient temple murals in Egypt show soldiers of Queen Hatshepsut bearing identical long-handled wooden staffs with shaped ends reminiscent

88 See chapter *From Spain with love.*

of battle axes. According to *Te Ara Encylopaedia of New Zealand* the *tewhatewha* is a long-handled staff shaped from a single piece of wood or bone with a spear point at one end and an axe-like part at the other. Blows, it says, were inflicted with the handle rather than the blade.

Outside New Zealand there seems to be no other depiction of such an instrument, except that found in the Hatshepsut mural. Research by the author suggests that anciently the weapon was used in close combat before the invention of body armour rendered it obsolete. Strangely, no such weapon can be traced to Taiwan, homeland of the fierce tribes to which Māori are genetically linked. Nor can it be found in the Pacific islands or the Indonesian archipelago, said to be the starting point for Melanesian dispersion into the Pacific.

However, since elsewhere Hatshepsut soldiers are depicted with metal spears it appears the mural is said to depict not troops but Punt trading expedition members returning to Egypt with examples of weapons found in that far off, and perhaps still at the time, Stone Age land in South America. Fact is the Bronze Age was already over 1,000 years old when the mural was painted.

Evidently, we all have much to learn about the true and ancient history of New Zealand and the world in which it was first settled. And for sure more artifacts and undeniable historical evidence will emerge in future years to support the case set out in this book.

The question is whether we New Zealanders have sufficiently open minds to receive it and rewrite our history in the light of it?

The End

INDEX OF KEY SUBJECTS

Ancient measurers:..............272-280

Archaeological evidence:.....11, 17, 87, 96, 103-108, 114, 134, 144, 160, 183, 191-195, 222, 281, 295, 302, 304, 306, 309, 311, 312, 319, 322, 325, 335-336

Ancient writing: 36, 38, 43, 270, 272, 276-278, 281-282, 295-297, 309-310, 316-317

Battles: 32-36, 49, 52, 54-56, 84, 118, 124-125, 128-130

Canoes:.................................196, 201, 209-210, 211-212

Cannibalism: 49-52, 54, 112-113, 118, 125, 128-130, 144-145, 169, 199

Celtic:...................................282, 285-286, 288-290, 292-294, 298, 300, 302-303

Chinese:................................194, 206, 223-249, 232, 250-252, 291

Climatic effects: 141-144

De Gonneville:....................253-267, 332

DNA:....................................43-44, 46, 197-199, 252

French connection:.............156-159, 253-267

Gospel preaching: 161-165, 166-171

Holocaust: 109-110, 111-112, 114, 123, 124-125, 130, 133, 138, 141-142

Māori:...................................8-9, 13-16, 22-23, 41, 44, 47-48, 111, 113-114, 127, 174, 181, 184-185, 187-188, 194, 197, 201, 206-207, 210-212, 252, 261, 264, 266, 315, 334, 335

Maps:....................................253, 255, 268, 275-276

Massacres:...........................27, 49, 54, 83-84, 109-110, 128-130, 131-133, 136-137, 151, 188

Melanesians: 45-47, 194-195, 197-204, 206-208, 210-212, 234, 252, 301, 334

Monica Matamua: 22-70

Moriori: 44, 188, 194-195, 204-212, 238, 250, 252, 262, 315

Ngapuhi: 177-178, 189, 195, 206

Navigation: 95-101, 253-267, 332

Patupaiarehe: 26, 47, 71-85, 89, 93-94, 98-100, 102-106, 122-124, 249, 252, 280, 288, 301, 303, 305, 319, 320

Peace and peacemakers: 18-20, 35, 48-49, 68, 112, 147-158, 161-165, 166-171

Phoenicians: 30-31, 34-35, 39, 286, 288, 290, 294, 296,-297, 300, 307-308, 310-311, 313

Radio carbon dating: 145, 239-240, 242-243

Ships and sailing: 30, 35-36, 40, 45-46, 99-100, 194, 207-208, 212, 217, 219, 221-222, 223-249, 254-263, 265-266, 270-271, 320-321, 325-327, 332

Suppressed truth: 131-133

Shipwrecks: 194, 223-249

Spanish connection: 206-208, 214-222, 385

Tangata whenua: 27, 29, 177

Te Upoko Ariki, Hori Kupenga Manuka Manuka: 173-190
(George Connelly)

Turehu: 47, 76, 232, 249, 252

Tuwharetoa: 22, 27, 29, 48, 51-55

Urekehu: 305, 313, 315, 318

Waitaha: 29, 39, 98, 156-159, 172-190, 194, 205, 235-236, 238, 249, 252, 259, 264, 301

The author

John Aldworth has had a wide and varied career in journalism. A former sub-editor on Britain's Daily Mail, in New Zealand he has variously edited The Accountants' Journal, The New Zealand Journal of Agriculture and the New Zealand Gardener.

A former business editor of the Waikato Times he has also worked for Wellington's Evening Post, The Dominion and Hamilton This Week.

The author of The Gentile Jesus, he contributes studies on belief in God to the website Day of Christ Ministries. He is married to Naomi, is the father of three children and has an ongoing passion for the truth of New Zealand's pre-history.

Contact him:

Phone: +64 7856 4566

Address: 17 Clark Place
Hillcrest, Hamilton 3216
New Zealand

Email: john.aldworth@hotmail.com

www.ingramcontent.com/pod-product-compliance
Ingram Content Group UK Ltd.
Pitfield, Milton Keynes, MK11 3LW, UK
UKHW020419250726
13967UKWH00007B/2716